SACRIFICE LOST

SACRIFICE LOST

The Dark Legacy of the Cross

Ashley Theuring

ORBIS BOOKS
Maryknoll, New York 10545

Founded in 1970, Orbis Books endeavors to publish works that enlighten the mind, nourish the spirit, and challenge the conscience. The publishing arm of the Maryknoll Fathers and Brothers, Orbis seeks to explore the global dimensions of the Christian faith and mission, to invite dialogue with diverse cultures and religious traditions, and to serve the cause of reconciliation and peace. The books published reflect the views of their authors and do not represent the official position of the Maryknoll Society. To learn more about Maryknoll and Orbis Books, please visit our website at www.maryknollsociety.org.

Copyright © 2024 by Ashley Theuring

Published by Orbis Books, Box 302, Maryknoll, NY 10545-0302.

All rights reserved.

Scripture quotations, unless otherwise noted, are from New Revised Standard Version Bible: Catholic Edition, copyright © 1989, 1993 National Council of the Churches of Christ in the United States of America. Used by permission. All rights reserved worldwide.

No part of this publication may be reproduced or transmitted in any form or by any means, electronic or mechanical, including photocopying, recording or any information storage or retrieval system, without prior permission in writing from the publisher.

Queries regarding rights and permissions should be addressed to: Orbis Books, P.O. Box 302, Maryknoll, New York 10545-0302.

Manufactured in the United States of America

Library of Congress Cataloging-in-Publication Data

Names: Theuring, Ashley, author.
Title: Sacrifice lost : the dark legacy of the cross / Ashley Theuring.
Description: Maryknoll, NY : Orbis Books, [2024] | Includes bibliographical references and index. | Summary: "Examines atonement theology in light of clergy perpetrated sexual abuse in the Roman Catholic Church"— Provided by publisher.
Identifiers: LCCN 2024034727 (print) | LCCN 2024034728 (ebook) | ISBN 9781626986152 (print) | ISBN 9798888660706 (ebook)
Subjects: LCSH: Atonement. | Child sexual abuse by clergy. | Catholic Church—Clergy—Sexual behavior.
Classification: LCC BT265.3 .T44 2024 (print) | LCC BT265.3 (ebook) | DDC 232/.3—dc23/eng/20240906
LC record available at https://lccn.loc.gov/2024034727
LC ebook record available at https://lccn.loc.gov/2024034728

*For the survivors who willingly shared their stories
and for all those who have yet to find the language*

Contents

Acknowledgments   ix

Introduction   xi

Part I
Unraveling the Cross:
Investigating Atonement Narratives

1. Sacrifice Empowered: Atonement and Salvation   3
2. Sacrifice Questioned: Critiques of the Classical Atonements   17
3. The Darker Side of Atonement Theories   35

Part II
The Crisis in Context:
Clergy Sexual Abuse

4. The Nature and History of the Clergy Sexual Abuse Crisis   63
5. Causes of the Clergy Sexual Abuse Crisis   75
6. The Fallout: Morally Injured Individuals and Communities   93
7. Recovery Needs for Individuals and Communities   110

Part III
Salvation Reimagined:
The Cross and Resurrection of Survivors

8. The Power of Trauma-Sensitive Passion Narratives: Purpose and Themes   131
9. A Narrative of the Crucifixion of Clergy Sexual Abuse   156
10. A Vision of Hope, Justice, and Resurrection   181
11. Looking toward a Survivor-Centered Future   208

Index   227

Acknowledgments

The journey to confront the clergy sexual abuse crisis through my work has been a long and complex one. Though the issue was initially too politically charged and emotionally raw for my early scholarship, my desire to address it through a trauma-informed lens has been a persistent calling. As a theologian, my vocation is to amplify the voices of those on the peripheries of our church communities, bringing them to the forefront where they belong. My work—in research, writing, and teaching—has been a continuous exploration of the sacramental dimensions in the lives of those who embody Christ most closely.

This book began to take shape in my mind during the fall of 2019. At the American Academy of Religions and Society of Biblical Literature conference, engaging discussions with ARC (Arts, Religion, and Culture) and Moral Injury working groups ignited my curiosity. Presenting on the panel "Creative Practice, Community Healing, and Trauma's Wake: Theopoetics in Conversation with Moral Injury" marked my initial attempt into integrating the concept of moral injury into my research.

In spring 2020, I embarked on a two-year research endeavor with a talented team of scholars from Xavier University, funded by the Taking Responsibility project at Fordham University. This interdisciplinary team, comprising theologians Dr. Marcus Mescher and Dr. Gillian Ahlgren, psychologist Dr. Anne Fuller, sociologist Dr. Kandi Stinson, and myself, aimed to explore the depths of moral injury within the context of the clergy sexual abuse crisis. Our work was supported by several graduate students from theology and psychology departments, notably Jonathan Hesford, Skyler Clark, Rachel Wolen, Giovanna Marin, Katie Saba, and Shannon Carley. Dr. Anne Fuller's expertise in statistical and quantitative analysis was invaluable in shaping this book's research backbone.

Parallel to this practical theological research, my constructive theological inquiries continued to evolve. Following the reception of my first book, *Fragile Resurrection: Practicing Hope after Domestic Violence*, I found myself delving deeper into christological questions that had surfaced. Encouraged by my colleague and mentor, Dr. Kristine Suna-Koro, I penned an article for *Dialog* titled "Fragile Crucifixion and Immigrant Survivors of Domestic Violence,"[1] which provided a platform to explore the interplay between my resurrection theology and a potential reexamination of the crucifixion narrative.

Xavier University's support was instrumental in this journey, granting me a Summer Research Fellowship in 2021 to begin outlining and drafting the initial chapters. A pretenure research sabbatical in the spring of 2023 afforded me the opportunity to complete a full first draft. The intellectual and emotional support of my colleagues was a constant source of encouragement and inspiration. Special thanks to Dr. Anna Miller, Dr. Gillian Ahlgren, Dr. Arthur Dewey, Dr. Martin Madar, Dr. Marcus Mescher, and Dr. Kristine Suna-Koro for their invaluable contributions, ranging from brainstorming sessions to meticulous draft reviews.

Lastly, I extend my deepest gratitude to my family, whose steadfast support made this project possible. My mother and mother-in-law, Beth and Cathy, were always there to spend time with their granddaughter, and my husband, Chris, patiently read my early drafts and often took over parenting duties to give me time to write. Their support has been crucial throughout this project.

---

1. *Dialog* 60, no. 3 (2021): 270–77.

Introduction

"I think the Protestant Reformation was a walk in the park compared to what they're facing now."
—Michael, survivor of clergy sexual abuse

When Michael was a mere eleven years old, he experienced abuse at the hands of his parish priest—a trusted figure in his tight-knit Catholic community.[1] Over the next three years, two more priests, both with prior accusations of abuse, likewise betrayed his trust in unimaginable ways. Michael grew up in a large Catholic family, in a predominantly Catholic part of the city. He'd been thrilled to serve as an altar boy, proudly donning his older brother's hand-me-down cassock. Yet the very institution he loved became the source of his deepest pain.

The two abusive priests had been moved to his parish after being accused of sexual abuse of children at their previous churches, and were subsequently moved several more times, with no intervention or accountability or justice being demanded of them. "[The church officials] let it happen," Michael, now in his fifties, told me with a heavy sigh. "They knew, and they let it happen. . . . No one knew more. No one did less than the church officials themselves."

Years after the abuse ended, Michael's journey toward healing has been fraught with obstacles, including alcoholism and PTSD. And as he battled his inner demons, his abusers lived out their days unpunished, residing in a retirement home specifically for priests accused of abuse. Calling it a "prayer and penance" program, Michael was frustrated by the lack of accountability, the absence of

---

1. The words of the survivor referred to as "Michael" throughout this book are from Survivor Transcript 10, taken from interviews with clergy abuse survivors done in the winter and spring of 2021 through research completed at Xavier University and supported by the Taking Responsibility grant through Fordham University.

justice, and the complete ignorance of most of the people within the church community. "It baffles me. Church officials in the Catholic Church are so divorced from reality—what is going on. It is scary.... They have absolutely no concept of what victims go through on a daily basis." Michael's faith, once a cornerstone of his identity, was shattered by the priests and by an institution that ignored his cries for justice. Though he no longer identifies as Catholic, he remains a spiritual individual, still seeking some form of divine peace.

How should testimonies from abuse survivors, such as Michael, shape our understanding of theology amid the clergy abuse crisis? Abuse by clergy is far more than a set of isolated incidents: it's symptomatic of deeper, systemic problems within modern church structures. What dark influences within our cultural and religious narratives enable such abuse? How does the abuse affect not only the survivors but the entire faith community? And why has church leadership's response often been shrouded in silence, shame, and guilt, with so little attention to the victims? This project will tackle the crisis from three perspectives: the contributing factors before the abuse, the consequences during the abuse, and the aftermath, which often includes a damaging silence by the church community toward victims and the larger community. This silence, used to protect abusers, ultimately stifles conversations around the behaviors and beliefs that permit such abuse to happen and go unpunished.

Michael is just one among hundreds of thousands of survivors in the United States, left in the shadows by an institution that proclaims a mission to protect the most vulnerable. This stark irony underlines the church communities' failure to safeguard those they vowed to defend. This book amplifies the voices and stories of these survivors, instead of ignoring or even actively thwarting them, insistently seeking insights that lead to healing, while demanding transformative reform within our church structures.

How Narratives Shape Our World and Faith

In her seminal work *She Who Is: The Mystery of God in Feminist Theological Discourse*, feminist theologian Elizabeth Johnson makes a compelling case that the way we talk about God matters, claiming that "the symbol of God functions."[2] This notion that our language

---

2. Elizabeth A. Johnson, "Female Symbols for God: The Apophatic Tradition

influences our perspective, shaping our worldview, is echoed across disciplines—from literature and cultural studies to psychology and sociology. Theorists have repeatedly found that our language structures, including vocabulary, grammar, and narratives, shape how we see the world, ourselves, and one another. For instance, research by Karen E. Dill-Shackleford and colleagues suggests that reading narrative fiction can actually make us more empathic and open-minded. This occurs, they find, through a process of a "dual empathy," defined as "simultaneously engaging in intense personal processing while also 'feeling through' characters."[3] Their study shows that narratives can have a powerful moral impact on individuals.

Why does this matter? Because, as neuroscientist Dr. Flavius Raslau puts it, "two people can look at the same world and yet not see the same world, merely on account of their lexicon."[4] Our culture, lived experience, and language all shape how we see and experience our world. This does not mean that objective truth is elusive. Rather, our grasp of it is always tinged by our subjective experiences. To put it simply, we learn and understand through metaphor. Again, Raslau explains that "to accept metaphor is not to deny that those concepts have an independent reality. Metaphor is simply how we get a grip on that reality."[5]

Today, a variety of language systems influence how we "get a grip" on our world. Christian theology, rich in its own set of narratives and metaphors, has profoundly influenced Western society. These are not mere words, but living, breathing concepts that help us wrestle with life's biggest questions, from the nature of God to the meaning of suffering. Sometimes, though, these living metaphors turn into fossilized ideas that no longer serve us. The task for modern theologians is to breathe new life into these ancient words, allowing them to resonate with the world we live in today.

---

and Social Justice," *International Journal of Orthodox Theology* 1, no. 2 (2010): 40–57, 40.

3. Karen E. Dill-Shackleford, Cynthia Vinney, and Kristin Hopper-Losenicky, "Connecting the Dots between Fantasy and Reality: The Social Psychology of Our Engagement with Fictional Narrative and Its Functional Value," *Social and Personality Psychology Compass* 10, no. 11 (2016): 634–46, 634.

4. Falvius Raslau, "Updated Christus Victor: A Neurotheological Perspective," *Journal of Psychology and Christianity* 40, no. 4 (2021): 329–43, 331.

5. Raslau, "Updated Christus Victor," 332.

Consider, for example, the concept of atonement—literally "at-one-ment." It's a centuries-old theological term that articulates how the life, death, and resurrection of Jesus reconciles humanity with the Divine. These narratives, filled with notions of good, evil, and sacrifice, shape our values and beliefs in profound ways we often don't even realize. Throughout history, the suffering of Jesus on the cross has been understood as an example of Christ's solidarity with our own experiences of suffering. Jesus's death on the cross is one of the ways in which Christians throughout history have connected to their faith. These narratives can offer comfort in times of hardship; for example, African Americans have found echoes of their own struggles against slavery and racism in the story of Jesus's suffering.[6]

Until recently, these effects were largely anecdotal. But psychologists have now begun to quantify the influence of atonement theories on mental well-being.[7] Researchers like Saima Riaz and Sabahat Nawaz have started to measure attitudes toward themes such as redemption and justice, while Curtis Abbott explores how the concept of atonement resembles psychological transference—the act of temporarily projecting one's pain and trauma onto another, a therapist, for example, while one engages in the work of healing.[8] This would point to the psychological healing potential in the narrative of atonement, where humanity transfers our pain, suffering, and guilt onto Jesus.

Raslau argues that atonement narratives can actually be an important way of understanding our own neuropsychology. They can serve as a framework for understanding—and healing—certain maladaptive psychological pathways. In essence, stories of atonement may offer a form of cognitive restructuring, helping us to break down destructive habits and replace them with healthier ones that "manifest the Spirit of God."[9]

---

6. James A. Noel and Matthew V. Johnson Sr., "Psychological Trauma, Christ's Passion, and the African American Faith Tradition," *Pastoral Psychology* 53, no. 4 (March 2005): 361–69, 361.

7. Saima Riaz and Sabahat Nawaz, "Development of the Attitude Atonement Scale for Adults," *Journal of Behavioral Sciences* 32, no. 1 (2022): 165–88.

8. Curtis Abbott, "The Blood of Recognition—Atonement and Transference in Psychoanalytically Based Pastoral Psychotherapy," *Journal of Spirituality in Mental Health* 10, no. 4 (2008): 265–307.

9. Raslau, "Updated Christus Victor," 336.

Introduction

Our atonement vocabulary and metaphors have the power to shape many of our contemporary worldviews. However, the power of these stories can also be misused. Rita Nakashima Brock warns that certain interpretations can exacerbate trauma by focusing on themes of guilt and fallenness.[10] In worse cases, they've been used to justify keeping women in abusive relationships.[11] In the chapters that follow, we'll explore these narratives, examining them through feminist, liberation, and nonviolent lenses. We'll ask the hard questions about how these ancient stories can be both liberating and limiting, and explore alternative ways in which they might resonate more positively with the challenges and opportunities of our contemporary world.

Enabling Abuse: The Underbelly of Atonement Theories

The clergy sexual abuse crisis within the Catholic Church serves as a distressing case study of how theological ideas, like those concerning atonement, can have real-world consequences. We will survey the full scope of this crisis in Part II of this book, but for now, let's grasp its enormous impact. In the United States alone, thousands of priests have been credibly accused of sexual abuse by tens of thousands of victims.[12] While most research focuses on child abuse, particularly against male children, emerging data suggests that adult abuse might also be pervasive but underreported.

This crisis affects not only survivors and perpetrators; it reverberates through the entire Catholic community. One in four U.S.

---

10. Rita Nakashima Brock, "Post Traumatic Stress, Moral Injury, and Soul Repair: Implications for Western Christian Theology," in D. Evers et al. (eds.), *Issues in Science and Theology: Do Emotions Shape the World?*, Issues in Science and Religion: Publications of the European Society for the Study of Science and Theology 3 (Cham, Switzerland: Springer, 2016): 27–40.

11. Augustus Nzioki Muthangya, Stephen Muoki Joshua, Tsawe-Munga Chidongo, and Francis Gikonyo Wokabi, "When Bible Becomes Harmful to Women: An Analysis of Textual Usages in Promoting Intimate Partner Violence among Christian Women of Kilifi County," *International Journal of Contemporary Applied Researches* 10, no. 1 (January 2023): 1–19.

12. John Jay College of Criminal Justice, "The Nature and Scope of the Problem of Sexual Abuse of Minors by Catholic Priests and Deacons in the United States" (New York, February 2004), 285, https://www.bishop-accountability.org/reports/2004_02_27_JohnJay_revised.

Catholics have scaled back their Mass attendance and donations to the Catholic Church due to the clergy sexual abuse crisis.[13] Despite systemic efforts to implement safety programs and best practices within church communities since the early 2000s, two-thirds of Catholics believe that clergy sexual abuse is still a current issue.[14]

While it is common to discuss sexual abuse in terms of trauma and post-traumatic stress disorder (PTSD), abuse within a religious setting adds another layer of complexity to an individual's suffering. Len Sperry introduces the term "sacred moral injury" to describe the unique suffering endured by survivors of clergy abuse. This goes beyond PTSD: it involves both the moral failure of the individual abuser and the systemic failure of the religious institution that enabled the abuse.[15]

Atonement theories can complicate survivors' experiences of abuse and the impact of "sacred moral injury." Our religious narratives influence how we think about sin, suffering, and redemption. So, when a survivor tries to make sense of the abuse, their understanding is often clouded by these existing beliefs about God, suffering, and human guilt, or, indeed, the perpetrator might even remind them of their sinfulness and guilt. Chapter 3 will explore specific examples of that; for now, it is essential to recognize that these narratives can make the healing process even more complex.

Atonement narratives do more than complicate healing: they can perpetuate the environment that allows such abuse to happen in the first place. Our classical interpretations of atonement are often tied to societal constructs like patriarchy and sexism, identified since the civil rights and feminist movements of the 1970s as underlying causes of sexual abuse. These traditional narratives tend to reinforce a hierarchical relationship between humanity and the Divine. Many trace their origins to medieval structures, such as serfdom, which were inherently oppressive. Moreover, they perpetuate the myth of perfection, implying that certain individu-

---

13. Pew Research Center, "Americans See Catholic Clergy Sex Abuse as an Ongoing Problem," June 11, 2019.

14. Pew Research Center, "Americans See Catholic Clergy Sex Abuse as an Ongoing Problem," June 11, 2019.

15. L. Sperry, "Psychotherapy Alone Is Insufficient: Treating Clergy Sexual Abuse and Sacred Moral Injury," *Spirituality in Clinical Practice* 10, no. 4 (2022): 350–57.

als or systems are exemplary, sinless, and above criticism. To put it bluntly, the language of atonement is not merely academic; it shapes attitudes and beliefs that can either challenge or perpetuate systemic abuse. Understanding this connection is crucial if we are to disentangle the harmful consequences of these deeply rooted narratives.

The Power and Pitfalls of Narratives in Trauma Healing

The language we use, especially in the realm of Christian atonement, shapes the experience of trauma and molds the path to healing. Psychologists have long investigated the effects of narratives on the mental health of individuals. In a meta-analysis of psychological literature on the topic, psychologist J. Llewellyn-Beardsley and colleagues discovered nine major dimensions to mental health recovery narratives.[16] Their work revealed that recovery stories are as diverse as they are nuanced—that there's no one-size-fits-all. Like trauma narratives themselves, recovery narratives are nonlinear and resist coherence. The psychologists concluded that clinicians should offer a spectrum of healing narratives to their patients, allowing for individualized recovery.

In the spirit of expanding those healing narratives, I investigate the ability for atonement narratives to act as narratives of healing. Christian teachings about atonement often center on Jesus's life and sacrifice as a source of healing—mending the rift between humans and the Divine. While this metaphor can offer comfort to survivors of abuse, it can also worsen their trauma by emphasizing guilt, shame, and self-sacrifice.

For atonement narratives to have a positive impact on trauma healing, they need to contribute to and encourage "post-traumatic growth," a term coined by psychologists Lawrence Calhoun and Richard Tedeschi.[17] Post-traumatic growth is a positive psychologi-

---

16. Including genre, positioning, emotional tone, relationship with recovery, trajectory, turning points, narrative sequence, protagonists, and use of metaphors. See Joy Llewellyn-Beardsley, Stefan Rennick-Egglestone, Felicity Callard, Paul Crawford, Marianne Farkas, Ada Hui, David Manley et al., "Characteristics of Mental Health Recovery Narratives: Systematic Review and Narrative Synthesis," *PloS ONE* 14, no. 3 (2019): e0214678.

17. Richard G. Tedeschi and Lawrence G. Calhoun, "The Posttraumatic Growth

cal change that can follow trauma. Studies indicate that survivors who adopt a "survivor identity" often experience significant personal growth.[18] For instance, a study involving 252 Israeli adults found a link between trauma exposure and higher reactive self-efficacy scores, emotional creativity, and divergent thinking.[19]

Research also supports the significance of positive self-narratives in fostering post-traumatic growth. Small studies on survivors of childhood abuse show that constructing a positive self-narrative, while acknowledging the lingering trauma, can be critical for post-traumatic growth.[20] Changes in societal attitudes and language can similarly affect how survivors perceive themselves, reinforcing that the stories we tell matter in both trauma and healing.[21]

As we'll explore in coming chapters, the idea that self-sacrifice is good and essential is one of the most controversial aspects of atonement narratives. Does growth necessitate suffering? Current research on both post-traumatic and post-ecstatic growth offers a resounding "No!" A meta-analysis by Judith Mangelsdorf, Michael Eid, and Maike Luhmann found that both good and bad experiences contribute equally to postevent growth.[22] The takeaway is twofold: suffering is not a prerequisite for growth, but, if it occurs, growth is still possible. This reframes how we should approach trauma and healing, questioning some of the core tenets of traditional atonement theories.

Inventory: Measuring the Positive Legacy of Trauma," *Journal of Traumatic Stress* 9 (1996): 455–71.

18. H. S. Bryngeirsdottir and S. Halldorsdottir, "'I'm a Winner, Not a Victim': The Facilitating Factors of Post-Traumatic Growth among Women Who Have Suffered Intimate Partner Violence," *International Journal of Environmental Research and Public Health* 19, no. 3 (2022): 1342, doi: 10.3390/ijerph19031342.

19. Hod Orkibi and Neta Ram-Vlasov, "Linking Trauma to Posttraumatic Growth and Mental Health through Emotional and Cognitive Creativity," *Psychology of Aesthetics, Creativity, and the Arts* 13, no. 4 (2019): 416–30.

20. Grace Sheridan and Alan Carr, "Survivors' Lived Experiences of Post-traumatic Growth after Institutional Childhood Abuse: An Interpretative Phenomenological Analysis," *Child Abuse & Neglect* 103 (2020): 104430, https://doi.org/10.1016/j.chiabu.2020.104430.

21. Sheridan and Carr, "Survivors' Lived Experiences," 9.

22. Judith Mangelsdorf, Michael Eid, and Maike Luhmann, "Does Growth Require Suffering? A Systematic Review and Meta-Analysis on Genuine Posttraumatic and Postecstatic Growth," *Psychological Bulletin* 145, no. 3 (2019): 302–38.

Introduction   xix

Methodology

A profound question raised by Lucy Tatman in her 1996 article "Atonement," featured in the book *An A to Z of Feminist Theology*, inspired me to research and write this book. Tatman zeroes in on a pressing issue: How can we understand atonement in a way that doesn't glorify suffering, yet still addresses the real pain and struggles people face every day?[23]

In response, I prioritize the Catholic liberation principle of focusing on society's most vulnerable—the "preferential option for the poor." My work, explored in depth in earlier writings,[24] aims to bridge the gap between long-standing religious traditions and the very real experiences of those who suffer today. Central to this book are survivors of clergy sexual abuse—a group whose anguish and trials must not be ignored.

For this particular practical theological project, using a blend of theological and ethnographic research methods, I collected survivors' stories and experiences of their abuse and healing. Thanks to a large research grant from Fordham University, under the Taking Responsibility project series, I was part of a research team that investigated this issue.[25] This funding enabled us to administer a pioneering survey studying moral injury among various groups, including university students, church staff, and abuse survivors. As part of this study, I personally interviewed fifteen survivors of clergy abuse. This blend of personal stories and hard data serves a dual purpose. First, it challenges established religious views on atonement. Second, it provides the foundation for a fresh narrative on the subject—one that is both relatable and transformative.

So, I am not just questioning old beliefs in this book, but proposing new ones, ones aimed at healing and growth. Through this book, I invite you to join me in taking a step toward changing how we—especially we in the church community—understand suffering, forgiveness, and spiritual renewal.

---

23. Lucy Tatman, "Atonement," in *An A to Z of Feminist Theology*, ed. Lisa Isherwood and Dorothea McEwan (Sheffield, England: Sheffield Academic Press, 1996), 12–15, 12.

24. Ashley Theuring, "Imagining a Sacramental Method: Divine Presence in the Lives of the Crucified Peoples," *Ecclesial Practices* 8 (2021): 11–25.

25. Research project website: https://takingresponsibility.ace.fordham.edu/measuring-moral-injury.

Chapter Summaries

In chapter 1, "Sacrifice Empowered: Atonement and Salvation," I survey major atonement theologies and their contemporary critiques, guided by the experience of a clergy sexual abuse survivor, Nathan. His story both frames our exploration and illuminates how Christian atonement concepts can offer healing, strength, and a means of making meaning. We examine three classical theories of atonement: *Christus Victor*, substitutionary atonement, and moral influence. In chapter 2, I present the modern critiques, largely from feminist, liberation, and nonviolent theological perspectives, to these three classical atonement theories. These critiques focus on issues surrounding theodicy and the concept of self-sacrifice.

Chapter 3, "The Darker Side of Atonement Theories," shifts the focus to the potentially harmful impact of classical atonement theories on trauma survivors, especially those who have suffered sexual abuse. This chapter presents a broad view of sexual abuse in the United States, integrating the specific experiences of clergy abuse survivors. Building on the critical perspectives introduced in chapter 2, this chapter considers the influence of these theologies on survivors' interpretations of their abuse. I conclude this chapter with a pressing call for the reimagining of contemporary cross narratives in the context of trauma theory and the experiences of abuse survivors, acknowledging their potential to inflict moral injury.

In Part II of the book, spanning chapters 4, 5, 6, and 7, I present a comprehensive exploration of the clergy sexual abuse crisis within the U.S. Catholic Church. This in-depth analysis sets the stage for later chapters where I will reconstruct the narrative of the crucifixion. Chapter 4, "The Nature and History of the Clergy Sexual Abuse Crisis," focuses on the intricate dynamics of abuse committed by priests, highlighting how their revered status can intensify the trauma for victims. Chapter 5 surveys the societal and personal factors that contribute to clergy abuse, emphasizing issues like clericalism and flaws in the formation of priests. Chapter 6, "The Fallout: Morally Injured Individuals and Communities," expands the conversation to include the wider impact of abuse, not only on individual victims but also on the entire faith community. Here, I introduce "moral injury" as a framework to understand the broader trauma inflicted by the abuse crisis, informed by insights from the Taking Responsibility project. Following, chapter 7 focuses on healing for individuals and communities. This chapter also contrasts the church leadership's historical response to the crisis with recognized best practices for managing sexual abuse within institutions, laying the groundwork for a reimagined understanding of the crucifixion in subsequent chapters.

The final section, including chapters 8 through 11, reimagines the narratives of crucifixion and resurrection through the experiences of clergy sexual abuse survivors. Chapter 8, "The Power of Trauma-Sensitive Passion Narratives: Purpose and Themes," revisits biblical passion narratives and contemporary theological writings, offering a critical analysis of the Gospel of Mark. This examination uncovers key themes for a modern understanding of the crucifixion, linking them to the concept of moral injury. In chapters 9 and 10, these renewed themes are woven into the narratives shared by survivors. This process results in a reenvisioned narrative of the crucifixion and resurrection, placing the experiences of survivors at the theological heart of the church.

The book culminates in chapter 11, "Looking toward a Survivor-Centered Future," where I discuss the broader implications of this work. This chapter brings the impact on academic discourse to the fore, particularly in feminist theology, by examining how atonement theories function in the lives of sexual abuse survivors. Theologically, it probes the implications for Christology and the significance of Jesus. Finally, I connect the book's major themes to the current landscape of trauma within the Catholic Church, emphasizing the urgent need for continued focus on clergy sexual abuse and paths toward healing and reform.

Part I

Unraveling the Cross

Investigating Atonement Narratives

1

Sacrifice Empowered

Atonement and Salvation

"If Jesus Christ can do what he did, entering Jerusalem on Palm Sunday, to a certain and known fate, then I can do this."
—Nathan, survivor of clergy sexual abuse

For many survivors of trauma, stories of suffering and healing offer crucial insights into their own journeys. Among these narratives, the crucifixion of Jesus in Christianity stands as a pivotal symbol of suffering, sacrifice, and salvation. Known in theological terms as "atonement," this concept has evolved over the past two millennia, shaped by historical forces like the Roman Empire and neocolonialism. To understand the potential impact of these narratives on survivors, let's delve into the story of Nathan, a survivor of clergy sexual abuse, whose profound connection with Jesus and the cross illuminates both the comforting and complex aspects of these narratives.[1]

In my interviews with survivors, I found that their references to the cross and Jesus varied widely, from sources of comfort to causes of distress. Nathan's account, however, offers a unique perspective. Despite enduring trauma at the hands of the church, he finds solace

---

1. The words of the survivor referred to as "Nathan" throughout this book are from Survivor Transcript 2, taken from interviews with clergy abuse survivors done in the winter and spring of 2021 through research completed at Xavier University and supported by the Taking Responsibility grant through Fordham University.

and strength in the narrative of Jesus's suffering and sacrifice. His journey, marked by a relentless quest for justice, mirrors the sacrifice he attributes to Jesus's mission. This connection, though laden with theological intricacies, provides Nathan with a framework to process his suffering and his fight for justice.

As we explore Nathan's story, we uncover the multifaceted nature of atonement theories and their profound impact on individuals grappling with deep-seated trauma. Nathan's experience exemplifies how atonement narratives, even when problematic, can help survivors make sense of their lives and find a semblance of healing. His relationship with Jesus and the cross, emerging as a beacon of hope in his struggle, is both complex and empowering. This narrative, while messy and far from straightforward, highlights the significant role such stories play in the healing process. Nathan's story will also reveal the intricate and often disturbing imperial influences that have shaped our contemporary understanding of salvation.

Nathan and His Sacrifice

Nathan's ordeal began in elementary school, continuing through high school. His abuser, a priest and teacher, groomed him from the age of ten, using the confessional's privacy to initiate inappropriate contact. This pattern of abuse extended to board-game nights at the rectory and altar-serving duties, with other adults seemingly oblivious to the wrongdoing.

As Nathan progressed through school, the abuse persisted, with other priests exploiting situations like locker rooms and even a mission trip to further their predatory behavior. This period left indelible scars on Nathan, yet he managed to pursue a semblance of normalcy in college, away from these traumatic experiences.

However, the shadow of his past loomed large, particularly as he approached his college graduation. In the following years, despite starting a family, Nathan grappled with deep-seated issues relating to his sexuality and mental health, even unknowingly reenacting aspects of his abuse.

It wasn't until 2002, with the widespread media coverage of clergy sexual abuse—including the *Boston Globe*'s Spotlight investigation and report on the abuse and coverup of sexual abuse in the Boston Archdiocese—that Nathan began to understand and confront his trauma. What followed was a decade-long struggle for healing, marked by unresponsive church authorities, debilitating panic attacks, and eventual job loss.

In seeking help from his church community, Nathan encountered denial and ostracism, which exacerbated his pain. "The biggest mistake I ever made was going to the Catholic Church for help," he confided. Now, years later, Nathan dedicates himself to survivor advocacy, hoping to prevent such tragedies for others, a testament to his resilience and strength.

Nathan's journey, emblematic of the varied paths of healing among survivors, oscillates between progress and enduring challenges. Despite gaining clarity and language to articulate his experiences, he remains deeply affected, with regular mental health challenges and difficulties in maintaining consistent work and relationships. His story poignantly shows the long-term impacts of such trauma.

In a striking contrast, Nathan's faith has not only endured but deepened. "I actually feel closer to Jesus Christ now than I ever have," he confides, drawing strength from perceived parallels between his advocacy for justice and Jesus's mission. This unexpected source of empowerment shows us the complex ways in which faith can provide solace and purpose in the aftermath of trauma.

Nathan views his advocacy as a missional continuation of Jesus's struggle against institutional oppression. "Jesus was fighting institutions. Jesus was crucified by a powerful institution. So how is [my experience] any different than what Jesus went through?" he questions. This identification with Jesus's suffering offers Nathan a powerful lens through which to understand and navigate his own journey of resistance and healing.

Furthermore, Nathan's grappling with his gender identity in the wake of abuse is telling. He associates sacrifice with traditional male roles, seeing his advocacy as part of a larger battle, akin to warfare. "The best aspects of being male is being sacrificed, and realizing, or willing to sacrifice yourself for a higher purpose," he muses, reflecting his struggle with sexual identity following the abuse and his effort to reconcile these feelings with societal expectations of masculinity. This interplay of personal struggle and societal expectations adds another layer to Nathan's complex narrative.

Yet, Nathan's story is not an isolated case. It represents a broader pattern of clergy sexual abuse sustained by a culture of secrecy and clericalism within church structures. His reliance on atonement narratives to make sense of his suffering raises important questions about the role of such narratives in processing trauma. While they offer a framework for empowerment, their implications are not straightforward, necessitating a critical reevaluation in light of contemporary ethical and experiential realities.

In conclusion, Nathan's journey is a testament to resilience and the human capacity to find meaning in the face of profound suffering. His story invites us to consider the ongoing significance and reinterpretation of theological concepts such as atonement, particularly in the context of modern challenges and traumas. His narrative, though deeply personal, touches on universal themes of suffering, healing, and the quest for meaning, resonating far beyond the confines of his individual experience.

Classical Theories of Atonement

Many survivors of trauma, Nathan included, gravitate toward familiar narratives as a way to frame and make sense of their suffering. These narratives not only provide language and scaffolding to articulate their experiences, but they often point toward a hopeful future. The power of the crucifixion narrative lies in its acknowledgment of profound suffering and in its promise of resurrection and renewal. For survivors like Nathan, connecting their personal struggles to such narratives offers a sense of strength and a hopeful outlook toward healing.

In Nathan's case, aligning his experience of abuse and his quest for justice with Jesus's mission and sacrifice infuses his own journey with purpose and hope. Through this narrative lens, Nathan sees his own self-sacrifice as meaningful. Similar themes of sacrifice, redemption, and ultimate triumph over adversity echo in the experiences of many survivors, mirroring their paths toward recovery. The atonement themes they draw upon often blend elements of classical atonement theories, though they might not align perfectly with systematic theological logic.

As we venture into constructing a renewed narrative of the crucifixion in the third and final part of this book, gaining an understanding of the most prominent classical atonement theories in Christian tradition will be invaluable. This knowledge enriches our perspective by providing a foundation for reimagining these narratives in a way that resonates with contemporary experiences of trauma and healing.

Christus Victor and Recapitulation Theories

The *Christus Victor* and recapitulation theories, the earliest systematic models of atonement in Christian theology, assert that Jesus's life, death, and resurrection were a victory over evil, death, and the devil. *Christus Victor*, or Christ's victory over death and sin, results in the restoration of humanity's unity with God, which had been hindered by sin and death. In some versions of this atonement model, Jesus is not just seen as victorious over death. He is seen as the new Adam, restoring humanity to its rightful nature. Recapitulation, or the summation of humanity in Jesus, focuses on the Incarnation's role in reversing the fall. The divine intervention of Jesus's Incarnation is what ultimately leads to victory, making these models popular in contemporary discussions about the significance of the Incarnation.

Historically, this model has its roots in both Hebrew and Christian Scriptures. In the Jewish tradition, the Passover and Exodus narratives set a precedent for salvation through divine intervention. In the book of Exodus, God intervenes through Moses to liberate the Israelites from Egyptian bondage. Through miracles and divine victory over Pharaoh and the Egyptians, in addition to the recommitment of the Israelites to God's law, the covenant is restored.

These motifs of captivity and liberation resonate through later Christian Scripture, particularly in Paul's writings and the Gospel of Matthew, portraying Jesus's mission as salvific. In the Letter to the Hebrews, Paul uses the language of bondage and liberation to describe Jesus's Incarnation and death.[2] He depicts humanity as

---

2. Heb. 2:14–15 (NRSV). See also N. T. Wright, "Get the Story Right and the Models Will Fit," in *Atonement: Jewish and Christian Origins*, ed. Max Botner et al. (Grand Rapids: Eerdmans, 2020), 112–30, 122; Reta Halteman Finger, "How Can Jesus Save Women? Three Theories on Christ's Atonement," *Daughters of Sarah* 14, no. 6 (1988): 14–18, 17.

enslaved by the fear of death. Jesus overthrows the power of death, held unjustly by the devil, by sharing in human flesh and blood. While Paul uses other metaphors and narratives of salvation that align with other classical theories, we see scriptural support here for the *Christus Victor* model.

Early theologians such as Irenaeus, Origen, and Augustine echoed this idea, linking Jesus's Incarnation and death to human salvation. In his work *Against Heresies*, Irenaeus argues that Jesus's Incarnation is so comprehensive that it restores humanity's image and likeness of God, which was lost in the fall of Adam. In solidarity with humanity, Irenaeus claims that Jesus also makes humanity divine.[3]

The modern revival of this model is largely credited to Lutheran Bishop Gustav Aulén's 1931 work, *Christus Victor*. Drawing on Irenaeus, Aulén argued that humanity's liberation from sin, death, and the devil was achieved through the Incarnation, which unifies the human Jesus with the divine Christ. In this version of the narrative, Christ's life, death, resurrection, and the works of the Holy Spirit all contribute to our salvation. This is possible because of the dual nature of Christ, embodying both the active divine reconciler and the passive reconciled human.[4]

This theory's focus on the Incarnation is one of its primary strengths. Jesus Christ's dual nature within his singular person provides a symbol of hope for humanity, a symbol of the repaired relationship between God and humanity. The Incarnation allows humanity to see themselves in Jesus, as Nathan does in his healing journey. By connecting to Jesus's humanity, Christians can see themselves already in unity with God. Christ was and is victorious, and we are promised salvation because of what has already happened.

Christus Victor theories also acknowledge both systemic and individual evil. Nathan's narrative, for example, reflects a belief in the reality of evil, including a vivid portrayal of Satan's role in the clergy sexual abuse crisis. Nathan lamented many Christians' "refusal to acknowledge the power of Satan." He believed that, by recogniz-

---

3. Irenaeus, "Against Heresies," preface to book 5, in *The Writings of Irenaeus*, vol. 2, ed. A. Roberts and J. Donaldson (Edinburgh: T. & T. Clark, 1869), 55.

4. Gustaf Aulén, *Christus Victor: An Historical Study of the Three Main Types of the Idea of the Atonement*, trans. A. G. Hebert (London: SPCK, 1970 [1931]).

ing Satan's role in the abuse and that "Satan is inside the Catholic Church," Christians could begin to participate in "this battle." The *Christus Victor* narrative offers a framework to identify and combat evil in both its personal and institutional forms.

Because of these strengths, *Christus Victor* has been embraced by feminist, Black, liberation, and nonviolent theologians in contemporary theologies of salvation. These modern interpretations, which we will examine in depth in chapter 8, adapt the theory to address current issues of systemic and individual evil. However, the theory faces criticism for not adequately addressing the *continued* presence of evil after Jesus's life and death.[5] While it declares Jesus as the victor over death and the devil, the persistence of evil, as evidenced in crises like clergy sexual abuse, challenges this narrative and suggests the need for a more nuanced understanding. We will explore these critiques further in the next two chapters.

Substitutionary and Satisfaction Theories

Substitutionary atonement theories, another cornerstone of Christian theology, posit that Jesus's crucifixion was a sacrifice that reconciled God and humanity. This theory views humanity's sinfulness as creating an insurmountable rift with God. Jesus, embodying both divinity and humanity, bridges this divide by sacrificing his life on the cross, thereby paying humanity's debt.[6] Similar to the *Christus Victor* and recapitulation theories, substitutionary theories rely on the Incarnation to overcome sin. But, unlike the previous theories, the healing of the human-God relationship is not complete until Jesus's sacrifice on the cross.

Substitutionary atonement theories also find their roots in both Hebrew and Christian Scriptures. In the Hebrew tradition, the concept of sacrifice, particularly evident in the Day of Atonement rituals, involved the use of a "scapegoat." This practice, deeply embedded in the Jewish understanding of atonement, is not about substituting the life of an animal for a human but is a means to express the intricate relationship between humanity and God. In these rituals, sacrifice serves various purposes: it could be given "in response to

---

5. Pamela Dickey Young, "Beyond Moral Influence to an Atoning Life," *Theology Today* 52, no. 3 (1995): 344–55.
6. Finger, "How Can Jesus Save Women?" 14–18.

distress, suffering, and sin, as well as situations of joy and happiness. Atonement and pleas for forgiveness were juxtaposed with celebrations of gratitude and recognition of divine blessing."[7] These practices were multifaceted, manifesting and solidifying the bond between the Divine and God's people.

In Christian Scripture, this language of sacrifice takes on new dimensions. The Gospel of Mark, for instance, refers to Jesus's mission as a ransom (Mark 10:45) and describes his blood as being "poured out for many" (Mark 14:24), suggesting a sacrificial purpose. Similarly, Paul's writings frequently emphasize the notion that Christ died "for" humanity,[8] underlining the substitutionary aspect of Jesus's death. Most strikingly, as we see in Rom. 8:3, Paul argues that Jesus takes on human sin so that the law might be fulfilled.[9] Substitutionary language is used in these passages, but interpretations of this language vary, reflecting the rich and diverse theological debates surrounding the concept of atonement.

Similar substitutionary language is found in several of the earliest Christian theologians such as Justin Martyr, Augustine, and Athanasius. However, Archbishop Anselm of Canterbury, in the late eleventh century, systematized this concept using the satisfaction models prevalent in medieval serfdom. In his work *Cur Deus Homo*, Anselm's innovative approach conceptualized atonement as a transaction between Jesus and God.

According to Anselm, humanity's sin and disobedience had dishonored God, creating a debt that humans, due to our inherent limitations, were incapable of repaying. The satisfaction required to restore God's honor was beyond human capacity since everything that humans had was already owed to God. Only Jesus, as both God and man, could make satisfaction by willingly offering his life in substitution for humanity. For Anselm, Jesus's willingness to die was an important aspect of his sacrifice. Anselm argued that the death of Jesus was not God's command, but rather this was Jesus's choice of obedience, even to death.[10] Thus, through this sacrificial act, the debt

---

7. Christian A Eberhart, "Atonement," in *Atonement: Jewish and Christian Origins*, ed. Max Botner, Justin Harrison Duff, and Simon Dürr (Grand Rapids: Eerdmans, 2020), 3–20, 11.

8. E.g., Rom. 14:15; 1 Cor. 8:11; 15:3–5; 2 Cor. 5:21; 1 Thess. 5:10.

9. Rom. 8:3 (NRSV).

10. Phil. 2:8 (NRSV).

was paid, the scales of justice were rebalanced, and the possibility of reunification between humanity and God was restored.[11]

Over a hundred years later, in the thirteenth-century Dominican priest Thomas Aquinas expanded Anselm's substitutionary theory of atonement. Aquinas's theological compendium, the *Summa Theologica*, outlines much of his own systematic theology. Most importantly for this conversation, in the Third Part of the *Summa Theologica*, Aquinas understands Jesus's death on the cross as uniquely salvific for several reasons that were not as explicitly included in Anselm's work.

For example, Aquinas finds the type, degree, and class of Jesus's suffering and death as significant to its salvific properties.[12] For Aquinas, Jesus's suffering on the cross is an example of a virtuous death, which connects to the Tree of Knowledge in the Garden of Eden, Noah's Ark, Moses's staff, and—while he didn't experience all types of suffering—Jesus endured the greatest suffering of all. Aquinas argues these points in a hopeful manner, attempting to allay any of humanity's fears of death. These tropes of Jesus's suffering as the greatest and the call for us to take courage in this reality will be significant in the coming chapters.

Like Anselm, Aquinas argues that Jesus died out of obedience to the Father. Aquinas also acknowledges three respects in which God did deliver up Christ to the passion. First, God preordained this passion for the deliverance of the human race. Second, God is responsible for Jesus's nature as someone who would choose this type of suffering and death. Third, God does not intervene, abandoning Jesus to suffer and die on the cross. Aquinas's interpretation here adds to the sense that God the Father is in some way responsible for Jesus's suffering and death.

Theologies of atonement continued to evolve in contextually relevant ways in the sixteenth century. Protestant reformer John Calvin further expanded the substitutionary theories of atonement by bringing in his own training in criminal law. Calvin uniquely applies the concept of "penalty" to the sacrifice of Jesus. In his work *Institutes of the Christian Religion*, Calvin reinforces the previous

---

11. Anselm of Canterbury, "Cur Deus Homo," in *Anselm of Canterbury: The Major Works*, ed. Brian Davies and G. R. Evans, Oxford World's Classics (Oxford: Oxford University Press, 2008), reissue edition.

12. Thomas Aquinas, *Summa Theologica*, III, q. 46.

ideas of atonement proposed by both Anselm and Aquinas, including Jesus's obedience to the Father, the importance of Jesus's divine and human natures, and Jesus as the new Adam. Calvin, in particular, focuses on the importance of Jesus's punishment and suffering on the cross as part of the penalty for sin.

In Calvin's narrative, Jesus must bear the weight of God's wrath. He must stand trial, suffer, and be punished. Using the language of pardon, Calvin believes Jesus must take on the role of a criminal in order to fully release humanity from our just punishment. Jesus subjects himself not just to death but to the cursed death of a criminal, experiencing the same punishment humanity would have endured.[13] Calvin writes, "For, in order to remove our condemnation, it was not sufficient to endure any kind of death. To satisfy our ransom, it was necessary to select a mode of death in which he might deliver us, both by giving himself up to condemnations and undertaking our expiation."[14] Calvin reaffirms Aquinas's claims about Jesus's unique suffering as the greatest suffering but frames it within a punishment model.

A fundamental strength of substitutionary atonement theories is their logical framework, which provides a systematic approach to understanding and engaging in the process of salvation. The emphasis on Jesus's humanity is central to this, fostering a sense of empowerment among believers by spotlighting their potential for an active, personal relationship with God.[15] For Anselm's contemporaries, living within a clearly defined hierarchical system, this concept likely offered a sense of comfort and participation.[16] They could perceive themselves as actively involved in their own salvation, not just as passive recipients of divine grace.

This notion of participatory salvation finds a powerful echo in modern narratives like Nathan's. In his journey, the act of self-sacrifice is not seen as a passive submission to suffering but is reframed as an active, purposeful, and empowering choice. Nathan's dedicated mission to raise awareness and hold church leaders accountable transforms into a personal sacrifice, one that

---

13. John Calvin, *Institutes of the Christian Religion*, 2.16.5, trans. Henry Beveridge (1845; repr., Grand Rapids: Eerdmans, 1989).

14. Calvin, *Institutes*, 2.16.6.

15. Flora A. Keshgegian, "The Scandal of the Cross: Revisiting Anselm and His Feminist Critics," *Anglican Theological Review* 82, no. 3 (2000): 475–92, 483.

16. Keshgegian, "The Scandal of the Cross," 486.

he believes will lead to meaningful change. This perspective allows Nathan, and others like him, to find a sense of agency and purpose in their struggles, resonating with the core tenets of substitutionary atonement, in which the act of giving oneself becomes a pathway to transformation and redemption.

While substitutionary atonement theories provide a structured understanding of salvation, they often struggle in translation to broader "popular theologies," at times reinforcing notions of coercive self-sacrifice and cultivating feelings of guilt and shame. Feminist theologians have critically engaged with these theories, noting how the overemphasis on suffering and sacrifice can perpetuate harmful narratives, especially in the context of gender dynamics and power structures.

The potential of these theories to downplay the importance of Jesus's life and the role of the Incarnation is a significant limitation.[17] By focusing predominantly on Jesus's death as the sole means of salvation, there's a risk of detaching the concept of salvation from its ethical dimensions and the teachings of Jesus.[18] This narrow focus can inadvertently render humanity passive in the face of ongoing injustice, offering little agency in addressing and rectifying systemic evils that pervade our interconnected lives.

Furthermore, similar to *Christus Victor* theories, substitutionary atonement theories often fail to adequately confront current suffering and oppression. They overlook the ongoing post-trauma and residual effects of systemic injustices that persist in the wake of the crucifixion.[19] This oversight shows how these theories need to evolve and incorporate a more holistic understanding of suffering, redemption, and the role of active human agency in combating injustice and facilitating healing in the modern world.

Moral Influence and Moral Example Theories

The third category of atonement theories is the moral influence and moral example theories, which emphasize Jesus's role as a moral

---

17. See Kathryn Tanner, "Incarnation, Cross, and Sacrifice: A Feminist-Inspired Reappraisal," *Anglican Theological Review* 86, no. 1 (2004): 35–56; Keshgegian, "The Scandal of the Cross," 475.

18. Nancy Pineda-Madrid, *Suffering and Salvation in Ciudad Juárez* (Minneapolis: Fortress Press, 2011).

19. Keshgegian, "The Scandal of the Cross," 475.

exemplar whose life and teachings guide humanity in overcoming ignorance and living ethically. These theories also tend to focus on the Divine's love and compassion for humanity, as opposed to God's wrath. These theories suggest that the separation between God and humanity stems from our lack of awareness of the Divine and our moral failings. By emulating Jesus, we can awaken to our God-consciousness and choose a moral path. This approach resonates in popular theological concepts, exemplified by the query, "What would Jesus do?," which prompts us to consider Jesus's actions in our circumstances and encourages emulation of his moral choices.

As with the previous atonement theories, moral influence and moral example theories have their roots in both Hebrew and Christian Scriptures. In the Hebrew Bible, there are traditions emphasizing social responsibility and the covenant's call to care for society's least fortunate, with the covenant acting as a moral code for maintaining a relationship with the Divine. In Christian Scriptures, Jesus's moral teachings and his vision of the Kingdom of God further establish this line of thought.

The theory was first notably advanced by Peter Abelard, in the eleventh century, presenting an alternative to his contemporary Anselm's substitutionary theory. Abelard argues for a "moral influence" atonement, where we are called by the immenseness of God's love to live a life of righteousness. In his comments on Rom. 3:19–26, Abelard focuses on the gift of divine grace and humanity's ability to live into this grace through our actions. Abelard depicts a redeemed world, where "we do all things out of love rather than fear."[20]

Later, Protestant reformer Faustus Socinus further developed Abelard's "moral example" theory of atonement. In his work, *De Jesu Christo servatore*, Socinus rejects the substitutionary and satisfaction atonement theories of other Protestants like Calvin, and instead puts forth the "moral example" theory, in which Jesus's life and death offers us an example of the perfect self-sacrificing life. For Socinus, Jesus is more than just an example of how much God loves us. He is a call to right action.

---

20. Peter Abelard, "Exposition of the Epistle to the Romans, Book II," in *A Scholastic Miscellany: Anselm to Ockham*, ed. Eugene R. Fairweather (London: SCM Press, 1956), 276–87, 280.

Nathan's theological perspective, emphasizing Jesus's mission and stance against injustice, aligns with these moral theories. Because he felt compelled to emulate Jesus, Nathan felt particularly troubled by the emphasis on the Eucharist as the source of salvation. Given Jesus's predominant focus on living a life of radical kindness and service, Nathan expressed discomfort with "justification by faith." Instead, he reflected a preference for "justification by deeds," mirroring the moral emphasis on ethical living as exemplified by Jesus.

These moral theories' primary strengths lie in their appeal to religious naturalists; they propose a morally guided life devoid of supernatural battles or transactions as a path to divine connection. Gaining popularity during the nineteenth-century scientific revolution, these moral theories of atonement sidestepped the supernatural elements prevalent in earlier atonement theories, focusing instead on Jesus's human nature and moral actions and humanity's choice to live a moral life.

However, they face criticism for potentially underestimating sin and evil's power over humanity. Can merely living morally adequately confront systemic evils like racism and sexism?[21] The clergy abuse crisis is certainly one of these systemic evils that defies resolution through individual moral choices alone. In Nathan's own descriptions of himself, his family, and his church community, there was no indication that their moral lives were lacking. While some appreciate these moral theories' deemphasis on the crucifixion, avoiding the problematic veneration of innocent suffering, others critique them for neglecting the cross's significance as an ultimate act of love and sacrifice worth emulating.

Conclusion

In conclusion, Nathan's own narrative gives us several examples of profound and multifaceted ways that atonement narratives can shape the healing processes for trauma survivors. There is empowering potential in viewing personal suffering through the lens of Jesus's sacrifice, offering a sense of purpose and resilience. As we have seen, Nathan's identification with Jesus's struggle against

---

21. Finger, "How Can Jesus Save Women?" 16.

institutional oppression provides a powerful framework for his advocacy and personal healing, demonstrating some of the enduring relevance of these theological concepts.

Yet, Nathan's experience also brings to light the complexities and potential pitfalls of classical atonement theories. While they offer valuable insights and a sense of solidarity, they can also perpetuate problematic narratives that may exacerbate feelings of guilt and shame. This dual nature of atonement narratives necessitates a careful and critical engagement, especially in light of contemporary ethical concerns and the lived experiences of survivors.

In the next chapter, we survey modern critiques of these classical atonement theories, examining how they intersect with current issues and evolving theological perspectives. By exploring these critiques, we aim to develop a more nuanced and compassionate understanding of atonement that resonates with today's diverse and complex realities. This ongoing dialogue will help us reimagine the crucifixion narrative in a way that honors both the historical significance and the contemporary needs for trauma healing and justice.

2

Sacrifice Questioned

Critiques of the Classical Atonements

"The best aspect of . . . being male . . . is being sacrificed, and realizing, or willing to sacrifice yourself for a higher purpose. If a situation is unacceptable, and you're capable of doing it, for whatever reason . . . bringing attention to [clergy abuse], and speaking up and out about it."
—Nathan, survivor of clergy sexual abuse

Nathan's story gives us an example of how classical atonement theologies continue to shape Christian understanding of salvation and the role of Jesus as the Christ.[1] These theologies, with their inherent strengths and weaknesses, influence Christian thought in varied and sometimes contradictory ways. In preparation for our exploration of moral injury and sexual abuse in the context of these narratives (chapter 3), this chapter presents an overview of general critiques that have emerged over the last fifty years against classical atonement theories. These critiques, mainly from feminist, womanist, and liberation theologians, argue that classical atonement theories were shaped—often exclusively—by the experiences of privileged male theologians and often ignored the real lives of most Christians at the time.

---

1. The words of the survivor referred to as "Nathan" throughout this book are from Survivor Transcript 2, taken from interviews with clergy abuse survivors done in the winter and spring of 2021 through research completed at Xavier University and supported by the Taking Responsibility grant through Fordham University.

Despite recent cultural shifts that have diversified theological voices, the field remains predominantly influenced by white, male perspectives of the past. This has rendered the task of challenging established traditions and questioning the status quo both risky and disruptive. Consequently, the critiques and systematic atonement work by the theologians discussed here are often dismissed as overly particular, context-driven, too spiritual, or lacking systematic rigor. For instance, feminist theologian Sally Alsford acknowledges the particularity of feminist theology in her own work, which primarily focuses on women's experiences. She writes that "[Feminist theology] begins from a concern with women's experience and directs its attention to women's experience, not generally claiming the status of a systematic theology."[2]

I argue that this particularity does not detract from the legitimacy or systematic nature of feminist's contributions. It is essential to recognize that the classical theological tradition itself has been implicitly shaped by specific cultural contexts, predominantly those of white, European males. The overview below presents various critiques from these liberation-focused, contextually aware voices. Their insights offer fresh perspectives on the landscape of atonement theology in Christianity, challenging us to reconsider traditional narratives in light of contemporary understandings of suffering, oppression, and social justice.

The Problem of Evil

Theodicy is often a problem at the root of classical atonement narratives. Theodicy grapples with a challenging question: If God is all-powerful, all-knowing, and wholly good, why does evil exist? This dilemma becomes especially pertinent when examining atonement theories. The central inquiry here is: if Jesus's death resulted in humanity's salvation, why do suffering and evil persist?

Feminist theologian Rosemary Radford Reuther encapsulates this paradox succinctly. She argues, "The God of omnipotent control over history and the God of good news to the poor are incompatible. . . . Divine goodness and divine omnipotence cannot be

---

2. Sally Alsford, "Sin and Atonement in Feminist Perspective," in *Atonement Today*, ed. John Goldingay (London: SPCK, 1995), 148–65, 160.

reconciled."[3] This critique is particularly relevant to the *Christus Victor* and substitutionary atonement theories, which highlight the death—and in some cases, such as those by Aquinas and Calvin, the suffering—of Jesus on the cross as the pivotal event for salvation.

The conceptualization of an all-powerful, wholly good, supernatural deity faced increasing scrutiny in the twentieth century, particularly post-World War II. Theologians in the "Death of God" movement, such as Dorothee Soelle, argue for a reevaluation of our understanding of God. They suggest moving away from traditional supernatural conceptions and toward recognizing the natural consequences of human actions. Soelle posits that evil deeds inherently breed their own repercussions, creating a cycle of consequences that manifest in our worldly experiences. She writes, "The liar deceived himself, the man who treats other men as prisoners is himself imprisoned. The loveless are bored."[4] The implication is that, instead of facing divine retribution after death, we endure the consequences of our actions in our lives.

In the context of clergy sexual abuse, where evil and suffering are clearly present, the problem of evil challenges the traditional narratives of atonement, urging a reconsideration of how we understand divine power, human suffering, and the role of Jesus's sacrifice. This critique paves the way for a nuanced understanding of salvation and divine justice, resonating deeply with contemporary theological and social sensibilities.

Glorified Suffering

Building on the problem of evil in atonement theories, a related critique emerges regarding how these narratives often elevate suffering as ultimately beneficial. The glorification of Jesus's suffering on the cross, integral to these atonement theories, presents a complex challenge for theologians who are sensitive to issues of oppression and injustice. In more contemporary or less nuanced interpretations of these atonement theories, there is a tendency to idolize Jesus's suffering, often portraying his death not as a tragedy to be lamented but as an essential, even exalted, element of God's plan.

---

3. Rosemary Radford Ruether, *Introducing Redemption in Christian Feminism* (Cleveland, OH: Pilgrim Press, 1998), 106.

4. Dorothee Soelle, *Christ the Representative: An Essay in Theology after the Death of God*, trans. David Lewis (Philadelphia: Fortress Press, 1967), 121.

This approach both diminishes the tragedy of Jesus's death and elevates his suffering to an almost morbid level of idolization, portraying it as both inevitable and unparalleled in its intensity.[5] With Aquinas, we saw the development of atonement thinking that painted Jesus's suffering as beyond any suffering experienced by humanity. This perspective is exemplified in the case of Nathan, who views sacrifice as central to Jesus's mission, masculinity, and his own healing process.

Feminist, womanist, and liberation theologians, while challenging the glorification of suffering as untenable, recognize that suffering is an inescapable aspect of life and inherently intertwined with our understanding of salvation. They confront a delicate theological balance: how do we acknowledge and name our suffering as Christic, reflecting the Christ-like experience of the passion, without glorifying, promoting, or seeking it?[6] This tension is an example of the need for a nuanced approach to understanding suffering in our Christologies. Many of these theologians assert that there is nothing liberating, salvific, or holy in suffering, including that of Jesus, and propose that there is nothing saving in the cross.[7] Instead, they encourage exploring other aspects of Jesus's life and Incarnation as sources of salvation, pointing to atonement theories more in line with the *Christus Victor* or moral theories.

However, the example of Nathan's healing illustrates that Jesus's suffering can symbolize solidarity, empowering survivors in their social justice endeavors. This raises an important theological question: can modern cross theologies move away from glorified suffering without losing Jesus's solidarity with the oppressed? Theologian Christina Baxter further explores this by questioning whether whether salvation must be experienced as "good" to be valid, using the Israelites' journey from Egypt to the desert as an example.[8] The

---

5. Pamela Dickey Young, "Beyond Moral Influence to an Atoning Life," *Theology Today* 52, no. 3 (1995): 344–55, 347.

6. Carter Heyward, "Suffering, Redemption, and Christ: Shifting the Grounds of Feminist Christology," *Christianity and Crisis* 49 (December 11, 1989): 381–89, 381.

7. See Heyward, "Suffering, Redemption," 384; Kathryn Tanner, "Incarnation, Cross, and Sacrifice: A Feminist-Inspired Reappraisal," *Anglican Theological Review* 86, no. 1 (2004): 35–56. And Delores S. Williams, *Sisters in the Wilderness: The Challenge of Womanist God-Talk* (Maryknoll, NY: Orbis Books, 2013).

8. See Christina A. Baxter, "Jesus the Man and Women's Salvation," in *Atonement Today*, ed. John Goldingay (London: SPCK, 1995), 131–47. Baxter uses the

difficulty of addressing suffering and evil in theology without prescribing suffering as a means to salvation remains today.

God as Divine Child-Abuser

Joanne Carlson Brown, a prominent feminist theologian, presents a challenging perspective on atonement theories. She argues that, while many scholars criticize atonement for endorsing suffering as part of oppression, they paradoxically accept Jesus's suffering as divinely ordained. She charges, "they want to end the suffering that is at the heart of oppression. They insist that all suffering must be regarded as negative and not ordained by God. All, that is, except Jesus's suffering!"[9] This critique, also expressed by theologians Rita Nakashima Brock and Rebecca Parker, leads to a disturbing portrayal of God as akin to an abusive father.[10] In ways that echo Calvin's penal substitution theory, viewing God as complicit in Jesus's suffering creates a harmful image of God and sets a problematic precedent for how suffering is perceived and justified within the Christian tradition.

The implications of this critique extend significantly, especially within the context of church structures' impact on women and children. Brown and her colleagues argue that, if Jesus's suffering and death are perceived as willed or sanctioned by God, this position inadvertently endorses a narrative that supports silent endurance of abuse and violence. "Thus many shaped by the Christian tradition feel that self-sacrifice and obedience are an integral part of what it means to be Christian."[11] This interpretation, they argue, frames self-sacrifice and obedience as virtues, dangerously echoing

---

example of the Israelites' suffering in the desert and their longing to return to the "safety" of slavery to question how, and more importantly *who*, defines salvation. Baxter's larger argument questions the possibility of a male savior providing salvation for women.

9. Joanne Carlson Brown, "Divine Child Abuse," *Daughters of Sarah* 18, no. 3 (1992): 24–28, 27.

10. See Rita Nakashima Brock, *Journeys by Heart: A Christology of Erotic Power* (New York: Crossroad, 1988); Joanne Carlson Brown and Rebecca Parker, "For God So Loved the World?," in *Christianity, Patriarchy, and Abuse: A Feminist Critique*, ed. Joanne Carlson Brown and Rebecca Parker (New York: Pilgrim Press, 1989); Brown, "Divine Child Abuse."

11. Brown, "Divine Child Abuse," 24.

the experiences of survivors of abuse. Brown starkly compares the church's relationship to women to that of an abusive partner, stating that the church community can be a sanctuary for women only if it actively confronts and disrupts cycles of abuse.[12] This critique gains a layer of irony when considering the experiences of individuals like Nathan, who, despite his own victimization within his church community, paradoxically gravitates toward the theme of self-sacrifice to interpret his suffering.

The "abusive Father-God" critique has sparked significant debate among theologians. Some, including feminist theologians, contend that this critique overlooks the trinitarian nature of the Divine, arguing that the Father and the Son in the Trinity should not be seen as distinct entities in this context.[13] They assert that a proper understanding of classical atonement theories should not lead to a perception of God as abusive but rather as part of a trinitarian relationship that works toward the restoration of justice and order. Notably, feminist theologian Flora Keshgegian, defending Anselm's theory of substitutionary atonement, emphasizes that the incarnational relationship between God and Jesus symbolizes a divine intervention on "behalf of humanity and for the sake of righting the disrupted order of justice."[14] This perspective suggests a more complex and nuanced interpretation of atonement theories, challenging the idea that they inherently portray God in a negative light.

Nathan's perspective, reflecting his personal experiences rather than formal theological training, notably omits the trinitarian aspect of Jesus. This highlights a key point: such theological narratives, particularly atonement theories, often permeate our lives without critical examination. Brock, Brown, and Parker draw attention to the potential harm of these theories, arguing that they can reinforce patriarchal structures by idolizing Jesus's obedience to an allegedly abusive Father figure. However, the "abusive father" critique is sometimes swiftly dismissed by theologians who favor interpretations grounded in historical context or biblical scholar-

---

12. Brown, "Divine Child Abuse," 25.

13. G. Margo, "Atonement and Abuse: An Alternate View," *Daughters of Sarah* 18, no. 3 (1992): 29–32.

14. Flora A. Keshgegian, "The Scandal of the Cross: Revisiting Anselm and His Feminist Critics," *Anglican Theological Review* 82, no. 3 (2000): 475–92, 480.

ship.[15] These scholars argue that a more nuanced understanding of classical atonement theories does not necessarily support a portrayal of God as abusive. Despite this, the underlying message of the critique remains significant: atonement theories, if unexamined, can perpetuate harmful narratives. As Brown aptly notes, "The glorification of anyone's suffering allows the glorification of all suffering."[16]

Jesus as Divine Victim

As we transition from the portrayal of God's potential complicity in suffering, we encounter another complex dimension of atonement theories: the concept of Jesus as a divine victim. This particular representation brings forth a multitude of critical issues that significantly influence our understanding of victimhood within the Christian narrative. The glorification of Jesus as a perfect, divine victim establishes an unrealistic benchmark, leaving real victims grappling with a standard they cannot possibly meet. The Christian tradition states, as represented by all of the classical theologies noted in chapter 1, that Jesus is human in all ways but sin. When this belief is combined with moral theories of atonement, victims may feel themself lacking in goodness. This idealization of Jesus inadvertently creates a troubling narrative: imperfection in victims could be misconstrued as a justification for their suffering or a reason to withhold aid.

The depiction of Jesus as an infallible victim, one who forgives and redeems his oppressors, sets an unattainable expectation on survivors. They are subtly encouraged to bear their suffering in silence, aspiring to a level of perfection in their victimhood that is inherently unachievable. If a survivor proves to be less than perfect, they "deserved suffering for guilt and the promise of becoming a Christlike agent of redemption for one's victimizers through inno-

---

15. See Stephen Finlan, *Problems with Atonement: The Origins of, and Controversy about, the Atonement Doctrine* (Collegeville, MN: Liturgical Press, 2005); Steve Jeffery, Michael Ovey, and Andrew Sach, *Pierced for Our Transgressions: Rediscovering the Glory of Penal Substitution* (Wheaton, IL: Crossway, 2007); I. Howard Marshall, *Aspects of the Atonement: Cross and Resurrection in the Reconciling of God and Humanity* (London: Paternoster, 2007).

16. Brown, "Divine Child Abuse," 27.

cent suffering."[17] For many of the survivors I interviewed, narratives of Jesus as a moral example left them with a deep sense of guilt and inadequacy, internalizing a distorted view of their abuse as deserved or indicative of their flawed nature. The language they use to describe themselves—often as "bad" or "troubled" children—reflects this internal conflict.

Moreover, classical atonement theories beyond those focused on Jesus's morality tend to portray Jesus as an obedient victim, a stance that can be manipulated to suggest suffering should be passively endured as an emulation of Christ. Challenging this notion, feminist theologians advocate for a recognition of Jesus's active role. While Jesus was a victim of his era's societal and political dynamics, he was far from passive. Acknowledging Jesus's human agency disrupts the narrative of mere endurance. He actively confronted and challenged oppressive systems, a journey that culminated in his death. Caryn Riswold's statement, "[Jesus] died because they killed him,"[18] poignantly emphasizes Jesus's resistance rather than a passive submission to his fate.

The debate extends to the interpretation of classical models, like *Christus Victor*, where the obedient Jesus is depicted as overthrowing oppressive powers.[19] The way this overthrow is conceptualized, particularly if it is tied to Jesus's self-sacrifice on the cross, raises concerns about promoting suffering as necessary for the oppressed.[20] In contrast, Keshgegian's interpretation of Anselmian atonement shows Jesus's active engagement, rejecting the idea of him as merely an obedient victim. She brings the incarnational aspect to the fore, portraying Jesus as an active participant in God's plan for reconciling humanity.[21]

The concept of self-sacrifice within Christian practice is also a subject of debate. Many of the classical atonements described above, particularly those of Aquinas and Calvin, stress the role of Jesus's

---

17. Rosemary Radford Ruether, *Introducing Redemption in Christian Feminism* (Cleveland, OH: Pilgrim Press, 1998), 100.
18. Caryn D. Riswold, *Coram Deo: Human Life in the Vision of God* (Eugene, OR: Pickwick Publications, 2006), 133.
19. Reta Halteman Finger, "How Can Jesus Save Women? Three Theories on Christ's Atonement," *Daughters of Sarah* 14, no. 6 (1988): 14.
20. Baxter, "Jesus the Man and Women's Salvation."
21. Keshgegian, "The Scandal of the Cross."

self-sacrifice in our salvation. While feminist critics warn against its portrayal as mandatory for the marginalized, theologians such as Hans Boersma emphasize its universal significance in Christian life. Boersma links self-sacrifice to the practice of hospitality, arguing that true hospitality requires self-giving love, making self-sacrifice integral to atonement, applicable to all, including the powerful.[22]

Nathan's narrative offers a reflective lens on this theological debate. His perception of self-sacrifice, viewed as empowering in his journey toward justice and holding the church accountable, provides a more dynamic understanding of this concept. His perspective offers a nuanced understanding of self-sacrifice. Rather than a passive acceptance of victimhood, it is an active engagement in seeking justice and transformation. This view resonates with the complexities and diverse interpretations within contemporary theological discourse.

Surrogates and Scapegoats

Building on the discussion of Jesus's active role in atonement, we now explore another significant critique, this time from the perspective of womanist theology. Delores Williams, a prominent womanist theologian, critically examines the use of surrogate language in classical atonement theories, particularly noting its detrimental impact on Black women.[23] In Calvin's development of the penal substitution theory, Jesus as a stand-in for humanity, taking on the role of the criminal in the court system of his day, was central to effecting salvation.

Williams contends that, throughout history, Black women have often been forced into roles of surrogacy. They have been mothers, sexual partners, and laborers during slavery, the Jim Crow era, and even in contemporary America. In portraying Jesus as the ultimate surrogate for humanity, these atonement theories inadvertently perpetuate the expectation for Black women to continue in these imposed roles. Williams boldly challenges the traditional focus on

---

22. Hans Boersma, *Violence, Hospitality, and the Cross: Reappropriating the Atonement Tradition* (Grand Rapids: Baker Academic, 2004), 118.

23. Delores S. Williams, "Black Women's Surrogacy Experience and the Christian Notion of Redemption," in *Cross Examinations: Readings on the Meaning of the Cross Today*, ed. Marit Trelstad (Minneapolis: Augsburg Fortress Press, 2006), 143–50.

the cross, asserting that "there is nothing Divine in the blood of the cross."[24] She posits that Jesus's conquest over sin was achieved during his wilderness experience, a narrative she parallels with Hagar's survival in the wilderness from the Hebrew Bible.

JoAnne Marie Terrell offers a contrasting viewpoint to that of Williams. Terrell rejects Aquinas's understanding of God's responsibility for Jesus's death. While agreeing with Williams "that God did not condone the violence of the cross or black women's surrogacy; nor yet does God condone this present state of affairs,"[25] Terrell expresses concern over completely removing the cross from atonement theology. She argues that doing so risks neglecting a significant part of the tradition that has enabled Black women to find meaning in their suffering and trauma.[26] Terrell questions the dismissal of any divine presence in Jesus's crucifixion.[27] She defends the importance of the cross not as the central purpose of Jesus's life but "rather, it was the tragic, if foreseeable, result of his confrontation with evil. This bespeaks a view of Jesus and the martyrs as empowered, sacramental, witnesses, not as victims who passively acquiesced to evil."[28] This perspective introduces a co-sufferer model of the cross, a theme that we will further explore in chapter 8.

This discussion naturally leads to the consideration of Jesus as a scapegoat in atonement theories. The metaphor of Jesus taking on the sins of the world and bearing humanity's punishment mirrors the surrogate language critiqued by Williams. Modern thinkers like René Girard and Mark Heim (more deeply engaged in chapter 8) have revisited this analogy, yet it remains susceptible to similar critiques. Societal practices that turn minorities and marginalized individuals into scapegoats problematizes these interpretations and notions that good can be derived from such suffering. This is reflected in Nathan's own theological reflections, where he reinterprets his suffering as a sacrificial act aimed at preventing further clergy sexual abuse and its cover-up.

---

24. Delores S. Williams, *Sisters in the Wilderness: The Challenge of Womanist God-Talk* (Maryknoll, NY: Orbis Books, 1993), 159.

25. JoAnne Marie Terrell, *Power in the Blood? The Cross in the African-American Experience* (Maryknoll, NY: Orbis Books, 1998), 121.

26. Terrell, *Power in the Blood?*, 125.

27. Terrell, 121.

28. Terrell, 142.

Necrophilic Atonements

Popular interpretations of classical atonement theories, particularly substitutionary atonement theories, often overemphasize Jesus's death as the pivotal moment of salvation. This perspective, unfortunately, tends to overshadow other essential aspects of Jesus's journey—his Incarnation, life, teachings, and resurrection. Such a narrowed focus is a direct consequence of overemphasizing the cross in atonement theology. When the cross is either centralized or perceived as the sole event of salvation in these theologies, we risk missing the broader narrative of Jesus's life and his message of the Kingdom of God.

The moral theories of Abelard and Socinus, for instance, emerged to challenge this undue fixation on Jesus's death. These theories shift the focus away from death, viewing it as just one facet of Jesus's life of love. Early Jesus followers' practices, like table fellowship and house-church gatherings, give us further insight into this perspective, indicating that Jesus's death was not originally seen as the central or only redemptive aspect of his life.[29]

This view resonates with Nathan's own story and understanding of salvation. Nathan doesn't name the cross as the defining element of his healing. Instead, he draws inspiration from Jesus's stance against the injustices of his time, finding empowerment in Jesus's active resistance.

Forgetting the Incarnation

Another issue arising from overemphasizing the cross in some atonement theories is the neglect of the Incarnation's significance. The dual nature of Jesus as fully human and fully divine is crucial in understanding why he is central to human salvation. However, the Incarnation, with its enigmatic nature, is frequently overlooked or misunderstood in mainstream interpretations of classical atonement theories.

For instance, the common Father–Son divide in many classical atonement narratives doesn't align well with a deeper comprehension of the Incarnation. If we acknowledge Jesus as God, then the depiction of his sacrifice in substitutionary atonement theories

---

29. See Ray, *Deceiving the Devil*.

becomes problematic. It's hard to reconcile the idea of Jesus paying a debt between God and humanity when Jesus himself is God.[30]

Feminist theologian Kathryn Tanner advocates for an atonement theory centered on the Incarnation. This approach aligns with the *Christus Victor* model, especially as expressed by Irenaeus, but it contrasts with other theories that solely emphasize Jesus's death as the crux of salvation. Tanner writes, "Humanity is at one with the divine in Jesus—on the cross as everywhere else in Jesus's life—and that is what is saving about it."[31]

This Incarnation-focused view, which we'll explore more deeply in chapter 8, recognizes the cross as significant, but the cross becomes, primarily, an illustration of the suffering and death from which humanity is being saved. "All those cruel and bloody features of the cross, which feminists and womanists are worried atonement theories find positive value in, are here identified in no uncertain terms with the world one needs to be saved from."[32] Tanner argues that salvation occurs through Jesus embodying human traits and transforming them within the divine essence. This transformative process encompasses Jesus's birth, life, death, and extends to his resurrection. It is an ongoing journey, not limited to a single moment of death, suffering, or self-sacrifice.[33]

Ignoring Suffering and Sin

As seen previously, feminist and womanist theologians have criticized classical atonement theories for their tendency to glorify suffering and overemphasize the cross. However, theories focusing solely on Jesus's Incarnation and life, such as *Christus Victor* and moral theories, also face scrutiny. The pervasive reality of suffering in our world is undeniable, and many believe and hope that this suffering can yield meaningful insights.

As seen in Nathan's story, Jesus's confrontation with injustice, leading up to his death on the cross, played a significant role in Nathan's healing journey and in finding meaning in his own suf-

---

30. Gustaf Aulén, *Christus Victor: An Historical Study of the Three Main Types of the Idea of the Atonement*, trans. A. G. Hebert (London: SPCK, 1970).
31. Tanner, "Incarnation, Cross, and Sacrifice," 43.
32. Tanner, 47.
33. Tanner, 46–47.

fering. Jesus's own experiences of suffering, which underline his humanity, resonate deeply with our own struggles. The crucifixion stands as the most profound narrative example of Christ's suffering.

In the moral theories of atonement, salvation is understood as embracing and emulating Jesus's moral life. However, this subjective approach can be problematic as it implies humans can somehow match Jesus's exemplary standards, overlooking our sin and the realities of systemic evil. Consequently, some theologians doubt humanity's capacity to truly imitate Christ.[34] Others argue for an emphasis on moral theories like Abelard's and Socinus's theories, which name the important role of God's love and grace. Instead of seeing Jesus's life as merely a model to follow, we could "accept it as the power and the possibility of changed relationships between oneself and God, oneself and other humans, oneself and the whole of creation."[35] A fundamental theological question is central to this debate: is humanity inherently doomed to sin?

The Problem of Sin

The concepts of sin and salvation are deeply intertwined, and our understanding of one significantly influences the other. As we broaden our definition and understanding of sin, it inevitably reshapes our atonement theories. Twentieth-century feminist theologians such as Valerie Saiving and Judith Plaskow started to challenge traditional interpretations of sin, primarily seen as pride and domination.[36] Saiving argued that this perspective was male-centric, overlooking that women, historically with less power to dominate, often erred on the side of self-negation. Understanding sin as an imbalance—whether through domination or self-negation—necessitates reimagining Jesus's sacrifice as "obedience unto death" in classical atonement theories.

---

34. Linda D. Peacore, *The Role of Women's Experience in Feminist Theologies of Atonement* (Eugene, OR: Pickwick, 2010), 159.

35. Young, "Beyond Moral Influence," 355.

36. See Judith Ellen Plaskow, *Sex, Sin, and Grace: Women's Experience and the Theologies of Reinhold Niebuhr and Paul Tillich* (Lanham, MD: University Press of America, 1979); Valerie Saiving Goldstein, "The Human Situation: A Feminine View," *The Journal of Religion* 40, no. 2 (1960): 100–112.

Furthermore, the evolution of our world into a more interconnected and globalized community brings the nature of sin to the fore: is it an individual or a relational phenomenon? Sally Alsford reframes this question eloquently, writing, "are we essentially individual souls and minds fallen and in need of salvation? Or is humanity essentially relational, and should we understand sin and salvation in a relational way?"[37] Traditionally, Christian theologians have primarily viewed sin as an individual concern. However, this view is inadequate in contexts like Nathan's, where suffering and sin arise from broader systems such as clericalism and child abuse, beyond just the individual sin of the abuser.

Karl Rahner, among other twentieth-century theologians, has recognized the interconnectedness of humanity and the systemic aspects contributing to sin. Rahner illustrated this through everyday examples, such as the ethical implications of buying a banana.[38] This simple act connects us to a chain of unethical labor and trade practices, from the underpaid laborers who harvested the banana to the grocery clerks struggling to pay for their student loans, astronomical rent, and childcare.

Similarly, in Nathan's case, the culpability extends beyond his abuser, encompassing church officials who concealed the abuse and parishioners who neglected or ostracized him and other survivors. In such a framework, we often find that we have very little choice or agency. Rather, individual sins are part of larger, systemic issues, suggesting that atonement theories focusing solely on individual salvation may not sufficiently address the complexities of sin in our world. The classical atonement theories, such as moral theories, can be interpreted to ignore the communal aspects of sin, instead focusing on the individual's salvation through moral action.

The "Maleness of Christ"

Many of these classical atonement theories and Christologies have been interpreted in ways that bolster male dominance within church hierarchy. Feminist theologian Mary Daly boldly asserts that a male symbol of salvation cannot surmount the deep-rooted, "original

---

37. Alsford, "Sin and Atonement in Feminist Perspective."
38. Karl Rahner, *Foundations of Christian Faith: An Introduction to the Idea of Christianity* (New York: Crossroad, 1978), 110–11.

sin" of sexism.[39] Instead, she argues, it often strengthens patriarchal structures rather than providing a transformative counterpoint. This gender dynamic is evident in Nathan's own experiences. In his interview, Nathan grapples with the concept of sacrifice, drawing parallels between Jesus's sacrifice for justice, Nathan's own actions for the same, and the traditional male archetype of soldiers in warfare. Although he intermittently clarified that his viewpoint was "not about gender," Nathan's reflections ultimately echo these conventional notions of male sacrifice.

Jesus's role as a symbol of salvation hasn't always been aligned with patriarchal values, nor is it an inevitable association. Feminist theologian Rosemary Radford Ruether critically examines this in "Can a Male Savior Save Women?"[40] She traces Jesus's evolution from a radical figure challenging societal norms to a symbol reinforcing patriarchy. Initially, Jesus's teachings about the forthcoming Kingdom of God were revolutionary, directly opposing nationalism and various forms of patriarchal dominance. However, as Christianity morphed into an imperial religion over the first five centuries, Christ's image shifted to align with the status quo. This transformation within church structures led to the exclusion of women from leadership roles and apostolic succession, with Jesus and his apostles' gender being cited as the primary reason for their marginalization. This rationale has persisted over time, even in the modern context of the Catholic Church. In 1976, the Vatican declared explicitly the exclusion of women, justifying the claim with women's inability to embody Christ.[41]

This historical precedent is problematic in several ways, particularly in how it relates to the concept of atonement through *Christus Victor*, recapitulation, or moral theories. Issues arise when our salvation hinges on either Jesus's summation of the human experience through the Incarnation or our ability to embody Christ, with gender being a part of that experience. If Jesus is perceived

---

39. Mary Daly, *Beyond God the Father: Toward a Philosophy of Women's Liberation* (Boston: Beacon, 1973), 71.

40. Rosemary Radford Ruether, "Christology and Feminism: Can a Male Savior Save Women," in *To Change the World: Christology and Cultural Criticism* (Eugene, OR: Wipf & Stock, 2001), 45–56.

41. Congregation for the Doctrine of the Faith, *Inter Insigniores: Declaration on the Question of Admission of Women to the Ministerial Priesthood*, October 15, 1976.

solely as representing the male aspect of humanity, it implies a troubling notion: women and nonmale individuals, by not being encompassed within the Incarnation, are excluded from salvation. This interpretation suggests that a male savior cannot save women. However, feminist theologians challenge this view, arguing that the specifics of Jesus's gender, race, and ethnicity represent his authentic humanity rather than elevating any particular identity over others.[42] This debate highlights a contradiction within Catholic Church tradition: "No-one who argues for male-only presidency at the eucharist is also arguing that only men are saved. So they are using the same person, the same event in two different ways, both exclusively and inclusively."[43]

Feminist theologians have raised questions about church leaders' and thinkers' emphasis on gender as an essential or ontological characteristic, while seemingly overlooking Jesus's race, culture, and religion. These elements play a significant role in shaping our understanding of atonement, yet it is clear that no individual can fully encapsulate the universality of Jesus. Radford Ruether introduces an alternative christological criterion, writing, "I believe Christians must affirm the particularity of Jesus, not only in gender, but also in ethnicity and culture, and the limitations of any single individual to be universally paradigmatic."[44] She emphasizes the inherent limitations any single individual has in being a universal exemplar. According to her, the essence of what makes Jesus a model for us lies not in his biological identity but in the embodiment of his teachings and actions—"person as lived message and practice."[45]

Jesus as Lone Superhero

In rethinking Christology and atonement, one approach is to move away from viewing Jesus solely as a male savior and toward considering his deeply interconnected community. Theologian Reta Finger suggests that Jesus's transformative relationships with

---

42. Baxter, "Jesus the Man and Women's Salvation."
43. Baxter, "Jesus the Man and Women's Salvation," 137.
44. Rosemary Radford Ruether, *Introducing Redemption in Christian Feminism* (Cleveland, OH: Pilgrim Press, 1998), 93.
45. Radford Ruether, *Introducing Redemption in Christian Feminism*, 93.

women challenge sexist norms and offer new paths for women in atonement narratives. Classical atonement theories, like *Christus Victor* and substitutionary theories, often stress the importance of Jesus's unique individuality. In the case of *Christus Victor*, they portray Jesus as a superhero-like figure, almost beyond humanity, who single-handedly conquers evil.[46] And, in the case of substitutionary theories, Jesus's unique experience of suffering is also important to our salvation. But these classical atonement theories often miss the significance of Jesus's community and humanity's interconnectedness. This misperception persists in modern liberation theologies up to the 1980s, which focus on Jesus's individual actions, his outreach to the impoverished, and his revolutionary message of the Kin-dom of God,[47] rather than the larger community that shaped Jesus and his mission.

Feminist theologian Rita Nakashima Brock advocates for a communally focused Christology in *Journeys by Heart: A Christology of Erotic Power*. This work critiques classical Christologies' individualistic history and proposes a communal model that encompasses Jesus's entire life context as integral to his formation and mission. This approach challenges the superhero narrative that has been critiqued by feminists for overlooking humanity's interconnectedness and perpetuating a patriarchal power structure. Thinkers like Brock, Elisabeth Schüssler Fiorenza, and Darby Kathleen Ray propose expanding Christology to encompass the *ekklēsia* (the church community) or Christa/community. Such an expansion would uncover shared power dynamics intrinsic to the Christian faith, moving beyond dominant individualistic interpretations.[48]

Considering the larger community in Jesus's life makes sense for understanding atonement. Just as sin manifests in both individual and systemic forms, atonement must address individual and communal aspects. Our evolving understanding of human persons and their interdependence necessitates that our narratives of atonement and Christology adapt accordingly. The adage "no person is an island" aptly applies to Jesus, suggesting his integral connec-

---

46. Brock, *Journeys by Heart*.
47. "Kin-dom of God" is a concept where God's reign is understood as a community of mutual care, contrasting with traditional hierarchically focused "kingdom" language.
48. Ray, *Deceiving the Devil*.

tion with the community. Thus, a robust atonement theory should encompass the formation of a new covenant community, extending beyond mere individual transformation.

Conclusion

Atonement theories and the crucifixion narrative offer powerful frameworks for understanding suffering and trauma. Through the lens of Nathan's story, we see how Jesus's life and death, marked by a steadfast resistance to injustice, can offer empowerment and healing to abuse survivors. However, it's crucial to balance our exploration with an acknowledgment of both the rich tradition we inherit and the above critiques. As noted by Hans Boersma, "In negotiating the relationship between our contemporary horizon and the biblical models of the atonement, we cannot simply ignore a large part of the theological tradition."[49] This calls for a nuanced approach as we deconstruct, examine, and reconstruct an atonement narrative in the context of the clergy sexual abuse crisis. Recognizing that both classical theological tradition and feminist critiques will significantly inform our journey ahead is essential. To further explore the impact of Christian atonement tradition on survivors of clergy sexual abuse, we must look at the specific aspects of how atonement narratives can problematically influence survivors of sexual abuse. Chapter 3 opens this critical dialogue, inviting us to confront and reassess these narratives in a new light.

---

49. Hans Boersma, "The Disappearance of Punishment: Metaphors, Models, and the Meaning of the Atonement," *Books & Culture* 9, no. 2 (2003): 3.

3

The Darker Side of Atonement Theories

"[Religion] was everything in my life as a child. I mean, we went to Novena. I went to mass every morning. It was our social life. It was the rhythm of our lives. You know, baptisms, first communions, Lent. Now . . . I think I'm spiritual, but religion plays no part in my life."
—Deborah, survivor of clergy sexual abuse

Previously, we've recognized the power of atonement theories and theologies of the cross in Christian life. These narratives deeply influence how we understand and talk about suffering. Such influence can be empowering, as illustrated by Nathan's story, where he finds strength in aligning his efforts for the church communities' accountability in the clergy sexual abuse crisis with Jesus's mission. However, this influence is not universally positive. Another survivor of clergy sexual abuse, Deborah, gives testament to the darker side of these narratives, where the line between sanctity and suffering is blurred by the very institutions meant to safeguard faith and morality.[1]

Deborah was raised in a devout Catholic environment where religious rituals and practices formed the rhythm of her life. She

---

1. The words of the survivor referred to as "Deborah" throughout this book are from Survivor Transcript 14, taken from interviews with clergy abuse survivors done in the winter and spring of 2021 through research completed at Xavier University and supported by the Taking Responsibility grant through Fordham University.

experienced a profound betrayal of trust when the very figures entrusted with her spiritual guidance exploited her innocence. From the time she was six years old until she was thirteen, Deborah was abused by the priests and religious leaders in her school. She suffered physical abuse and deeply spiritual abuse, with her abusers manipulating religious doctrine to justify their actions and to instill in her a pervasive sense of sin and unworthiness. This manipulation extended to the sacraments, turning what should have been sources of comfort and reconciliation into further instruments of control and shame.

After her childhood experience of abuse, Deborah largely suppressed these memories. About twenty years later, working in a Catholic school, Deborah came face to face with clergy sexual abuse again. This time as a teacher, she became the advocate for several children who were being victimized by a priest. After fighting for over a year with the diocese to remove the abusive priest, church leaders relocated him to another school. He remained a priest and nothing more was done. Her father's sudden death triggered a resurgence of memories about her own abuse, propelling her into activism. She joined a survivors' network, where she became an employee, eventually serving as the executive director. Her commitment to the movement was fueled by her experiences as both a survivor and a witness to abuse within her church community.

These compounding experiences of betrayal have left Deborah's faith in the Catholic Church shattered. As an adult, Deborah grapples with the long-lasting effects of her abuse, including a fractured relationship with religion and an enduring struggle with the concepts of sin, atonement, and divine justice. Her story is a poignant illustration of the devastating impact that clergy abuse can have on an individual's spirituality, sense of self, and worldview.

Deborah's journey through the labyrinth of spiritual abuse and betrayal offers a visceral insight into the troubling intersection of spirituality and sexual assault. Her narrative is a stark illustration of what feminist theologian Susan Ross observes: often, atonement theologies, instead of offering solace or understanding, perpetuate a spirituality that coerces acceptance of suffering without challenging its source or legitimacy.[2] When Christian survivors of sexual

---

2. Susan A. Ross, "Feminist Theology and the Clergy Sexual Abuse Crisis," *Theological Studies* 80, no. 3 (September 2019): 632–52.

abuse search for language to contextualize their trauma, they often turn to the narratives of the cross. However, if they encounter interpretations that are toxic and reinforce victimhood, this can substantially hinder their healing process. In Deborah's world, the sacred narratives of the cross, trust in God, and sacrifice became tools of manipulation that were wielded by those she was taught to trust unconditionally.

In witnessing Deborah's experiences, we confront unsettling questions about the prevalence and acceptance of harmful interpretations of atonement and suffering within our religious and societal structures. Modern academic discussions about atonement and the cross have grown to include these traditional views alongside insights from the Bible, human growth, and society.[3] This broader perspective is common in scholarly circles. Defending a specific atonement theory called penal substitution, scholars Steve Jeffery, Michael Ovey, and Andrew Sach argue against harmful interpretations that portray God as an abuser and Jesus as a passive victim, calling them a gross misinterpretation of Christianity. They continue, writing, "It must be said, however, that such distortion of the gospel does not appear to be widespread in mainstream Christian writing. In fact, we have been unable to locate a single example. If this sadistic misappropriation of the gospel exists at all, it seems not to have a wide following."[4]

However, many theologians, such as Ross, challenge this idea. She questions whether these advanced, thoughtful academic discussions are as widespread and influential in everyday Christian beliefs, especially in the United States today. This leads me to ask: how much do these scholarly views actually shape the common Christian understanding today? Deborah's story forces us to reconsider the scope and influence of scholarly theological debates on the everyday lives of believers, especially those who, like Deborah, find their faith and identity under siege by the very doctrines meant to offer refuge and understanding.

---

3. Ross, "Feminist Theology."
4. Steve Jeffrey, Michael Ovey, and Andrew Sach, *Pierced for Our Transgressions: Rediscovering the Glory of Penal Substitution* (Wheaton, IL: Crossway, 2007), 322.

Popular Stories of Purposeful Suffering

In a society where popular Christian literature often paints suffering as a divine mandate for personal growth and spiritual maturation, Deborah's narrative emerges as a powerful counternarrative. It challenges us to reflect on the implications of a theology that glorifies suffering and demands unquestioning obedience, even in the face of egregious moral and spiritual violations. In my classroom, when students read and reflect on activist Sr. Dianna Ortiz's harrowing journey as a torture survivor, an inevitable discussion emerges: does everything happen for a reason? This dialogue often reveals a mix of emotions. While some students express anger and frustration toward this mentality, many more seem to embrace it, suggesting a belief that God permits suffering as part of a larger plan—a plan in which even our deepest pains serve a purpose. I suggest that my students' class discussions are not isolated opinions. Rather, they are a microcosm of wider American societal views.

My students' sentiments, that everything that happens is part of God's larger plan, resonate with the themes found in popular Christian literature. Bestselling authors like Lysa TerKeurst and Max Lucado, through works such as TerKeurst's *It's Not Supposed to Be This Way: Finding Unexpected Strength When Disappointments Leave You Shattered* and Lucado's *You'll Get through This: Hope and Help for Your Turbulent Times*, have profoundly influenced Christian pop culture.[5] These books, often topping Amazon's lists in categories like "Christian Bible Study Guides," "Christian Women's Issues," "Hebrew Bible," and "Old Testament Meditations," shape the narrative that suffering, according to Christian belief, is part of a divine plan for personal growth and understanding.

A common idea in these popular Christian books is the belief that suffering serves a greater purpose. Echoing thoughts from early Christian thinkers, these modern authors suggest that enduring suffering helps us grow spiritually, bringing us closer to being Christ-like. TerKeurst warns her reader, "The process of acquiring

---

5. Lysa TerKeurst, *It's Not Supposed to Be This Way: Finding Unexpected Strength When Disappointments Leave You Shattered* (Nashville, TN: Thomas Nelson, 2018); Max Lucado, *You'll Get Through This: Hope and Help for Your Turbulent Times* (Nashville, TN: Thomas Nelson, 2013).

these good qualities doesn't usually feel good at the time, but it will be good in time."[6] She explains that, while God doesn't cause our suffering, he allows it to help us grow and avoid becoming too self-reliant or distant from him. In her words, "God doesn't want you or me to suffer. But He will allow it in doses to increase our trust. Our pain and suffering isn't to hurt us. It's to save us. To save us from a life where we are self-reliant, self-satisfied, self-absorbed, and set up for the greatest pain of all . . . separation from God."[7]

These authors argue that suffering happens for a reason—to develop positive qualities like obedience and trust. TerKeurst points to Jesus as an example. While Jesus's divine nature was complete, his human nature "grew and matured and learned how to be obedient" through suffering.[8] In this view, qualities like obedience and trust are more valuable than human needs for safety, comfort, and health. As TerKeurst writes, "His humanity suffered. Really suffered. . . . His humanity said, please not this. His humanity cried for something different. His humanity begged for another way. But this obedience He learned from suffering compelled Him to trust God beyond what His physical eyes could see."[9] In other words, TerKeurst claims Jesus's suffering, including on the cross, taught him complete trust in God. And she argues it can teach us the same.

Jesus's obedience and trust in God becomes our goal. Even amid pain and suffering, imitating Jesus in these moments becomes the sole, faithful choice, according to TerKeurst. She repeatedly points readers to the importance of *imitatio Christi*. As she writes, "This is what Jesus did. This is what Jesus modeled. To be like Jesus, we must become more and more saturated with Him and less and less saturated with our human ways of processing circumstances."[10] In other words, we must reject our embodied senses telling us things are wrong and trust and obey instead. Authors like TerKeurst argue this is not too much to ask because Jesus exemplified how humans can do this. Author Max Lucado makes a similar point, arguing God would not ask anything of us that Jesus did not experience

---

6. TerKeurst, *It's Not Supposed to Be This Way*, 184.
7. TerKeurst, 45.
8. TerKeurst, 43.
9. TerKeurst, 43.
10. TerKeurst, 184.

himself. As Lucado states, "He exacts nothing from us that he did not experience himself."[11] And we should not expect any further explanation, according to this view.

At the core of this push to "trust in God" is the belief in a larger divine plan beyond human comprehension. God is orchestrating this plan, and trusting in it becomes an act of faith.[12] Moments of suffering are necessary evils in the present, serving to avoid even greater suffering down the road, these authors argue. As TerKeurst repeatedly states, "God loves me too much to answer my prayers at any other time than the right time and in any other way than the right way."[13] This plan is not ours to question. Lucado echoes this, writing that even if God provided a reason, "what makes us think we would understand it?"[14] He implies the problem lies more in our limited perspective than God's actions.

At times, these authors even compare questioning amidst suffering to the Genesis story of the Fall, where eating the apple represented indulging dangerous doubts. Doubting God's vision in our pain gives in to the Devil's influence. Lucado both reassures and warns, "What is coming will make sense of what is happening now. Let God finish his work. Let the composer complete his symphony. The forecast is simple. Good days. Bad days. But God is in all days. He is the Lord of the famine and the feast, and he uses both to accomplish his will."[15]

Lucado argues that moments of suffering are "ingredients" that God will bring together to create something good. Comparing suffering to the hot water used to make coffee, Lucado muses that hot water alone does not taste good. In his view, suffering itself is not good, but "God will mix [it] with other ingredients and bring good out of them." However, "we must let God define good." Our human definition centers on health, comfort, and recognition. Yet, in the case of Jesus, God defined Christ's good life as one with "struggles, storms, and death." Still, God worked it all toward the greatest good: "his glory and our salvation."[16] So, our suffering plays a role

---

11. Lucado, *You'll Get Through This*, 84–85.
12. TerKeurst, *It's Not Supposed to Be This Way*.
13. TerKeurst, 45.
14. Lucado, *You'll Get Through This*, 84–85.
15. Lucado, 87.
16. Lucado, 83.

in the good life that God plans for us, even if we cannot see how. The call is to trust God's ultimate plan.

Both Lucado and TerKeurst believe suffering serves a divine purpose and that we are chosen by God to endure both suffering and blessings. To illustrate this point, both authors utilize the narrative of Jesus healing the blind man (John 9:1–7). They employ the metaphor of a "sign" to describe the man's disability, suggesting that his life of suffering becomes a canvas for "displaying the works of God." The man's deposition is further likened to a metaphorical "billboard for Jesus's power to heal."[17] Reflecting on this biblical story, TerKeurst prompts her readers to consider the idea that the most challenging aspects of their lives are "actually gateways to the very best parts you'd never want to do without."[18]

These popular interpretations, as exemplified by Lucado and TerKeurst, reveal a deep-seated ableism and problematic lack of sensitivity to trauma in their portrayal of the blind man. In these narratives, the blind man is diminished to an object without personal agency, his suffering exploited merely as a display of Jesus's miracles. This approach not only objectifies individuals with disabilities but also undermines their dignity and humanity, perpetuating harmful ableist narratives.

Moreover, these interpretations encourage a broader acceptance of powerlessness and suffering as divinely ordained, glorifying suffering as both inevitable and spiritually beneficial. This theology, emphasizing passive obedience to God, extends its harmful impact beyond the disabled community. It dissuades individuals, regardless of their circumstances, from actively seeking solutions or advocating for change. This narrative inadvertently supports a faith of passivity in the face of adversity and injustice.

The harmful impact of narratives that portray suffering as a divine act is evident in Deborah's survivor account. She remembered being told as a child, "If you pray to God with a pure heart, nothing can hurt you because God would never let an innocent child suffer." This belief deeply influenced Deborah as she endured her abuse, leading her to view her pain and suffering as purposeful and a consequence of her own guilt. Reflecting on these memories, she shared, "I always felt like I had control of the abuse because if I

---

17. TerKeurst, *It's Not Supposed to Be This Way*, 134.
18. TerKeurst, 134.

had memorized the prayer, if I had you know, not done something evil . . . then the abuse wouldn't take place."

It is not my intention to critique Lucado and TerKeurst as academic scholars; such a comparison would be inappropriate given their roles as popular religious figures and pastors and my position as a theologian. However, I present their perspectives as examples of widespread Christian interpretations of suffering and atonement. These popular understandings, while not overtly harmful, subtly support more problematic theological concepts such as glorified suffering and self-sacrifice. These narratives, often critically unexamined, shape our cultural and religious contexts. They contribute to a culture that fosters shame, guilt, and abuse, resulting in a society that tolerates abuse and a church community that further traumatizes survivors.

As we explore the ramifications of atonement and the cross, especially in the context of clergy sexual abuse, it's vital to first understand the broader spectrum of sexual abuse in the United States. This understanding forms a vital foundation for analyzing the specific ways in which atonement theologies uniquely impact survivors of sexual abuse. It will also help us to further define the dynamic relationships between faith, moral injury, and abuse.

Overview of Sexual Abuse

At this point, you may find yourself thinking, "How prevalent is sexual abuse within my community?" This is a crucial inquiry, especially as we contemplate whether our understanding of the cross and atonement should be shaped by the experience of abuse survivors.

Sexual abuse is tragically common. Picture your church gathering on a Sunday morning or imagine being among friends and family. Statistically, one in every three women and one in four men you see is a survivor of physical sexual abuse.

Beyond these alarming numbers, our Christian faith, particularly within the Catholic tradition, teaches us to prioritize the poor and oppressed. This preferential option for the poor involves more than just addressing their needs or dismantling systems of inequality. It calls us to actively listen to and prioritize their experiences in life. For those of us grappling with theological truths, integrating the voices of survivors into our understanding is not just a matter of compassion—it is an ethical imperative.[19]

Statistical Prevalence

Sexual abuse in the United States is alarmingly prevalent. Currently, 43.6 percent of women (over 52 million) and 24.8 percent of men (over 27 million) have experienced physical sexual abuse in their lifetimes.[20] This includes the harrowing statistic that one in five women in the United States will face rape or attempted rape.[21] When we expand our definition of sexual abuse to encompass harassment, the numbers rise staggeringly to 81 percent of women and 43 percent of men impacted.[22]

While sexual abuse spans all demographics, women predominantly bear the brunt of these assaults. Notably, the prevalence of sexual abuse among women does not significantly vary across different demographics, with two exceptions: disability status and sexual orientation. Women who identify as disabled, lesbian, or bisexual face a higher risk of sexual assault. Among men, marginalized groups—those who are low-income, men of color, gay or bisexual, or living with a disability—are more likely to report physical sexual abuse.[23] Most survivors, both women (81.3 percent) and men (70.8 percent), encounter their first experience of rape or attempted rape before the age of twenty-five, with the age range of fourteen to seventeen being particularly vulnerable (27 percent of women and 20 percent of men).[24]

The impact of sexual assault on survivors is profound and varied,

---

19. Ashley Theuring, "Imagining a Sacramental Method: Divine Presence in the Lives of the Crucified Peoples," *Ecclesial Practices* 8, no. 1 (2021): 11–25.

20. S. G. Smith, X. Zhang, K. C. Basile, M. T. Merrick, J. Wang, M. Kresnow, J. Chen, "The National Intimate Partner and Sexual Violence Survey: 2015 Data Brief—Updated Release" (Atlanta: Centers for Disease Control and Prevention, 2018).

21. Smith et al., "The National Intimate Partner and Sexual Violence Survey."

22. Holly Kearl, "The Facts behind the #MeToo Movement: A National Study on Sexual Harassment and Assault (Executive Summary)," 2018, https://www.nsvrc.org/resource/facts-behind-metoo-movement-national-study-sexual-harassment-and-assault, pp. 7-8.

23. Kearl, "The Facts Behind the #MeToo Movement."

24. Kearl, "The Facts Behind the #MeToo Movement."

leading to an increased frequency and severity of psychopathologies such as post-traumatic stress disorder (PTSD), stress-related conditions, suicidality, depression, anxiety, disordered eating, bipolar disorder, obsessive-compulsive conditions, and substance abuse or dependence.[25] The severity of these disorders is influenced by factors like the individual's psychosocial health, the trauma of the assault, postassault responses, previous traumas, and societal norms.[26] Notably, many of these disorders, such as PTSD and anxiety, often overlap. The relationship between these psychopathologies and sexual assault is complex, with ongoing research exploring whether conditions like depression or anxiety are direct results of the assault, are heightened by PTSD resulting from the assault, or are influenced by a combination of genetic predispositions and other unknown variables. Even conditions traditionally believed to be primarily genetic, like bipolar disorder, can be exacerbated by sexual assault.[27]

Survivors of sexual assault face a uniquely severe risk of suicidal ideation and attempts, a risk that is notably higher than that faced by individuals with PTSD from nonsexual traumas. This heightened vulnerability may be tied to the stigma and shame so often associated with sexual assault.[28] Self-blame plays a critical role in this context, both at the individual and the cultural levels. For the individual, self-blame is linked to higher rates of PTSD and depression. Additionally, encountering victim-blaming responses from others, including family members, healthcare providers, and law enforcement, exacerbates PTSD symptoms. At a broader cultural level, rape myths and victim-blaming attitudes profoundly impact survivors' experiences of trauma.[29]

In Deborah's story, the intertwining of blame and guilt is stark. She repeatedly expressed feeling responsible for the abuse that she endured. As a child, she was indoctrinated with the belief that

---

25. Emily R. Dworkin, Suvarna V. Menon, Jonathan Bystrynski, and Nicole E. Allen, "Sexual Assault Victimization and Psychopathology: A Review and Meta-Analysis," *Clinical Psychology Review* 56 (2017): 65–81.

26. Rebecca Campbell, Emily Dworkin, and Giannina Cabral, "An Ecological Model of the Impact of Sexual Assault on Women's Mental Health," *Trauma, Violence, & Abuse* 10, no. 3 (2009): 225–46.

27. Dworkin et al., "Sexual Assault Victimization and Psychopathology."

28. Dworkin et al., "Sexual Assault Victimization and Psychopathology."

29. Campbell et al., "An Ecological Model."

"God would never let an innocent child suffer," leading her to conclude that her suffering was a consequence of her own guilt. This belief, exploited by her abuser, kept her silent, too frightened to confide in her parents or anyone else. Deborah described her childhood as feeling "like I'm just tumbling down into this huge hole with no way out." Later in life, she grappled with guilt for not having disclosed the abuse earlier, both as a child to stop it and as an adult to prevent its continuation. Her efforts later in life as a teacher to have the abusive priest removed from her workplace were met with victim-blaming, epitomized in a confessional where a priest condemned her, saying, "You have ruined a priest's life. That's a mortal sin." The profound impact of shame and guilt, often rooted in survivors' spiritual and religious beliefs, plays a crucial role in shaping their perceptions and narratives of abuse.

Spirituality and Sexual Assault: An Inscrutable Relationship

The relationship between religion, spirituality, and trauma is multifaceted. This is especially true in cases of sexual assault, when religion and personal spirituality can play a dual role for survivors as both supportive and burdensome. Survivors' religious coping methods significantly influence their psychological well-being. Negative religious responses, like feeling disappointed or angry with God, tend to worsen mental health outcomes. In contrast, integrating faith into rape-awareness programs can be beneficial, helping survivors process their trauma, affirm their identity, and foster healing.[30]

The impact of trauma on religious identity is equally complex. Survivors often feel abandoned by God or their community, leading to a diminished or rejected religious identity. A study focusing on Jewish survivors of sexual assault revealed that about half

---

30. For more on this relationship see the following texts: Ashley Theuring, "A Brief History of Domestic Violence and Theology," in *Fragile Resurrection: Hope after Domestic Violence* (Eugene, OR: Cascade Books, 2021), 57–92; Lisa Rudolfsson, "Religious Victims of Sexual Abuse," in *Sexual Crime, Religion and Spirituality*, ed. I. Levy and E. Eckhaus (Leiden: Brill, 2020), 163–94; I. Levy and E. Eckhaus, "Rape Narratives Analysis through Natural Language Processing: Survivor Self-Label, Narrative Time Span, Faith, and Rape Terminology," *Psychological Trauma: Theory, Research, Practice, and Policy* 12, no. 6 (2020): 635–42.

became more secular post-trauma.[31] This tendency toward secularization might be even more pronounced in cases of religiously related trauma. Deborah's experience shows the complex interplay between her Catholic faith and the trauma of sexual abuse by clergy. Her abuse, starting from a young age, was intertwined with religious manipulation, leading to a deep sense of being evil and unworthy. The perpetrators used religious authority to justify their actions, deeply impacting her spiritual life and leading to a significant loss of faith and trust in the Catholic Church. After having grown up in a strongly religious and culturally Catholic household, Deborah now describes religion as playing no part in her life. In our qualitative study of fifteen clergy sexual abuse survivors, 60 percent (nine out of fifteen) no longer identified as Catholic.

Furthermore, survivors of abuse in a religious context, like Deborah, often suffer more severe mental health issues, including heightened symptoms of depression, anxiety, hostility, psychosis, paranoia, and somatization, compared to those abused in a nonreligious context. Beyond these mental health impacts, survivors of clergy sexual abuse also endure existential and spiritual traumas, often describing their experience as challenging the very meaning of life.[32]

When a survivor's traumatic experiences, like a violent assault, starkly contrast with their fundamental beliefs and worldviews, it can trigger a crisis. For example, the belief in a protective and benevolent God may be deeply challenged in the aftermath of an assault, as was the case for Deborah, who was told and believed God would not let innocent children suffer. The erosion of trust between the survivor and their religious beliefs often has broader implications, extending to their religious life and leading to a decreased engagement with their faith communities.[33]

Religious settings can be triggering for some survivors. Liturgical language around sacrifice, male-dominated authority struc-

---

31. Menachem Ben-Ezra, Yuval Palgi, Dina Sternberg, Dina Berkley, Hadar Eldar, Yael Glidai, Liron Moshe, and Amit Shrira, "Losing My Religion: A Preliminary Study of Changes in Belief Pattern after Sexual Assault," *Traumatology* 16, no. 2 (2010): 7–13.

32. See Rudolfsson, "Religious Victims of Sexual Abuse"; D. P. Farrell, "Sexual Abuse Perpetrated by Roman Catholic Priests and Religious," *Mental Health, Religion & Culture* 12 (2009): 39–53.

33. See Rudolfsson, "Religious Victims of Sexual Abuse."

tures, or unexamined concepts of forgiveness can evoke feelings of shame, guilt, and alienation. The lack of awareness and training in sexual abuse issues among church leaders often leaves survivors feeling unsafe. This shows us the need for trauma-informed and sensitive practices in religious contexts, including healing rituals and discussions on sensitive topics like forgiveness. Inclusivity in liturgical planning, especially involving survivors, is crucial to avoid reinforcing feelings of exclusion and shame.[34]

Conversely, many survivors find that their religious narratives and worldviews become crucial for their healing process. Some survivors find significant support in their religious communities, leading to a revitalized religious identity post-trauma.[35] Among the fifteen survivors we interviewed, six continued identifying as Catholic. They, like Nathan, the survivor from the previous chapter, drew on religious narratives to find meaning in their suffering.

Finally, shifting focus from how abuse impacts faith, it's crucial to consider how a survivor's religious beliefs and worldview might shape their vulnerability to and experiences of abuse. Many survivors report that their religious and conservative upbringing made them more susceptible to victimization.[36] The narratives of obedience and trust in God and the church, often found in Christian texts, can inadvertently create environments conducive to abuse, as was the case for Deborah. High religiosity has been linked to victim-blaming and acceptance of rape myths, potentially depriving survivors of the agency needed to seek help or stop the abuse.[37] Such victim-blaming can lead to severe mental health repercussions, including shame and guilt. This, in turn, may result in "moral injury," where survivors grapple with deep questions about their own goodness and the nature of morality.

---

34. Lisa Rudolfsson and Fredrik Portin, "It's Almost Impossible to Speak about It: Sexual Abuse, Forgiveness, and the Need for Restitution Rituals," *Religions* 9, no. 12 (2018): 421.

35. See Rudolfsson, "Religious Victims of Sexual Abuse."

36. A. Barker and R. V. Galliher, "Young Women's Sexual Assault Experiences: Exploring Conservative Socialisation Experiences as an Important Contextual Factor," *Sex Education* 20, no. 5 (2020): 477–93.

37. Emma G. Heath and Kathryn Sperry, "A Religious Paradox: Can Priming Ideas of God Reduce Rape Victim Blame?," *Sex Roles* 84 (2021): 196–207.

Sexual Abuse and Moral Injury

Building on the understanding of how abuse impacts a survivor's religious beliefs and their vulnerability, we now turn to the concept of moral injury. A critical topic in the fields of psychology and trauma studies, moral injury was first recognized in military veterans. It involves the betrayal of deeply held moral beliefs, often by an authority figure in high-stakes situations, leading to profound psychological and spiritual distress. Moral injury's relevance to sexual abuse becomes evident when considering how religious upbringing and narratives can foster environments where abuse occurs. This section will explore the comprehensive effects of moral injury on survivors of sexual abuse, including the complex roles of guilt, perpetration, and witnessing acts that violate moral beliefs.

The concept of moral injury first emerged in the works of Jonathan Shay, a doctor and clinical psychiatrist focusing on veterans. Shay defines moral injury as a betrayal of what's right by someone in a position of legitimate authority in a high-stakes situation.[38] This definition reflects the experiences of veterans who exhibited symptoms of moral injury due to their exposure to human suffering and violence in the military.

Moral injury's scope was later broadened to include not only the immoral acts of superiors but also the actions of individuals themselves. Brett Litz, a psychiatric professor and researcher, expands moral injury to the wider enduring psychological, biological, spiritual, behavioral, and social impacts of perpetrating, failing to prevent, or bearing witness to acts that violate one's moral beliefs.[39] This definition includes the holistic nature of trauma and, specifically, moral injury. It also recognizes the complexities of perpetration, guilt, and the roles of enablers and bystanders in violence.

While initially observed in veterans, the concept of moral injury has expanded to encompass various nonmilitary contexts. It can occur whenever an individual's actions conflict with their core moral values, leading to guilt and shame. Though studied in diverse fields like education, nursing, and during crises such as pandemics,

---

38. J. Shay, "Moral Injury," *Psychoanalytic Psychology* 31, no. 2 (2014): 182–91, 183.

39. B. T. Litz, N. Stein, E. Delaney, L. Lebowitz, W. P. Nash, C. Silva, and S. Maguen, "Moral Injury and Moral Repair in War Veterans: A Preliminary Model and Intervention Strategy," *Clinical Psychology Review* 29, no. 8 (2009): 695–706, 697.

research remains predominantly focused on military experiences, with a notable lack of civilian-specific measurement tools.[40]

While not new to the human experience, moral injury is a developing concept in psychological and sociological theory, still being defined, measured, and treated. Debates continue even over its causation, with differing views on whether it stems from natural cognitive processes or physical trauma to the brain.[41] These discussions, including whether moral injury is a subset of trauma or PTSD, or a distinct mental disorder, I'll happily leave to the experts at the American Psychiatric Association.

Symptoms of Moral Injury

Moral injury, whether viewed as a condition with specific symptoms or as a constellation of maladaptive cognitive processes, remains a complex phenomenon. Its symptoms, however, are crucial for distinguishing it from other trauma-related conditions, such as PTSD. While PTSD and moral injury share many symptoms and can be triggered by similar events, a key difference lies in the nature of their impact. Those experiencing moral injury often grapple with intense feelings of guilt and shame, irrespective of their role in the event. PTSD typically arises from events threatening one's life or

---

40. For more on the expansion of moral injury beyond military contexts, see E. A. Dombo, C. Gray, and B. P. Early, "The Trauma of Moral Injury: Beyond the Battlefield," *Journal of Religion & Spirituality in Social Work* 32, no. 3 (2013): 197–210; Meira Levinson, "Moral Injury and the Ethics of Educational Injustice," *Harvard Educational Review* 85, no. 2 (2015): 203–28; J. McCarthy and R. Deady, "Moral Distress Reconsidered," *Nursing Ethics* 15, no. 2 (2008): 254–62; Jennifer Middleton and Amber McDonald, "Creating Sanctuary: Trauma-Informed Change for Survivors of Sex Trafficking and Commercial Sexual Exploitation," in *The Palgrave International Handbook of Human Trafficking* (Cham, Switzerland: Palgrave Macmillan, 2020), 583–600; Wendy Haight, Erin P. Sugrue, and Molly Calhoun, "Moral Injury among Child Protection Professionals: Implications for the Ethical Treatment and Retention of Workers," *Children and Youth Services Review* 82 (2017): 27–41; Suzanne Shale, "Moral Injury and the COVID-19 Pandemic: Reframing What It Is, Who It Affects and How Care Leaders Can Manage It," *BMJ Leader* 4 (2020): 224–27.

41. For more on this debate, see J. K. Farnsworth, J. A. Nieuwsma, K. D. Drescher, R. B. Walser, and J. M. Currier, "The Role of Moral Emotions in Military Trauma: Implications for the Study and Treatment of Moral Injury," *Review of General Psychology* 18, no. 4 (2014): 249–62; and W. P. Nash, "Commentary on the Special Issue on Moral Injury: Unpacking Two Models for Understanding Moral Injury," *Journal of Traumatic Stress* 32, no. 3 (2019): 465–70.

safety, embodying an existential threat. In contrast, moral injury challenges a person's moral framework, threatening their sense of "goodness" and ethical integrity. This distinction underlines why conventional PTSD treatments may not fully address the complexities of moral injury.[42]

Survivors suffering from moral injury may exhibit a range of symptoms, including guilt, shame, spiritual or existential conflicts (like questioning life's purpose), and various psychological issues (depression, anxiety, anger, intrusive memories, self-destructive behaviors, and suicidal tendencies). Social difficulties, such as loss of trust and isolation, are also common. Many of these symptoms overlap with PTSD. PTSD and moral injury often occur together, especially in military veterans, where the event itself is both traumatic and causes deep moral and ethical distress. However, these overlapping symptoms are not exclusive to military contexts; similar patterns of overlap between moral injury and PTSD can also emerge in civilian experiences.[43]

Cultural and Spiritual Context of Moral Injury

Continuing research is beginning to clarify the relationship and differences between moral injury and PTSD, particularly as we give more attention to the role of cultural and spiritual contexts. Key questions arise: how do our surroundings shape our perceptions of blame, guilt, and shame? In our discussion about the trauma of sexual abuse, especially focusing on clergy sexual abuse, understanding the distinct symptoms of moral injury, such as shame and guilt, is crucial. Historically, sexual abuse has been linked to PTSD, a connection made well known by Judith Herman in her influential book, *Trauma and Recovery*.[44]

---

42. Harold G. Koenig, Donna Ames, Nagy A. Youssef, John P. Oliver, Fred Volk, Ellen J. Teng, Kerry Haynes, Zachary D. Erickson, Irina Arnold, Keisha O'Garo, and Michelle Pearce, "The Moral Injury Symptom Scale—Military Version," *Journal of Religion and Health* 57, no. 1 (2018): 249–65.

43. See Jeremy D. Jinkerson, "Defining and Assessing Moral Injury: A Syndrome Perspective," *Traumatology* 22, no. 2 (2016): 122–30; B. T. Litz et al., "Moral Injury and Moral Repair in War Veterans," 697; Kent D. Drescher, David W. Foy, Camilo Kelly, Amy Leshner, Karen Schutz, and Brett Litz, "An Exploration of the Viability and Usefulness of the Construct of Moral Injury in War Veterans," *Traumatology* 17, no. 1 (2011): 8–13.

44. Judith Lewis Herman, *Trauma and Recovery: The Aftermath of Violence—From Domestic Abuse to Political Terror* (London: Hachette, 2015).

However, it's only recently that theorists have begun to explore the concept of moral injury in relation to sexual abuse. Deborah's story shows a clear link between her sexual abuse and her sense of her moral self. When asked about her sense of self growing up after her abuse, she frequently remarked that she felt "less than," not "good enough," or like a "failure." The sexual nature of clergy abuse introduces complex layers of cultural and religious interpretations of guilt, shame, sex, consent, and our own bodies.

Social philosopher Sarah Clark Miller asserts that the impact of rape on survivors extends beyond personal suffering, leading to the wider stripping of dignity and a loss of voice within entire communities. Her work with survivors of rape in genocides and ethnic cleansing in Darfur revealed that moral injury, often experienced as overwhelming shame and guilt, leads to a collective degradation in the survivors' perspective. Cultural perceptions of the body, sex, women, and consent profoundly influence the interpretation of rape by the individual.[45] In Deborah's account, she recalls her childhood confusion about sex and consent, perceiving only the sinfulness of the act and her implicated guilt. Both Miller's research and Deborah's narrative illustrate how survivors' shame and guilt are deeply embedded in societal beliefs and myths about the act of rape itself.

Shame, both emotionally and conceptually, is profoundly shaped by cultural views on dignity and virtue. An individual's cultural beliefs about sex and the body significantly influence their interpretation of sexual abuse and the extent of moral injury it can cause. This effect also extends to the survivor's personal spirituality. Studies show that individuals who experience considerable spiritual distress as part of their moral injury often had stronger religious or spiritual beliefs prior to their trauma, indicating that one's faith deeply affects how they interpret traumatic events and their susceptibility to moral injury.[46]

Deborah's story embodies this truth. She recalls her childhood as deeply rooted in her faith, with cherished memories of midnight

---

45. S. C. Miller, "Moral Injury and Relational Harm: Analyzing Rape in Darfur," *Journal of Social Philosophy* 40, no. 4 (2009): 504–23, 504.

46. J. M. Currier, J. D. Foster, and S. L. Isaak, "Moral Injury and Spiritual Struggles in Military Veterans: A Latent Profile Analysis," *Journal of Traumatic Stress* 32, no. 3 (2019): 393–404.

Mass and its music. However, she also expresses a profound sense of loss, mourning what was taken from her. Her experience, alongside the above research, suggests that sexual abuse within a religious context, like clergy sexual abuse, is likely to be a deeply morally injurious event, with a high risk of harmful religious coping mechanisms.

Clergy Sexual Abuse and Moral Injury

As we investigate the causes and consequences of the clergy sexual abuse crisis and its cover-up in the coming chapters, our focus narrows to the specific way sexual abuse within our churches can lead to moral injury. This understanding stems from in-depth interviews I conducted with fifteen survivors of childhood clergy sexual abuse during the winter of 2021 and spring of 2022. These interviews, part of Fordham University's Taking Responsibility project, were conducted by a multidisciplinary team from Xavier University. Our exploration included both qualitative survivor interviews and broader quantitative surveys, enriching the insights presented in this book.[47]

Deborah's story, emblematic of this struggle, reveals the deep moral conflict and shame that many survivors faced. A profound sense of moral confusion was central to the experiences of clergy sexual abuse survivors, significantly impacting their sense of self-worth and agency. This confusion stemmed from a stark contradiction between their deeply held beliefs about God, the church, and the world, and the reality of their traumatic experiences. Survivors like Deborah struggled to articulate their pain, lacking the language and frameworks to fully understand their abuse. Deborah describes feeling trapped in a moral paradox, unable to reconcile her image of God, as someone who would "not let an innocent child suffer," with the reality of her abuse.

---

47. Of the fifteen survivors interviewed, five were women and ten were men. All fifteen identified as having been raised in the Catholic Church prior to being abused. The survivors' ages at the start of the abuse ranged from six to sixteen years old, with an average age of 10.8 years. The duration of the abuse experiences ranged from four months to ten years, with an average length of 3.6 years. At present, six survivors still identify as Catholic, five identify as spiritual, and four identify as nonreligious/nonspiritual.

This moral confusion, a recurrent theme across our interviews, emerged from the dissonance between survivors' beliefs and their experiences. For some, it was the shattered belief in the inherent goodness of priests, the safety of the church, or the authority of adults. This internal conflict eroded their sense of self, engendering feelings of shame and unworthiness, and left them grappling with a sense of helplessness and diminished agency.

In their journey toward healing, many survivors we interviewed identified resolving their core moral confusion as crucial to their recovery. This process often involved cultivating moral clarity by reevaluating and sometimes reimagining their previously contradicted beliefs. For Deborah, achieving moral clarity meant rejecting the misconception that suffering is a measure of one's goodness and reshaping her own story through a trauma-informed lens.

Articulating their experiences became a crucial step for survivors in regaining a sense of power and agency. Deborah's involvement in survivor advocacy and her connections with other survivors significantly boosted her self-esteem. She realized that she was no longer bound by the oppressive expectations and rules that had constrained her during her childhood. This newfound voice and perspective marked a turning point in the healing process for many survivors, transforming how they saw themselves and instilling a profound sense of empowerment. These stories underscore the transformative power of storytelling in healing, demonstrating how redefining one's past can lead to a renewed sense of self and purpose.

Atonement Implications

Survivors of sexual abuse, such as Deborah, navigate through complex layers of trauma, one of which is moral injury. As we saw above, the extent of this moral injury often hinges on factors such as cultural and religious contexts, the nature of the abuse, and the effectiveness of their support systems. In cases of clergy sexual abuse, the religious context intensifies the trauma, making it particularly susceptible to moral injury. This is in part due to how the church's extensive tradition, spanning over two millennia, profoundly shapes how trauma survivors perceive and articulate their suffering. Atonement theology is a significant element of this tradition.

Atonement narratives, beyond their obvious potential to trigger survivors of sexual abuse, also exert a profound cultural and spiritual influence on individuals. This impact is clearly seen in the narratives from top-selling books in Christian theology and spirituality, as analyzed earlier. These texts often promote a toxic spirituality that frames suffering as divinely sanctioned and formative. Followers are encouraged to mirror Jesus's acceptance, trust, and endurance in the face of suffering. A similar pattern emerged in Deborah's story, where religious narratives were manipulated to associate suffering with virtue. Such narratives deeply influence how individuals interpret life events, echoing theologian Elizabeth Johnson's observation that "the symbol of God functions" or that our God language shapes our lives.[48] In essence, our atonement narratives mold our perceptions of right and wrong, and, significantly, they shape how individuals process their experiences of sexual abuse.

I argue that these harmful narratives contribute to a cultural and religious context that heightens the likelihood of moral injury in survivors of sexual abuse, like Deborah. They do this by framing suffering in a way that often invalidates or exacerbates the survivors' traumatic experiences

The Problem of Evil

Evil presents a significant challenge within the Christian worldview. The question arises: if God is all-powerful, good, and loving, why does evil persist? Throughout history, individuals and communities have grappled with this dilemma. Figures like Irenaeus have posited that while God doesn't cause evil, God permits it as a means to enrich our souls and serve the greater good. However, these theological interpretations are problematic. They imply that suffering should be endured rather than used to address the underlying evils in our society.[49]

---

48. Elizabeth A. Johnson, "Female Symbols for God: The Apophatic Tradition and Social Justice," *International Journal of Orthodox Theology* 1, no. 2 (2010): 40–57, 40.

49. For more on this, see Marie M. Fortune, "The Transformation of Suffering: A Biblical and Theological Perspective," in *Violence against Women and Children: A Christian Theological Sourcebook*, ed. Carol J. Adams and Marie M. Fortune (New York: Continuum, 1995), 85–91.

For survivors of sexual abuse, like Deborah, such interpretations frame their suffering as divinely permitted, potentially beneficial even. This perspective can lead to several adverse effects. First, if survivors don't perceive their abuse as having "strengthened" them, they might feel a sense of personal failure. This was certainly the case for Deborah, who suffered with feelings of failure and unworthiness long after her abuse. Second, this narrative could discourage them from seeking change in their abusive situations, under the misguided belief that enduring suffering will somehow better them spiritually. This is particularly troubling in cases of sexual abuse. While many survivors do find ways to "make meaning" from their experiences, the notion that they are spiritually enhanced by such trauma is deeply flawed and offensive.

Feminist theologian Marie Fortune firmly rejects this "endurance" model of interpreting evil. Instead, she advocates for a theology centered on "transformation"—focusing not on the reasons for suffering or the existence of evil, but on aiding people to transform suffering through hope and empowerment. Fortune states, "by refusing to endure evil and by seeking to transform suffering, we are about God's work of making justice and healing brokenness."[50] Thus, interpretations of the crucifixion that suggest that God allowed Jesus's suffering and death for a greater purpose can be particularly harmful and triggering for survivors of violence. The notion that everything, including the traumatic experience of sexual assault, happens for a reason is, at best, a naïve understanding of the complex realities of suffering.

The Problem of Sin

The concept of sin, especially when linked to experiences of violence, becomes particularly problematic for survivors, and even more so for those who have endured sexual violence, like Deborah. The Christian tradition has often focused on personal sin, framing it as an act of disobedience against God, a matter to be resolved between the individual and the Divine. This interpretation, which characterizes sin as a "rebellion against God," overlooks the impact on the victims and fails to address the needs that are essential for their healing. A view of sin that neglects the social and systemic

---

50. Fortune, "The Transformation of Suffering," 91.

aspects of sin falls short in addressing the complexities of rape culture and the pervasiveness of sexual abuse.

In Deborah's story, she was frequently told by her abusers and bystanders that she had caused a priest to sin. This response not only blamed Deborah for her abuse but turned the abuse into the priest's personal sin against God. Sexual abuse must be understood as both a personal sin against a victim and a social sin that is supported by broader systems of sexism, clericalism, secrecy, and a lack of accountability. In this context, rape culture implicates everyone. Survivors of sexual abuse are not merely observers of a perpetrator's sin against God. Our understanding of sin must mature, recognizing the collective harm inflicted on the victim.

Additionally, the Christian tradition's relationship with sexuality complicates the issue. Since the 1980s, feminist theologians such as Lisa Cahill and Margaret Farley have urged the tradition to develop more comprehensive approaches to sexuality and sexual ethics. However, historically, a purity culture that is focused on abstinence and marital procreation has dominated Christian thought. The church community's historical reticence about sex has allowed rape culture to flourish unchecked. A morality that is obsessed with obedience and sexual purity fosters internalization and perpetuation of rape myths, including victim-blaming and misconceptions about rape.

Marie Fortune advocates for a redefinition of sin, calling it "sin-as-harm-done-to-others." This perspective on sin, especially in cases of sexual violence, acknowledges victimization and stresses the need for accountability for those causing harm. Sexual assault, under this framework, is a sin by the perpetrator as it violates another person, inflicting physical and/or emotional harm through the denial of autonomy and choice. This understanding does not absolve perpetrators but rather explicitly recognizes the violence as a sin against the victim. It opens the door for accountability and potential consequences for the perpetrator, and, crucially, justice and healing for the victim.[51]

In a similar vein, Marjorie Suchocki, in *The Fall to Violence*, redefines sin as "participation through intent or act in unnecessary vio-

---

51. Marie Fortune, "The Conundrum of Sin, Sex, Violence, and Theodicy," in *The Other Side of Sin: Woundedness from the Perspective of the Sinned-Against*, ed. Andrew Sung Park and Susan L. Nelson (New York: Paulist Press, 2001), 123–42.

lence that contributes to the ill-being of any aspect of earth or its inhabitants."[52] Moving beyond the traditional Augustinian definition of sin as rebellion against God, Suchocki argues that sin is a rebellion against creation itself, encompassing both God and the victims.

By expanding the concept of sin beyond a mere individual act against God to include broader social contexts, the victim, and all implicated parties, we can reclaim the language of sin in a way that is meaningful and powerful. Recognizing sexual abuse as both a social and a personal sin paves the way for paths of accountability, retribution, and healing. Unfortunately, the persistence of purity culture and rape myths within the popular Christian imagination continues to inflict psychological harm on survivors of sexual assault.

Glorified Suffering

One of the most problematic interpretations of the cross, particularly for trauma survivors, is the justification or glorification of suffering. Common narratives surrounding the crucifixion often depict Jesus's suffering as essential for humanity's salvation, even suggesting that Jesus endured the "greatest" suffering, a self-sacrifice that redeems us. This portrayal, frequently amplified in popular reenactments, media, and passion narratives, fixates on the extreme violence and torture of the crucifixion. By portraying Jesus's pain as beyond human understanding and labeling it as necessary, trauma survivors are often left in a troubling dilemma: they must either diminish their own pain or see it as a necessary, even beneficial, experience.

For survivors of sexual abuse, like Deborah, depictions of Jesus's pain as uniquely horrific and necessary can be particularly triggering. The emphasis on violence and the notion that Jesus suffered the most not only resonates painfully with their own experiences but also implicitly suggests that their suffering is comparatively less significant. This approach risks delegitimizing the profound pain and trauma survivors have endured.

Moreover, glorifying Jesus's self-sacrifice as noble and salvific presents another challenge. It implies that suffering, like Jesus's,

---

52. Marjorie Suchocki, *The Fall to Violence: Original Sin in Relational Theology* (London: A & C Black, 1994), 12.

is justifiable if it leads to some greater good, or conversely, it is a source of shame if it does not yield such benefits. For survivors, this perspective can create an untenable situation: either they view their suffering as beneficial, which can pressure them into embracing further self-sacrifice, or they feel shame and guilt for not finding redemptive value in their trauma. This is particularly distressing for survivors of sexual abuse, like Deborah, where issues of consent, guilt, and shame are already so prevalent. To suggest that their abuse was a "chosen sacrifice" is to overlook the fundamental absence of agency and consent inherent in acts of sexual violence.

Addressing the glorification of suffering is a complex task, both theologically and practically. Trauma theorists and mental health professionals recognize the therapeutic value in survivors finding meaning in their suffering and incorporating their trauma narratives into their lives. A large part of healing for Deborah was becoming part of and, later, leading her survivors' network. However, the challenge lies in finding purpose without justifying or glorifying the trauma, which can retraumatize survivors or contribute to victim coercion. Feminist theologians Joanne Carlson Brown and Rebecca Parker poignantly highlight this dilemma, observing that women have often been persuaded that their suffering is justifiable. Their skepticism about the capacities of church leadership and thinkers to transform their interpretation of suffering and the cross is stark, likening the situation of women in church communities to victims remaining in abusive relationships.[53]

Brown and Parker argue forcefully that Christianity must outright reject the notion that suffering is redemptive. They contend that any glorification of suffering perpetuates abuse and leads to the justification of victim suffering. Their bold assertion that equating salvation solely with the cross turns God into a "divine sadist and a divine child abuser"[54] is a provocative wake-up call. The next step

---

53. Joanne Carlson Brown and Rebecca Parker, "For God So Loved the World?," in Carol J. Adams and Marie Fortune, eds., *Violence against Women and Children: A Christian Theological Sourcebook* (London: A & C Black, 1995), 36. Originally printed in Joanne Carlson Brown and Rebecca Parker, "For God So Loved the World?," in *Christianity, Patriarchy, and Abuse: A Feminist Critique,* ed. Joanne Carlson Brown and Rebecca Parker (New York: Pilgrim Press, 1989).

54. Brown and Parker, "For God So Loved the World?," 53.

for feminist theologians who seek to remain within their church communities is to reinterpret the cross, Jesus's suffering, and their role in salvation in a way that resonates with and is sensitive to the experiences of trauma survivors.

God as Divine Child-Abuser

Substitutionary interpretations of the crucifixion often center the roles of God and Jesus as Father and Son, respectively. In these narratives, humanity is depicted as God's sinful children, contrasting with Jesus, the perfect Son. God, the omnipotent Father, sacrifices his flawless Son for the redemption of humanity. Jesus is portrayed as the obedient and willing participant in this divine plan, embodying submission to his Father's will.[55] This portrayal, however, raises profound issues, especially in the context of sexual abuse.

The emphasis on obedience and submission in these narratives becomes particularly troubling in the context of sexual abuse, where power imbalances and control are central. Sexual abuse often involves subjugation, and framing it within the language of obedience and submission can dangerously distort the reality of the abuse. In such a theological context, personal agency and well-being are overshadowed by the demand for obedience, which can be misused as a tool of abuse. Deborah's experience illustrates this vividly. She recalled the intense pressure she and her friends faced to obey their priests, leading to one of her friends being beaten by her mother for disclosing the abuse.

This issue is further complicated in cases of incest or clergy sexual abuse, where the abuser typically assumes a "fatherly" role. Deborah's account reflects this dynamic: "Father's this holy being. You can't talk about him like that," she said with the reverence and fear instilled in her by the clergy. Fortune and James Poling's theological investigation of clergy sexual abuse views this through the lens of incest. They note the similarity between the relationship of a male clergy abuser and a female parishioner or child and that of a patriarchal God with an obedient, self-sacrificing Jesus, symbolic of sinful humanity.[56]

---

55. Marie M. Fortune and James Newton Poling, *Sexual Abuse by Clergy: A Crisis for the Church* (Eugene, OR: Wipf & Stock, 2008), 29–43.

56. Fortune and Poling, *Sexual Abuse by Clergy*, 39.

This substitutionary narrative, portraying God as an abusive parent, essentially legitimizes abuse in our lives, particularly for children. It metaphorically reenacts the crucifixion, persuading victims that their suffering is required by divine decree. Fortune and Poling critically assess this viewpoint, urging Christians to reconceptualize their understanding of God. Moving away from traditional theistic perceptions of God as omnipotent and perfect is crucial, especially for survivors of sexual abuse. For them, such a depiction of God is not only misleading but also potentially damaging.

Conclusion

In the opening chapter, we explored how atonement theories and theologies of the cross can serve as potent healing narratives, aiding individuals in finding meaning amidst suffering. Positive religious narratives and worldviews often correlate with beneficial mental health outcomes, yet, as we learned from Deborah's story and supporting scientific research, there's a contrasting side. Negative religious coping mechanisms, narratives imbued with shame, guilt, and obedience, can inflict profound damage, especially on survivors of sexual abuse within religious contexts. Atonement theologies centered on violence, self-sacrifice, and human sin not only trigger survivors but can also exacerbate their mental health challenges through moral injury.

Moving forward, the next part of this book focuses on the context of clergy sexual abuse. We will examine its prevalence, history, and root causes. The intersection of religious context and the prevalent themes of shame in the clergy sexual abuse crisis provides a complex and challenging environment for reevaluating atonement theologies and theologies of the cross. Given that 4 percent of women and 2 percent of men have endured sexual abuse in religious settings, this investigation is essential. In understanding this context, we aim to reconstruct a theology of the cross that resonates with and is sensitive to the experiences of survivors like Deborah, providing a pathway for healing and transformation.

Part II

The Crisis in Context

Clergy Sexual Abuse

4

The Nature and History of the Clergy Sexual Abuse Crisis

"Who would believe that the hands of [a priest]—that were raised over us in blessing—would ever harm a child of God."

—Michael, survivor of clergy sexual abuse[1]

As we continue to navigate the complex interplay between atonement theologies and the lived experiences of those who have survived sexual trauma, revisiting and reflecting upon the stories of Michael, Nathan, and Deborah are crucial. Their narratives anchor our theological explorations and illuminate the deeply personal and systemic nature of the clergy sexual abuse crisis that has profoundly impacted the Catholic Church in the United States over the last fifty years.

Michael, in his fifties, embodies the journey of someone who, while distancing himself from institutional religion, remains deeply engaged in the survivor community. As a spiritual but not religious individual, his work as a communications coordinator for a survivor network symbolizes the critical role that connection and advocacy play in healing and reform.

---

1. The words of the survivor referred to as "Michael" throughout this book are from Survivor Transcript 10, taken from interviews with clergy abuse survivors done in the winter and spring of 2021 through research completed at Xavier University and supported by the Taking Responsibility grant through Fordham University.

Nathan's story offers a contrasting yet equally compelling narrative. As a practicing Catholic, he grapples with the tension of maintaining his faith amidst personal struggles with employment, depression, and strained family relationships. His commitment to advocating for justice for survivors gives us insight into the complex relationship many have with their faith and the institution that betrayed their trust.

Deborah, a retired schoolteacher, represents a powerful voice of advocacy and resilience. Having witnessed abuse within her professional environment, in addition to her own childhood abuse experience, her decision to no longer identify as Catholic does not diminish her dedication to supporting survivors. Her story spotlights the pervasive impact of clergy abuse affecting victims, educators, families, and communities at large.

By integrating the experiences of Michael, Nathan, and Deborah into our exploration of the clergy sexual abuse crisis, this chapter contextualizes the staggering data and historical analysis while also humanizing the discussion of clergy sexual abuse. Their stories serve as a reminder of the real, individual lives behind the statistics and reports, guiding our examination in this chapter of the nature, history, prevalence, and underlying causes of clergy sexual abuse. Subsequently, in the next chapter, we will explore the different causes—both systemic and individual—of clergy sexual abuse.

Sexual Abuse under the Halo of Religion

At its core, sexual abuse is an exercise of power and control rather than a matter of sexual desire. This understanding is crucial when addressing clergy sexual abuse, where the abuser's religious authority intensifies the power imbalance. Often, the narrative wrongly frames such abuse as a breach of celibacy or an adulterous act, oversimplifying and misdirecting the issue. This approach reduces the problem to individual failings, ignoring the systemic roots in church culture and patriarchal structures. Furthermore, this reduction muddies the waters by equating violence with consensual acts.

Marie Fortune, a pioneering feminist theologian, challenges this misconception by classifying clergy sexual abuse as a violation of the seventh commandment, "You shall not steal," underscoring the theft of innocence and potential from the victims, which results in profound and enduring harm.[2] Echoing this sentiment, Michael shares his experience of abuse in terms of theft. Having been victimized by three different priests, Michael articulates the loss of his innocence, faith, and trust in church figures as irrevocable, giving us another example of the profound impact such violations have on survivors' lives.

In 1983, Marie Fortune illuminated the inherent power imbalances that make consensual sexual relationships between priests and parishioners impossible. Her seminal work, *Sexual Violence: The Unmentionable Sin*, marked a pivotal early contribution to discussions on clergy sexual abuse. Power disparities are intrinsic to therapeutic and mentorship roles, including those held by pastors, clergy, or therapists, demanding openness and vulnerability from parishioners or clients. However, such imbalances, while ubiquitous in relationships like those between parents and children or mentors and mentees, do not inherently spell dysfunction. The crux lies in the more powerful party's capacity to uphold clear boundaries, distinguishing their needs from those they serve. Fortune's critique challenges us to discern these dynamics within the context of religious authority, where the abuse of power can have devastating effects.[3]

The authority of clergy is expressed through various means: their attire, the rituals they perform, the symbols they carry, and their presence at the pulpit. Such elements can inadvertently foster narcissistic traits, leading to a disparity in how clergy view and engage with others. At the heart of their influence lies the sacramental role they embody, acting as intermediaries to the Divine, akin to the

---

2. Marie M. Fortune, "Ethics and Legalities: A Response to Fr. Donald B. Cozzens," in *Sexual Abuse in the Catholic Church: Trusting the Clergy?*, ed. Marie M. Fortune and W. Merle Longwood (Binghamton, NY: Haworth Pastoral Press, 2003), 53–58.

3. Marie M. Fortune, *Sexual Violence: The Unmentionable Sin* (New York: Pilgrim Press, 1983), 106–9; see also Andrea Celenza, "Sexual Misconduct in the Clergy," in *Sexual Boundary Violations: Therapeutic, Supervisory, and Academic Contexts* (Lanham, MD: Jason Aronson Publishers, 2007), 77–92; Stefan Gärtner, "Powerful and Dependent: Ambivalence in the Religious Leader," in *Religious Leadership and Christian Identity*, ed. Doris Nauer, Rein Nauta, and Henk Witte (Münster: LIT Verlag, 2004), 157–67, 166; Cristina L. H. Traina, *Erotic Attunement: Parenthood and the Ethics of Sensuality between Unequals* (Chicago: University of Chicago Press, 2011), 363.

"*alter Christus*" concept.[4] This sets the stage for a complex dance of power between God, the clergy, and the congregation, rendering a truly equitable relationship challenging. Deborah's experience of clergy abuse was especially impacted by the conflation of clergy with the Divine. Her abuser frequently told her that he was sent by God to save her soul because she was an evil child. This type of spiritual abuse compounded Deborah's trauma, adding layers of shame and guilt on top of the physical abuse.

Despite the inherent power imbalances between clergy and laity, there's an expectation for the priest and parishioners of a parish to cultivate a community grounded in vulnerability, a state that inherently exposes individuals to potential harm.[5] The spiritual dimension deeply intensifies the vulnerability inherent in the power-imbalanced relationships with clergy, rendering any breach of this trust profoundly traumatic. During life's pivotal moments—birth, illness, death—we invite religious leaders into our lives as embodiments of both the community and divinity.[6] The symbols and traditions surrounding clergy bring God into every space they inhabit. However, when this sacred space turns harmful, the consequences are dire, with God perceived as a silent bystander, if not an unwitting accomplice.[7]

This dynamic of vulnerability affects everyone, adults and children alike, though it impacts them differently due to variations in power, age, and maturity. Such breaches of trust carry grave spiritual repercussions, underlining the critical need for safe and

---

4. Neil Ormerod and Thea Ormerod, "Events of Abundant Evil," in *History and Presence* (Cambridge, MA: Belknap Press of Harvard University Press, 2016), 215–48.

5. See Gärtner, "Powerful and Dependent," 157–67; Celenza, "Sexual Misconduct in the Clergy," 77–92; Ormerod and Ormerod, "Events of Abundant Evil," 215–48; Carter Heyward and Beverly Wildung Harrison, "Boundaries: Protecting the Vulnerable or Perpetrating a Bad Idea," in *Boundary Wars: Intimacy and Distance in Healing Relationships*, ed. Katherine Hancock Ragsdale (Philadelphia: Westminster Press, 1996), 111–28; Donald R. Hands and Wayne L. Fehr, *Spiritual Wholeness for Clergy: A New Psychology of Intimacy with God, Self and Others* (Washington, DC: Alban Institute, 1993).

6. Barbara J. Blodgett, *Lives Entrusted: An Ethic of Trust for Ministry* (Minneapolis: Fortress Press, 2008).

7. Ormerod and Ormerod, "Events of Abundant Evil," 215–48.

respectful clergy-parishioner relationships.[8] For both Michael and Deborah, their abuse and the subsequent lack of support from their church communities influence their decisions to no longer identify as Catholic. Having grown up in close Catholic communities, they both mourned this acute loss.

The priest–parishioner dynamic sets the stage for the abuse and for the obstacles that victims face in acknowledging and reporting their trauma. The perceived holiness of the abuser blurs recognition of the abuse and heightens fears of disbelief or reprisal from the community. When he shared his story of clergy abuse with his friend, the auxiliary bishop, Nathan was told that he must be mistaken, because the bishop knew the accused priest, and "he could never do anything to hurt a child." A deep-seated reverence for clergy that often impedes accountability efforts and skepticism toward survivors' accounts in the Catholic Church are revealed in this response.

Trust in clergy, endorsed by both the laity and the church hierarchy, has shifted from trust in individuals toward blanket trust for institutional policies. This evolution reflects a long-standing tradition of clericalism and a hierarchical structure, which feminist theologian Susan Ross critiques as a form of "unchecked, divinely sanctioned patriarchal power," with profound and damaging implications.[9]

---

8. See Celenza, "Sexual Misconduct in the Clergy," 77–92; and Claire M. Renzetti and Sandra Yocum, eds., "Don't Call It an Affair: Understanding and Preventing Clergy Sexual Misconduct with Adults," in *Clergy Sexual Abuse: Social Science Perspectives* (Boston: Northeastern University Press, 2013), ebook; and Mary Gail Frawley-O'Dea, "God Images in Clinical Work with Sexual Abuse Survivors: A Relational Psychodynamic Paradigm," in *Spiritually Oriented Psychotherapy*, ed. Donald F. Walker, Christine A. Courtois, and Jamie D. Aten (Washington, DC: American Psychological Association, 2015), ebook.

9. See Susan A. Ross, "Feminist Theology and the Clergy Sexual Abuse Crisis," *Theological Studies* 80, no. 3 (September 2019): 632–52; Maria José Rosado-Nunes and Regina Soares Jurkewicz, "Sexual Violence in the Catholic Church," in *Violence against Women in Contemporary World Religion: Roots and Cures*, ed. Daniel C. Maguire and Sa'diyya Shaikh (Cleveland, OH: Pilgrim Press, 2007), 212–30; and Ormerod and Ormerod, "Events of Abundant Evil," 215–48; and Beth Ann Gaede, ed., *When a Congregation Is Betrayed: Responding to Clergy Misconduct* (Herndon, VA: Alban Institute, 2005); and Blodgett, *Lives Entrusted*.

History of Clergy Abuse in the United States Catholic Church

Tracing the history of clergy sexual abuse within the Catholic Church presents challenges due to evolving understandings of sexuality, power, and childhood. Historically, the terminology describing child and adult sexual abuse has varied widely. However, scholars note references to such issues in church documents as early as the fourth century. During the medieval period, instances of clergy abuse were often categorized under "sodomy," a term prevalent in medieval and early modern discourse. Theologian Mark Jordan argues that terms like "sodomy" served to stigmatize individuals as deeply corrupted, casting them as scapegoats. *Damian's Book of Gomorrah*, addressed to Pope Leo IX (1048–1054), detailed sexual abuses by bishops against their mentees, hinting at a secretive hierarchy that shielded clergy and obscured their sexual abuses against laypeople. Additionally, the Spanish Inquisition (1530–1819) recorded 223 cases of "solicitation," where confessors exploited their unsupervised access to religious women, often on a daily basis.[10]

The discussion on clergy abuse in the United States, while rooted in history, became pronounced in 1984 with the case of Fr. Gilbert Gauthe in Louisiana's Diocese of Lafayette. Facing both civil and criminal charges, Gauthe's widely publicized trial revealed his admission of abusing thirty-seven children, sparking varied reactions within and outside church communities. In response, F. Ray Mouton, Gauthe's lawyer, along with Rev. Thomas P. Doyle, a canon lawyer, and Rev. Michael R. Peterson, the director of St. Luke Institute, crafted "The Manual." This document aimed to brief the United States Conference of Catholic Bishops (USCCB) on the crisis and recommend actions.

Despite its intentions, "The Manual" was sidelined at the USCCB's June 1985 meeting. By December, a disheartened Peterson distributed "The Manual" and supplementary materials to all

---

10. See Mark D. Jordan, "Chapter Five: Memoirs of Priestly Sodomy," in *The Silence of Sodom: Homosexuality in Modern Catholicism* (Chicago: University of Chicago Press, 2000), 113–40; and Mark D. Jordan, *The Invention of Sodomy in Christian Theology* (Chicago: University of Chicago Press, 1997); and Stephen Haliczer, *Sexuality in the Confessional: A Sacrament Profaned* (New York: Oxford University Press, 1996).

U.S. ordinaries, marking a crucial moment when church hierarchy could no longer ignore the widespread issue of clergy sexual abuse. This effort by Mouton, Doyle, and Peterson underscored the pressing need for leaders in church structures to confront and address the systemic abuse within its ranks.[11]

Before 1985, the bishops were predominantly advised that priests facing abuse charges could be cured, with spiritual interventions like prayer considered effective for rehabilitation.[12] This perspective slowly changed with the public release of "The Manual" and the later establishment of the USCCB's Ad Hoc Committee on Sexual Abuse in 1994. At the time, the committee was formed mainly to rebuild trust in the aftermath of emerging sexual abuse allegations, and focused on addressing and mitigating the crisis.[13] But the church community was soon met with an even larger scandal.

The year 2002 marked a pivotal moment in the Catholic Church's history with the clergy sexual abuse crisis. *The Boston Globe*'s investigation into the Archdiocese of Boston exposed a systemic practice of concealing and defending abusers within church structures, providing evidence sufficient for convicting five priests in the process of its investigation. This revelation significantly shifted public awareness and trust, showing the urgency of addressing the crisis.[14]

In response, the USCCB convened in Dallas in June 2002 and adopted the Charter for the Protection of Children and Young People, establishing the National Review Board to take the place of the Ad Hoc Committee on Sexual Abuse, and commissioning a comprehensive study by John Jay College. Completed in 2004, the study,

---

11. See Michael R. Peterson, Thomas P. Doyle, and F. Ray Mouton Jr., *The Problem of Sexual Molestation by Roman Catholic Clergy: Meeting the Problem in a Comprehensive and Responsible Manner*, BishopAccountability.org, 2004 (originally created in 1985).

12. Karen J. Terry, Margaret Leland Smith, Katarina Schuth, James R. Kelly, Brenda Vollman, and Christina Massey, *The Causes and Context of Sexual Abuse of Minors by Catholic Priests in the United States, 1950–2010: A Report Presented to the United States Conference of Catholic Bishops by the John Jay College Research Team* (Washington, DC: United States Conference of Catholic Bishops, 2011).

13. John F. Kinney and Bishops' Ad Hoc Committee on Sexual Abuse, *Restoring Trust: A Pastoral Response to Sexual Abuse*, vol. 1 (Washington, DC: National Conference of Catholic Bishops, 1994).

14. Investigative Staff of the *Boston Globe*, *Betrayal: The Crisis in the Catholic Church* (Boston: Little, Brown and Company, 2002).

which encompassed data from a vast majority of the clergy (including 98 percent of all diocesan priests, 60 percent of religious communities, and 80 percent of religious priests in the US), unveiled 10,667 allegations of child sexual abuse against 4,393 priests for the period of 1950–2002. A 2006 follow-up by the John Jay Research Team noted the role of media in encouraging survivors to come forward and identified education on sexual abuse as a critical measure for creating safer environments.[15]

Parallel to the John Jay study, the National Review Board scrutinized the Catholic Church's internal systems, focusing on both the failure to screen for abusive priests and the response of the bishops to allegations of abuse. The board's findings noted systemic failures, including secrecy, a bias toward accused priests, and an adversarial stance toward victims. Recommendations called for stricter screening, improved formation and oversight, and enhanced accountability for church leaders.[16]

In light of both the John Jay and National Review Board studies, the Charter for the Protection of Children and Young People was revised in 2005 and 2006. The revisions aimed at bettering healing processes, setting standards for responding to allegations, and establishing accountability measures. A 2007 review by the National Review Board acknowledged some progress but criticized the church community's internal collaboration level and noted clericalism and hierarchical issues as significant obstacles. Advocacy groups like the Survivors Network of those Abused by Priests (SNAP) were noted for their more effective response and change efforts.[17]

The spotlight on the U.S. Catholic Church due to abuse allegations did not wane after 2002. Repeated public revelations of decades-long clergy abuse severely damaged the church's public

---

15. John Jay College Research Team, *The Nature and Scope of Sexual Abuse of Minors by Catholic Priests and Deacons in the United States, 1950–2002: Supplementary Data Analysis* (Washington, DC: United States Conference of Catholic Bishops, 2006), 54.

16. National Review Board for the Protection of Children and Young People, *A Report on the Crisis in the Catholic Church in the United States* (Washington, DC: United States Conference of Catholic Bishops, 2004).

17. Michael R. Merz, "Was Archimedes an Insider or an Outsider?," in *Sexual Abuse in the Catholic Church: A Decade of Crisis, 2002–2012*, ed. Thomas G. Plante and Kathleen L. McChesney (New York: Bloomsbury Publishing, 2012), 79–90.

trust. A glaring example was the systemic cover-up documented in subsequent reports, including the 2004 "Report to the People of God" by the Archdiocese of Los Angeles, which publicly acknowledged the mishandling of the clergy sexual abuse crisis and admitted that a culture of silence had failed many victims. Similarly, the 2018 Pennsylvania Grand Jury Report unveiled abuse of over a thousand children by more than three hundred priests across six dioceses, suggesting the actual number of victims could be much higher. The same year, the Vatican initiated an investigation into allegations against Fr. Theodore McCarrick, former archbishop of Washington, DC, resulting in his laicization in 2019, followed by a comprehensive report in 2020.

In the period leading up to the COVID-19 pandemic, the Catholic Church saw a significant surge in reported abuse allegations, with 4,434 cases filed in 2019–2020, tripling figures from previous years. This rise is anticipated to persist as states enact look-back laws and repeal statutes of limitations on sexual abuse claims. By December 2020, the U.S. Catholic Church had logged seventeen thousand complaints and disbursed approximately four billion dollars in compensation to victims since the 1980s.[18]

Prevalence

Grasping the scope of clergy abuse through statistics presents challenges because of inconsistent reporting and elusive accurate figures. Estimates suggest that between 3 percent and 6 percent of priests are involved in child abuse, yet these numbers barely scratch the surface of the issue. The majority of abuse survivors report their experiences years, sometimes decades, after the incidents, with only 13 percent coming forward within a year of the abuse's commencement. Astonishingly, a quarter wait more than thirty years to make their allegations.[19]

The John Jay College Report sheds light on the duration and frequency of this abuse. It reveals that, while a significant portion of the abuse lasts under four years, a distressing 10.2 percent endures

---

18. Maryclaire Dale, "DOJ Probe of Catholic Church Abuse Goes Quiet 2 Years Later," APNews.com (December 13, 2020).

19. For all findings, see John Jay College Research Team, *The Nature and Scope of Sexual Abuse.*

between five and nine years, with a small fraction extending beyond a decade. Most abusers were ordained between 1950 and 1979, showing a historical trend of abusive behavior. While over half (56 percent) of the abusive clergy targeted a single child, 3.4 percent were responsible for abusing ten or more children, accounting for 26 percent of all victims during the studied period.

The age of victims plays a crucial role in understanding the nature of this abuse. Two kinds of age-related abusers are prevalent in the data: pedophiles, those who prey on children under fourteen, and ephebophiles, those who choose to target adolescents between fourteen and eighteen. This distinction helps clarify that the majority of clergy abusers fall into the latter category, abusing adolescents between fourteen and eighteen years of age. Furthermore, this distinction points to a specific pattern of victimization, focusing on fewer victims and a different type of fixation compared to pedophiles.[20]

While the conversation often centers on child victims, the abuse of adults, particularly women, by clergy is a significant yet underexplored aspect of this crisis.[21] Marie Fortune estimates that between 10 to 25 percent of male clergy engage in sexual misconduct with parishioners, a number often overshadowed by the focus on male adolescent victims.[22] Stephen Edward de Weger advocates

---

20. Gerard J. McGlone, "The Pedophile and the Pious: Towards a New Understanding of Sexually Offending and Non-Offending Roman Catholic Priests," in *The Victimization of Children: Emerging Issues*, ed. Janet L. Mullings, James W. Marquart, and Deborah J. Hartley (Binghamton, NY: Haworth Maltreatment & Trauma Press, 2004), 115–31, simultaneously published in *Journal of Aggression, Maltreatment and Trauma* 8, no. 1/2 & 3 (2003): 115–31.

21. There is a lack of statistical research on the clerical abuse of adults, but when rates of pedophilia in nonclerical populations are compared with rates of abusers of adults, one can extrapolate that adults, especially adult women, are likely victims of clergy abuse as well, and most likely at higher rates than children. See Thomas W. Haywood and Jack Green, "Cleric Serial Offenders: Clinical Characteristics and Treatment Approaches," in *Serial Offenders: Current Thought, Recent Findings*, ed. Louis B. Schlesinger (Boca Raton, FL: CRC Press, 2000), 247–62; and Len Sperry, *Sex, Priestly Ministry, and the Church* (Collegeville, MN: Liturgical Press, 2003), 186.

22. See Marie M. Fortune and James Newton Poling, *Sexual Abuse by Clergy: A Crisis for the Church* (Eugene, OR: Wipf & Stock, 2008), 29–43; Kathryn A. Flynn, *The Sexual Abuse of Women by Members of the Clergy* (Jefferson, NC: McFarland & Company, 2003), 296.

for framing clergy sexual misconduct against adults as professional misconduct, emphasizing the abuse of power at its core rather than framing it as consensual affairs gone wrong.[23]

This narrative tends to spotlight child victims, perceived as entirely innocent and blameless. However, the binary thinking of victims as either wholly blameless or entirely at fault oversimplifies the complex dynamics of sexual abuse, which often involves grooming, coercion, and guilt. Adult survivors, facing myths of impeachable agency, struggle against significant power imbalances in their relationships with clergy, challenging the notion that any semblance of consent could exist in such contexts.[24]

Gender dynamics further complicate the landscape of clergy abuse. While the majority of reported victims are male, this statistic may obscure the reality of female victimization, which is potentially underreported due to historical and cultural biases. Studies indicate that a notable percentage of women in religious communities have faced unwanted sexual advances from church leaders, pointing to a broader issue of abuse and power exploitation that transcends age and gender.[25]

Survivors of clergy sexual abuse, regardless of their gender, encounter stigma, disbelief, and pervasive misconceptions. The patriarchal structure of both the church hierarchy and society at large often frames female survivors as complicit or seductive, undermining the severity of their trauma. Yet, research shows that women who experience clergy abuse suffer profound, long-lasting, psychosocial distress.[26] Deborah, for instance, faced intrusive ques-

---

23. Stephen Edward deWeger, "Unchaste Celibates: Clergy Sexual Misconduct against Adults—Expressions, Definitions, and Harms," *Religions* 13 (2022): 393, https://doi.org/10.3390/rel13050393.

24. See Jennifer L. Dunn, *Judging Victims: Why We Stigmatize Survivors, and How They Reclaim Respect* (Boulder, CO: Lynne Rienner Publishers, 2010).

25. See Mary Ann Tolbert, "Where Have All the Young Girls Gone?," in *Gay Catholic Priests and Clerical Sexual Misconduct: Breaking the Silence*, ed. Donald L. Boisvert and Robert E. Goss (Binghamton, NY: Harrington Park Press, imprint of Haworth Press, 2005), 199–207; and Mark Chaves and Diana Garland, "The Prevalence of Clergy Sexual Advances toward Adults in Their Congregations," *Journal for the Scientific Study of Religion* 48, no. 4 (2009): 817–24.

26. See Kathryn A. Flynn, "In Their Own Voices: Women Who Were Sexually Abused by Members of the Clergy," in *Understanding the Impact of Clergy Sexual Abuse: Betrayal and Recovery*, ed. Robert A. McMackin, Terrence M. Keane,

tions about her alleged complicity in the abuse when she bravely came forward. Moreover, she encountered skepticism from those who clung to the mistaken belief that only young boys fell victim to such atrocities. A bishop's shocking response upon learning that her abuse began at six years old was, "Well, you must have been sexually developed very early." Horrified, Deborah could only think, "I was six. I didn't have front teeth."

On the other side of the gender spectrum, Nathan and Michael grappled with issues of sexuality and gender identity intertwined with their trauma. Michael hesitated to disclose his experiences, fearing the label of being gay as a consequence. Nathan, on the other hand, faced enduring confusion about his gender identity stemming from the abuse, a struggle that persisted into adulthood. These narratives reveal the complex layers of misunderstanding and prejudice that survivors must navigate based on their gender, underscoring the need for a more empathetic and informed response to their suffering.

Conclusion

As we move to explore the prevalence of clergy sexual abuse, it becomes clear that this crisis is not merely a series of isolated incidents. Rather it is a systemic issue that is deeply rooted within the fabric of church structures. To fully understand the enduring crisis, we must turn our attention to the underlying social causes, particularly the pervasive culture of clericalism and the patriarchal values that have become entrenched within the Catholic Church. These factors not only facilitate the perpetuation of abuse, they also hinder the processes of accountability and healing.

---

and Paul M. Kline (London: Routledge, 2009), 20–41; and Deborah Sauvage and Patrick O'Leary, "Child Sexual Abuse in Faith-Based Institutions: Gender, Spiritual Trauma and Treatment Frameworks," in *The Sexual Abuse of Children: Recognition and Redress*, ed. Yorick Smaal, Andy Kaladelfos, and Mark Finnane (Clayton, Victoria, Australia: Monash University Publishing, 2016), 146–59.

5

Causes of the Clergy Sexual Abuse Crisis

> "The fact that there are people within the Catholic Church, in the hierarchy and even in the priesthood, who would follow such an order, says really devastating things about the current state of the Catholic Church. . . . If you're gonna follow an illegal or immoral order, what other kind of stuff will you turn a blind eye to?"
> —Nathan, survivor of clergy sexual abuse

The clergy sexual abuse crisis in the Catholic Church is not merely a series of isolated incidents—or "a few bad apples." It is a complex and systemic issue that is deeply rooted in broader institutional, social, and individual dynamics. Understanding the causes of this crisis requires a multifaceted exploration of social and cultural factors within church structures that have allowed such abuses to persist and be concealed. In addition to these systemic causes, individuals' choices to use the priesthood to gain power and control over others cannot be ignored as a factor in the abuse crisis.

Nathan's remarks at the beginning of this chapter give one interpretation of the fundamental problem within the Catholic Church: the willingness of individuals within the hierarchy to follow immoral or illegal orders. Obedience to corrupt authority within the Catholic Church highlights the devastating effects of clericalism and the abuse of power within the hierarchy. These words invite us to consider the broader culture of complicity and silence that enables abuse to continue unchecked in addition to the specific acts of abuse themselves.

In this chapter, we explore the underlying causes of clergy sexual abuse, focusing on the patriarchal structures within the Catholic Church, the culture of clericalism, and the individual factors that contribute to this pervasive problem. By examining these elements, we aim to uncover the systemic and personal dynamics that have perpetuated abuse and hindered accountability within the church. In the next chapter, we will examine the healing journeys of survivors and communities, as well as the responses of church leaders and communities.

Social Causes: Patriarchy in the Church

Clergy abuse, like all forms of abuse, is rooted in a wider issue that affects our whole society: the unequal power dynamics between genders, often called patriarchy. This means that, in many areas of life—whether it's at home, at work, or in this case, within a church—certain groups hold more power than others. This imbalance makes it easier for those in power to abuse it. In the context of church communities, this abuse isn't just about individual wrongdoings but is tied to bigger problems within the system.

Initially, when experts began studying clergy abuse, they thought it was similar to cases of abuse within families, where the abusive priest acted in the role of an incestual or abusive parent. This view mainly focused on male leaders in churches, who misused their authority over others, particularly women, to demonstrate and exercise their power.[1] Critics of this view argue that this comparison to family abuse doesn't fully capture the broader setting in which this abuse happens for two main reasons:

First, comparing clergy abuse to family abuse oversimplifies the issue. It suggests that, if we just remove the abusive individuals, the problem is solved. But it's more complicated than that. Clergy abuse is part of a larger issue that includes not just individual actions but also cultural and systemic factors that churches and society haven't fully addressed. As long as the response is focused only on dealing with perpetrators on a case-by-case basis, without challenging the

---

1. See Janet L. Jacobs, "Charisma, Male Entitlement, and the Abuse of Power," in *Bad Pastors: Clergy Misconduct in Modern America*, ed. Anson Shupe, William A. Stacey, and Susan E. Darnell (New York: New York University Press, 2000), 113–30.

wider culture that allows abuse to happen, mistakes and cover-ups will continue.[2]

Second, viewing church communities as isolated from the rest of society misses the mark. Churches don't exist in a vacuum. They're part of larger social, economic, and governmental systems. These systems, while separate, both influence and are influenced by churches. Many people, including religious leaders and others with power in society, have a stake in keeping things as they are because it benefits them. Some theorists, such as Anson Shupe and Peter Iadicola, suggest that religious elites work together with other powerful groups to maintain their control.[3] This discussion sets the stage for understanding how clergy abuse is connected to deeper issues of power and control within churches and society.

Catholic Church Culture

Recognizing clergy sexual abuse as a systemic issue challenges the notion that it is merely the result of actions by a few misguided individuals. While this problem pervades various institutions, it's crucial to understand that the Catholic Church, with its distinctive cultural and theological practices, presents a particularly complex case. This isn't to say that other institutions are free from blame or that they don't face similar challenges. However, the Catholic Church's unique hierarchical structure, combined with specific doctrines and practices, renders it especially vulnerable to perpetuating and concealing abuse.

The Catholic Church's structure is marked by a system of "clericalism," the privileging of clergy over laity. This includes rigid obedience to male authority, deference to church structures as holy, privileging of the priesthood, and a denial of sexual complexity. These structures of clericalism have historically fostered an environment where secrecy, unilateral decision-making, and the abuse of laity are perpetuated.[4]

---

2. Marie M. Fortune and James Newton Poling, *Sexual Abuse by Clergy: A Crisis for the Church* (Eugene, OR: Wipf & Stock, 2008), 60.

3. See Anson Shupe and Peter Iadicola, "Issues in Conceptualizing Clergy Malfeasance," in *Bad Pastors*, ed. Shupe, Stacey, and Darnell, 13–38.

4. Karen J. Terry, Margaret Leland Smith, Katarina Schuth, James R. Kelly, Brenda Vollman, and Christina Massey, "The Causes and Context of Sexual Abuse

The stories of Michael, Nathan, and Deborah all shed light on clericalism's role in fostering an environment where power imbalances can lead to abuse. Michael's statement, "who would believe that the hands ... that were raised over us in blessing would ever harm a child of God," highlights the dissonance between the clergy's revered status and his own harrowing experiences. Similarly, Nathan expresses his dismay at the potential for violence and sin within the clerical system, asking, "If you're gonna follow an illegal, or immoral order, y'know, what other kinds of stuff will you turn a blind eye to?" Echoing this sentiment, Deborah reflects on her childhood experience of abuse with resignation, saying, "whatever Father said was law," indicating a deep-rooted belief in the clergy's unassailable authority.

The Catholic Church's approach to clericalism is deeply intertwined with certain theological beliefs that, while profound and at times liberating, can be misinterpreted in ways that exacerbate abuse. A sacramental worldview—seeing the divine in all aspects of life and suggesting that our everyday existence, practices, and institutions are reflections of the sacred—sits at the core of these beliefs. This perspective is meant to empower the church community to embody God's Kingdom on Earth. However, when misapplied, it grants churches and their clergy an untouchable status, making them seem beyond reproach.

Furthermore, the doctrine of the church as one, holy, catholic, and apostolic, as affirmed by the First Council of Constantinople in 381, sets the church apart from the world.[5] "The church" and the Roman Catholic hierarchy are not one and the same. When this separation is ignored, church leadership is conflated with divine infallibility, blurring the lines between human organization and divine will and perfection. This confusion complicates efforts to address and rectify the Catholic Church's mishandling of sexual abuse cases. The reality is that churches, as institutions, must

---

of Minors by Catholic Priests in the United States, 1950–2010," report presented to United States Conference of Catholic Bishops, Washington, DC, 2011.

5. Erik Borgman, "Theological Aspects of the Sexual Abuse Crisis," in *Sacramentalizing Human History: In Honour of Edward Schillebeeckx (1914–2009)*, ed. Erik Borgman, Paul D. Murray, and Andrés Torres Queiruga; Concilium 2012/1 (London: SCM Press, 2012), 123–29.

acknowledge their imperfections and the necessity for change to restore trust and ensure accountability, moving beyond the status quo where scandals continue to erode faith and credibility.

When the sacramental worldview and doctrine of the church combine, the sacramental view of the priesthood, suggesting a profound change in those ordained, can lead to beliefs that priests are incapable of sin or that their reconciliation automatically restores them if they do sin. This belief often results in church hierarchy siding with abusive priests over victims, prioritizing the priests' "moral spiritual state" over justice for those harmed.[6] The clericalism at play here is supported not only by the religious elite but also by liturgical practices that enhance the authority of the priesthood, such as confession and celibacy.

For Michael, Nathan, and Deborah, the act of confession was not just a religious duty. It was a setting for their abuse. Michael described his experiences in the confessional as "sadistic, spiritual counseling," primarily serving as a pretext for further psychological and spiritual violation. The role of confession in perpetuating the abuse crisis has been a subject of critique among theologians and scholars. John Cornwell, a writer and journalist, specifically challenges the mandatory nature of childhood confessions.[7] He links its widespread practice in the twentieth century to an increase in sexual abuse, arguing it created both a pretext and a psychological framework conducive to abuse.

Celibacy, another scrutinized practice within the clergy, is often misunderstood in its contribution to the abuse crisis. The Catholic Church tradition's stance on celibacy, rather than causing sexual

---

6. See John C. Gonsiorek, Claire M. Renzetti, and Sandra Yocum, "The Interplay of Psychological and Institutional Factors in Sexual Abuse by Roman Catholic Clergy," in *Clergy Sexual Abuse: Social Science Perspectives*, ed. Claire M. Renzetti and Sandra Yocum (Boston: Northeastern University Press, 2013), 37–59; Eamonn Conway, "Operative Theologies of Priesthood: Have They Contributed to Child Sexual Abuse," in *The Structural Betrayal of Trust*, ed. Regina Ammicht-Quinn, Hille Haker, and Maureen Junker-Kenny; Concilium 2004/3 (London: SCM Press, 2004), 72–86; Sandra Yocum, "The Priest and Catholic Culture as Symbolic System of Purity," in *Clergy Sexual Abuse: Social Science Perspectives*, ed. Claire M. Renzetti and Sandra Yocum (Boston: Northeastern University Press, 2013), 90–117.

7. See John Cornwall, *The Dark Box: A Secret History of Confession* (New York: Basic Books, 2014).

abuse directly, has inadvertently fostered a culture shrouded in secrecy and mystique. Celibacy is perceived as a marker of clerical power, rooted in the admirable but daunting vow to renounce all sexual pleasure for service to others.[8] Psychotherapist and researcher A. W. Richard Sipe estimates that only about half of priests maintain their vow of celibacy, suggesting that this perception of clerical power potentially exacerbates the culture of secrecy.[9] When clergy break their vows, it intensifies a cycle of hidden transgressions, preserving their own and each other's secrets. For example, Michael told me he felt much of his life was spent in secret, ruefully saying, "They taught me how to be silent about the bad things that were happening in my life."

Noting this culture of secrecy and mystique gives us insights into how deeply ingrained practices contribute to the problematic structures enabling the ongoing abuse crisis. Clericalism, with its emphasis on authority and exclusivity, further entrenches these issues, creating an environment where accountability is obscured and reform becomes challenging. As we investigate clericalism, we'll explore how this emphasis on hierarchical power perpetuates a cycle of silence and suppression, further complicating efforts toward transparency and healing.

Clericalism: Enabling the Problem

Clericalism, characterized by the concentration of power and privilege in the hands of a select group of leaders, has significantly contributed to the toxic dynamics within the Catholic Church. This practice, deeply rooted in the belief that the church and its clergy are divinely sanctioned, demands unwavering deference from the laity, leading to a harmful structure of clericalism. Psychologist Thomas Plante writes on the destructive nature of clericalism, noting its impediment to essential checks and balances and its

---

8. See Gonsiorek, Renzetti, and Yocum, "The Interplay of Psychological"; A. W. Richard Sipe, "Scandal versus Culture: Mother Church and the Rape of Her Children," in *Sexual Abuse in the Catholic Church: A Decade of Crisis, 2002–2012*, ed. Thomas G. Plante and Kathleen L. McChesney (New York: Bloomsbury Publishing, 2012), 117–30.

9. See A. W. Richard Sipe, "How Do Those Who Profess Celibacy Practice It?," in *Celibacy in Crisis: A Secret World Revisited* (New York: Brunner-Routledge, 2003), 43–56.

stifling of the critical feedback that is necessary for any institution's growth and ethical decision-making.[10] The elevation of clerics fosters a culture of secrecy and unattainable expectations for clergy while also discouraging the admission of fallibility, paving the way for a system where denial, deceit, and suppression thrive unchallenged.

This pervasive culture of secrecy and unattainable holiness, problematic at the level of individual priests, also hinders the development of healthy leadership and accountable decision-making within church structures. The current system encourages local priests to defer to their bishops, who, then, look to archbishops and, ultimately, the pope, in a chain of command that dilutes accountability and fosters an environment ripe for denial and cover-ups. Moreover, this inward-looking approach isolates churches from external oversight, granting bishops excessive autonomy in handling abuse allegations. Such a closed system both obstructs justice and perpetuates the very secrecy that shields abusers, undermining efforts to foster a culture of openness and accountability.[11]

This shield of secrecy leads the church communities and leaders to view outsiders with doubt and suspicion. These communities and leaders then take a defensive posture against the insights and critiques from the behavioral, social, and medical sciences. Responding with a "siege mentality,"[12] church leaders are reluctant to open up to external scrutiny, preferring instead to address issues alone. Such a stance has enabled church leaders to discreetly relocate abusive priests—either to new dioceses or to clinical treatment facilities—without facing public accountability. Consequently, clericalism insulates church leaders from necessary checks and bal-

---

10. See Thomas Plante, "Clericalism Contributes to Religious, Spiritual, and Behavioral Struggles among Catholic Priests," *Religions* 11, no. 5 (2020): 217, https://doi.org/10.3390/rel11050217.

11. See Gonsiorek, Renzetti, and Yocum, "The Interplay of Psychological"; Theresa Krebs, "Church Structures That Facilitate Pedophilia among Roman Catholic Clergy," in *Wolves within the Fold: Religious Leadership and Abuses of Power*, ed. Anson Shupe (Piscataway, NJ: Rutgers University Press, 1998), 85–100.

12. A "siege mentality" is a sociological phenomenon where a community takes on defensive, and even paranoid, positions against others who are seen as enemies wanting to oppress the community. See Daniel Bar-Tal, "Siege Mentality," in *The Encyclopedia of Peace Psychology*, vol. 1, ed. Daniel J. Christie (Hoboken, NJ: John Wiley & Sons, 2011), 996–99.

ances and allows them to manage scandals internally, keeping the laity and the public in the dark. This secretive handling of abuse cases adds to the systemic failure to protect the vulnerable and to confront the issues transparently.[13]

The ongoing crisis of sexual abuse within the Catholic Church is not actually a consequence of outdated Canon Law. It stems from a failure to effectively implement existing laws. Despite efforts over the past two to three decades to introduce institutional reforms, the essence of the crisis, as articulated by Paul Lakeland, has been simmering for over two centuries. This period has seen church structures become increasingly "bureaucratized and centralized," adopting a defensive stance against the tides of modernity.[14] Such evolution has rendered the church's hierarchy opaque, self-serving, and sluggish in its responses.

Despite notable reforms, clericalism continues to undermine the Catholic Church's commitment to accountability. Lakeland further elaborates on the consequences of this defensive approach, showing how it has led to the emergence of a professional clerical class. This class, self-sustaining and self-regulating, stands detached from the lay faithful, shielded by their distinct lifestyle and monopolization of authority. According to Lakeland, the grievous issue of sexual abuse, while seemingly an isolated phenomenon, is, in fact, a direct, albeit secondary, outcome of this entrenched bureaucracy.[15]

Alongside the systems of bureaucracy, secrecy is a powerful tool of control that supports clericalism. Secrecy binds the clerical system, preventing the introduction of necessary checks and balances.[16] This culture of silence extends to the laity as well, especially when their silence is deemed necessary for their church's image. Laity, when approaching bishops with reports of ethical misconduct, have been led to believe that their participation in the cover-up serves

---

13. See John Gonsiorek, "Barriers to Responding to the Clergy Sexual Abuse Crisis within the Roman Catholic Church," in *Sin against the Innocents: Sexual Abuse by Priests and the Role of the Catholic Church*, ed. Thomas G. Plante (Westport, CT: Praeger, 2004), 139–54; Krebs, "Church Structures," 85–100.

14. See Paul Lakeland, "Understanding the Crisis in the Church," in *Church Ethics and Its Organizational Context: Learning from the Sex Abuse Scandal in the Catholic Church*, ed. Jean M. Bartunek, Mary Ann Hinsdale, and James F. Keenan (Lanham, MD: Rowman & Littlefield, 2006), 3–16.

15. Lakeland, "Understanding the Crisis in the Church," 3–16.

16. Sipe, "Scandal versus Culture."

the church's greater good.[17] When Deborah courageously came forward with her account of abuse and endeavored to raise awareness about the broader crisis, she encountered profound losses, not only in her personal relationships but also facing resistance from numerous church members and leaders. These individuals, prioritizing the church's image above the truth, perceived Deborah's act of speaking out as a threat, labeling it as detrimental to the church's reputation and, by extension, an act against the church itself.

Intertwining secrecy with the theological mystique that surrounds the clergy and sacramental rituals complicates matters. While a certain level of unknown in the religious experience is often accepted by the laity, the prevailing "culture of confidentiality and secrecy" has hindered the ability of nonoffending clergy and laity to openly address instances of clergy sexual abuse.[18] Moreover, clericalism's exclusion of laity from church matters is problematic. The participation of laity provides essential avenues for women and children to voice their perspectives and concerns within the larger church community. Denying this participation through increased clericalism not only silences these voices. It risks the church's failure to authentically embody the people of God. This reflects a historical legacy where Christian churches, mirroring societal norms of the Roman Empire, relegated women and children to inferior statuses, acknowledging full moral autonomy only for elite freeborn men.[19]

Despite modern advancements in our understanding of childhood, psychology, and evolutionary sciences, remnants of this leg-

---

17. Thomas P. Doyle, "Clericalism and Catholic Clergy Sexual Abuse," in *Predatory Priests, Silenced Victims: The Sexual Abuse Crisis and the Catholic Church*, ed. Mary Gail Frawley-O'Dea and Virginia Goldner (Mahwah, NJ: Analytic Press, 2007), 35–57.

18. Brendan Geary, "'A Strip of White with the Might of an Empire behind It': Contributions of the Catholic Hierarchical System to Sexual Abuse of Children," in *The Dark Night of the Catholic Church: Examining the Child Sexual Abuse Scandal*, ed. Brendan Geary and Joanne Marie Greer (Stowmarket, Suffolk, England: Kevin Mayhew Publishers, 2011), 71–108; Mark D. Jordan, "The Confusion of Priestly Secrets," in Frawley-O'Dea and Goldner, *Predatory Priests*, 35–57.

19. Mary Rose D'Angelo, "Feminist Ethics and the Sexual Abuse of Children: Reading Christian Origins," in *A Just and True Love: Feminism at the Frontiers of Theological Ethics: Essays in Honor of Margaret A. Farley*, ed. Maura A. Ryan and Brian F. Linnane (Notre Dame, IN: University of Notre Dame Press, 2007), 234–72.

acy of subordination linger, particularly in the diminished value and agency that is historically ascribed to children within scriptural contexts. This historical view, which saw male children as valuable primarily as property of their parents and subject to punitive discipline, starkly contrasts with contemporary approaches to child welfare, including a more enlightened understanding of sexual abuse.[20]

The ongoing impact of patriarchy and clericalism in the Catholic Church has both permitted and intensified the clergy sexual abuse crisis. However, these factors are not the sole contributors to this issue. The crisis of sexual abuse spans various denominations and societal structures, reflecting a broader problem. In the era of "Me Too," the prevalence of sexual abuse in numerous settings, including beyond the Catholic Church, is increasingly recognized. Nevertheless, the specific cultural dynamics within churches, such as the privilege afforded to male clergy, a culture of secrecy, and the marginalization of lay members, have created conditions that enable sexual abuse of women, children, and other adults to thrive, along with the concealment of such abuses internally.[21]

Theologians and researchers in other disciplines concur that, as long as churches maintain their patriarchal structures, abuse will persist.[22] Studies reveal a direct correlation across Christian denominations: the more centralized the power within a church, the higher the incidence of clergy abuse, its normalization, and its denial. Conversely, churches that embrace dispersed power and shared governance report fewer such incidents.[23] The Catholic Church urgently needs to undergo theological and systemic transformations that emphasize mutuality, equality, and a collaborative contribution from both clergy and laity. However, implementing such profound structural reforms is challenging and often met with resistance, as it threatens the entrenched power dynamics within existing churches. This resistance is illustrated by the experience of Penny Jamieson, the first female bishop in New Zealand,

---

20. Ron O'Grady, *The Hidden Shame of the Church: Sexual Abuse of Children and the Church* (Geneva: WCC Publications, 2001).

21. Susan A. Ross, "Feminist Theology and the Clergy Sexual Abuse Crisis," *Theological Studies* 80, 3 (September 2019): 632–52.

22. Fortune and Poling, *Sexual Abuse by Clergy*, 60.

23. See Shupe and Iadicola, "Issues in Conceptualizing Clergy Malfeasance," 13–38.

who described her efforts to address clergy sexual abuse within her church as akin to "firing an open torpedo shot at the underlying and still very well-functioning patriarchal structure of the church."[24]

Individual Causes: Screening and Formation

In addition to the structural and systemic conditions that facilitate clergy sexual abuse, individual factors, including the psychological profiles and training of abusive priests, play a crucial role. The National Review Board noted two key aspects for safeguarding the laity: rigorous screening of clergy candidates and a formation process designed to mitigate, not exacerbate, potential issues.[25] The challenge lies in determining whether the priesthood inadvertently draws individuals prone to abusive behaviors or if certain aspects of its formation process and institutional structure contribute to such tendencies. It's probable that both elements interact. Importantly, research indicates that abuse cannot be predicted based on individual characteristics like race, mental health history, or education. Instead, social and cultural factors are more telling predictors of abuse.[26]

Screening to Prevent Abusers Becoming Priests

In the crucial process of screening potential clergy, a primary objective is to identify and exclude individuals who exhibit psychological and behavioral patterns typical of sex offenders. This task, however, presents significant challenges. The tools currently available for predicting abusive behavior lack the definitive accuracy required for such a critical issue.[27] Moreover, psychological and behavioral

---

24. Penny Jamieson, "The Abuse of Power," in *Living at the Edge: Sacrament and Solidarity in Leadership* (London: Mowbray, 1997), 106–24, 123.

25. James Martin, S.J., "How Could It Happen? An Analysis of the Catholic Sexual Abuse Scandal," in Frawley-O'Dea and Goldner, *Predatory Priests*, 35–57.

26. Karen J. Terry, Katarina Schuth, and Margaret Leland Smith, "Incidence of Clerical Sexual Abuse over Time: Changes in Behavior and Seminary Training between 1950 and 2008," in Plante and McChesney, *Sexual Abuse in the Catholic Church*, 17–32.

27. See A. W. Richard Sipe, "The Problem of Prevention in Clergy Sexual Abuse," in *Bless Me Father for I Have Sinned: Perspectives on Sexual Abuse Committed by Roman Catholic Priests*, ed. Thomas G. Plante (Westport, CT: Praeger, 1999), 111–135; and Terry et al., *The Causes and Context of Sexual Abuse*.

concerns may not become apparent until after the initial screening, during the period of clergy formation.

Early discussions in the 1990s, led by psychologists and psychotherapists such as Stephen Rosetti, highlighted that child abuse often stems from an inability to reconcile sexual desires and aggressive tendencies with one's lifestyle. For clergy, who are bound by vows of celibacy and principles of nonviolence, fully integrating these aspects with their inner needs and desires can prove particularly difficult.[28] Since these initial discussions, our understanding of the psychological underpinnings of pedophilia and related abusive disorders has evolved, becoming more nuanced and complex.

Forensic psychologist John Gonsiorek has identified key behavioral and developmental factors that could assist in the screening of clergy candidates. He suggests that a history of using abusive behaviors—whether emotional, verbal, physical, spiritual, or sexual—to dominate others can be a warning sign of the potential to abuse. Such patterns may reveal themselves as a cycle of aggressive outbursts followed by remorseful behavior. Gonsiorek's research shows the importance of developmental history, including insecure parental attachment, exposure to emotional or physical abuse, and witnessing abuse, as critical red flags.[29] This is supported by other psychologists who affirm that a background of abuse, particularly within environments where shame and guilt are prevalent, significantly raises the risk of future abusive behavior.[30]

Moreover, the experience of abuse, either in childhood or during seminary formation, can predispose individuals to develop abusive tendencies. This includes the less-discussed but significant issue of sexual abuse within the seminary setting, where novices may be victimized by their superiors, potentially perpetuating a cycle of abuse and secrecy.[31]

---

28. Stephen J. Rossetti, "A Challenge to the People of God," in *Slayer of the Soul: Child Sexual Abuse and the Catholic Church*, ed. Stephen J. Rossetti (Mystic, CT: Twenty-Third Publications, 1990), 185–99.

29. John C. Gonsiorek, "Forensic Psychological Evaluations in Clergy Abuse," in Plante, *Bless Me Father*, 27–58.

30. Gerald E. Kochansky and Murray Cohen, "Priests Who Sexualize Minors: Psychodynamic, Characterological, and Clerical Considerations," in Frawley-O'Dea and Goldner, *Predatory Priests*, 35–57.

31. Mark D. Jordan, "Reproducing 'Father,'" in *The Silence of Sodom: Homosexuality in Modern Catholicism* (Chicago: University of Chicago Press, 2000), 141–78.

In examining populations of abusers, a prevalent narrative is their history of having been abused. A comprehensive assessment involving over 150 individuals—clergy, lawyers, and licensed health professionals accused of sexual misconduct or offenses and participating in the Professional Assessment Program—revealed that more than 80 percent reported a history of abuse.[32] However, research focusing on such populations often limits its scope to those already within the criminal justice system, which complicates our understanding of causation.[33] We must recognize that, while a history of childhood abuse might increase the risk of becoming an abuser, it does not predetermine one's future actions. Recognizing a history of abuse is vital in the screening process for priesthood candidates; yet, it should not automatically disqualify someone. Instead, it necessitates a nuanced approach in formation programs to address and heal these wounds, ensuring those with such histories are given the support and intervention needed to foster healthy relationships.

One deeply entrenched and dangerous myth is the notion that adults who commit abuse against children are motivated by homosexual attraction. This misperception distorts reality and diverts attention from the actual root causes of clergy sexual abuse. The erroneous association of gay priests with the abuse crisis undermines the critical examination of systemic issues such as clericalism, secrecy, and patriarchal structures within churches.[34] It is well established among psychologists that there is no inherent connection between homosexual orientation and abusive behavior; these are distinct and separate realities.[35] To conflate the two displays

---

32. Richard Irons, "Inpatient Assessment of the Sexually Exploitative Professional," in *Breach of Trust: Sexual Exploitation by Health Care Professionals and Clergy*, ed. John C. Gonsiorek (Thousand Oaks, CA: Sage Publications, 1995), 163–75.

33. Judith Herman, *Truth and Repair: How Trauma Survivors Envision Justice* (Hachette, UK: 2023), 169.

34. Mark D. Jordan, *Telling Truths in Church: Scandal, Flesh, and Christian Speech* (Boston: Beacon, 2003); William Glenn, "Neither Do I: A Meditation on Scapegoating," in *Gay Catholic Priests and Clerical Sexual Misconduct: Breaking the Silence*, ed. Donald L. Boisvert and Robert E. Goss (Binghamton, NY: Harrington Park Press, an imprint of Haworth Press, 2005), 199–207; Mary Gail Frawley-O'Dea and Virginia Goldner, "Abusive Priests: Who They Were and Were Not," in Frawley-O'Dea and Goldner, *Predatory Priests*, 35–57.

35. Stephen J. Rossetti and Leslie M. Lothstein, "Myths of the Child Molester," in Rossetti, *Slayer of the Soul*, 1990), 9–18.

a profound misunderstanding of sexual identity and unjustly stigmatizes and scapegoats gay clergy. In truth, sexual identity and abusive behavior are complex phenomena that do not have a causal relationship.[36] Acknowledging this distinction is crucial for addressing the real causes of abuse and fostering more inclusive and understanding church environments.

Forming Nonabusive Priests

The formation of clergy emerges as the next crucial junction in preventing abuse, necessitating significant evolution in how churches approach this topic. The current curriculum for clergy training starkly ignores the inherent power imbalance between clergy and laity, failing to establish clear guidelines for maintaining ethical and professional relationships. Clergy face "the extraordinary challenges of maintaining personal and professional boundaries in the clergy role.... The role that they are expected to fill is the most complex and 'boundary strained' of any helper role."[37] As we explored above, this critical boundary is often shrouded in mystique, rarely addressed openly or constructively.

The inadequate training on psychological nuances such as these issues of power is a glaring deficiency in clergy formation. This is particularly important for clergy in managing transference and countertransference—where the emotional dynamics between clergy and those they counsel can lead to unhealthy attachments and attractions. This gap leaves clergy ill-equipped to handle these natural interactions that have been observed in counseling in a healthy or professional way.

Furthermore, the formation process sorely lacks in imparting "emotionally integrated, morally coherent, and humane perspec-

---

36. Robert Miller, "The Church and Gay Men: A Spiritual Opportunity in the Wake of the Clergy Sexual Abuse Crisis," in *Sexual Abuse in the Catholic Church: Trusting the Clergy?*, ed. Marie M. Fortune and W. Merle Longwood (Binghamton, NY: Haworth Pastoral Press, 2003), 87–102; Thomas J. Gumbleton, "Homosexuality in the Priesthood Does Not Contribute to Child Sexual Abuse," in *The Catholic Church*, ed. Mary E. Williams (Detroit: Greenhaven Press, 2006), 83–91, reprinted from Thomas J. Gumbleton, "Yes, Gay Men Should Be Ordained," *America* 187 (September 2002); and Mary Gail Frawley-O'Dea and Virginia Goldner, "Abusive Priests: Who They Were and Were Not," in Frawley-O'Dea and Goldner, *Predatory Priests*, 35–57.

37. Gonsiorek, Renzetti, and Yocum, "The Interplay of Psychological," ebook.

tives on human sexuality."[38] Insights from Kate Ott, drawing on a seminary survey, reveal a stark educational void: only one in six seminaries mandates courses on sexual ethics. Consequently, the vast majority of clergy step into their roles without fundamental education on human sexuality, despite most clergy (80 percent) expressing a desire for training on sexual harassment prevention.[39]

This educational shortfall perpetuates a shame-based narrative around sexuality, keeping clergy from being able to address issues of sexuality in safe and healthy ways. Instead, clergy often feel fear and despair, being forced to navigate a system preoccupied with purity and abstinence, to the detriment of acknowledging and embracing human sexuality.[40] Combined with the practice and philosophy of celibacy, the dearth of comprehensive training in sexuality contributes to the pressing need for a paradigm shift in how churches prepare their clergy. Embracing a more developed, mature approach to sexuality and boundary maintenance is essential for fostering a healthy, nonabusive environment within churches.

Responding to Perpetrators

A church's approach to managing sexually abusive priests is pivotal in confronting and rectifying the clergy sexual abuse crisis. Historically, the Catholic Church's method—relocating or briefly institutionalizing abusive priests before reassigning them, all while keeping the laity and public in the dark—failed to establish accountability. This absence of accountability allowed perpetrators to continue their abusive behaviors unchecked. The debate over whether it is possible to safely reintegrate sexually abusive priests into ministry remains unresolved.

---

38. Gonsiorek, Renzetti, and Yocum, "The Interplay of Psychological."

39. Kate M. Ott, *Sex and the Seminary: Preparing Ministers for Sexual Health and Justice* (New York: Religious Institute on Sexual Morality, Justice, and Healing, and Union Theological Seminary, 2009).

40. See Donald R. Hands, "Beyond the Cloister—Shamed Sexuality in the Formation of Sex-Offending Clergy," in *The Sex Offender: Theoretical Advances, Treating Special Populations, and Legal Developments*, ed. Barbara K. Schwartz and Henry R. Cellini (Kingston, NJ: Civic Research Institute, 2002), 29.1–8; and A. W. Richard Sipe, "The Crisis of Sexual Abuse and the Celibate/Sexual Agenda of the Church," in Plante, *Sin against the Innocents*, 61–72.

According to some psychological evaluations, a significant number of these priests might be reintegrated after undergoing extensive rehabilitation for addictive behavior, typically spanning twelve to twenty-four months.[41] Most of these assessments concentrate on priests who abuse children. These types of child abuse behaviors are often likened to addictions, akin to alcoholism, which are not resolved or cured but managed with continuous efforts at sobriety.[42] Consequently, it's argued that these individuals should avoid any ministry settings that could present them with their specific triggers, such as access to children.

Most psychologists concur that deciding whether to reintegrate a perpetrator into the general population post-treatment is contingent upon the specifics of each case. However, one truth remains certain: accountability is imperative. Absent this accountability, merely relocating or laicizing clergy, effectively ostracizing them from their church community, merely displaces the problem, allowing their abusive behaviors to manifest elsewhere.

Churches must adopt proactive systems of accountability to safeguard both victims and perpetrators alike. Marie Fortune insightfully notes, "for perpetrators, the most loving response may be the development of systems of accountability and consequences that stop their destructive behaviors."[43] Despite their actions, abusers remain human beings and members of church communities. They warrant our compassion, which indispensably includes holding them accountable.

Establishing systems of accountability should effectively involve leveraging support networks beyond church communities. It's essential for church leaders and communities to collaborate closely with social workers, crisis intervention specialists, and counselors. Such partnerships aim to educate both clergy and laity about abuse awareness and the implementation of best practices in accountabil-

---

41. Alan J. Placa, "Legal Aspects of the Sexual Abuse of Children," in Rossetti, *Slayer of the Soul*, 166–69; Frank Valcour, "The Treatment of Child Sex Abusers in the Church," in Rossetti, *Slayer of the Soul*; and Irons, "Inpatient Assessment," 45–66.

42. Valcour, "The Treatment of Child Sex Abusers in the Church."

43. Marie M. Fortune and James Poling, "Calling to Accountability: The Church's Response to Abusers," in *Violence against Women and Children: A Christian Theological Sourcebook*, ed. Carol J. Adams and Marie M. Fortune (New York: Continuum, 1995), 451–63, 451.

ity networks. Engaging openly with police, legal professionals, and the justice system ensures that priests are held accountable for their actions, both within the ecclesiastical framework and in broader society.[44]

Another critical facet of accountability involves providing abusive priests with necessary training, counseling, and rehabilitation. Their well-being and ability to engage in healthy relationships must be a priority, irrespective of their potential return to ministry. This approach also facilitates the healing process within the parish community, helping congregation members navigate their mixed feelings about a priest's removal by reassuring them that the individual is receiving the support that they need, thus smoothing the transition and fostering congregational healing.[45]

The public dimension of clergy sexual abuse adds significantly to its complexity. Exposing or removing an abuser from their role, of course, impacts the perpetrator and victim. It also resonates throughout the entire congregation, creating a ripple effect of trauma. This collective hurt extends beyond the church doors, subjecting the parish community to external scrutiny and judgment. Seeking an accountable response to this widespread damage, advocates are turning to restorative justice practices for their potential to address and alleviate the communal and individual suffering.

Restorative justice, which seeks the rehabilitation of the offender through reconciliation efforts with the victims and the broader community, offers an inclusive approach where all affected parties participate in the healing process. Traditionally perpetrators, victims, and community members all have a seat at the table in deciding how that reconciliation happens. While only a few theorists have ventured to apply restorative justice to the context of clergy sexual abuse, they advocate for its ability to foster beneficial outcomes for everyone involved. However, theorists also caution against the possibility of underplaying the gravity of sexual abuse or inadvertently causing further trauma to survivors through their interactions with the perpetrator.[46] The agency and accountability

---

44. Fortune and Poling, "Calling to Accountability," 460.

45. E. Larraine Frampton, "Responding to the Offender Family," in *When a Congregation Is Betrayed: Responding to Clergy Misconduct*, ed. Beth Ann Gaede (Herndon, VA: Alban Institute, 2005), 156–62.

46. Anne-Marie McAlinden, "Are There Limits to Restorative Justice? The Case

provided to all parties through this process have great potential for healing individuals and communities. The collaborative model of atonement and healing found in a restorative justice approach gives us significant insights into our crucifixion and resurrection narratives, explored in more depth later in this book.

Conclusion

The history, causes, and responses to the clergy sexual abuse crisis provide crucial context for the perspectives of survivors. Survivors seek narratives of suffering and healing to comprehend and navigate their trauma within this framework. The forthcoming chapter explores the profound impact of clergy sexual abuse on individuals and the broader community, exploring in greater depth the moral injury inflicted on survivors and the church community at large. It will also detail the specific needs of survivors and others embarking on the journey toward healing. The act of meaning-making is central to the healing and recovery process, returning us to this book's core question: how can we narrate the cross and atonement in a way that acknowledges the pain of clergy abuse survivors, while simultaneously empowering them and charting a path forward for the entire church community?

---

of Child Sexual Abuse," in *Handbook of Restorative Justice: A Global Perspective*, ed. Dennis Sullivan and Larry Tifft (Abingdon, Oxfordshire, England: Routledge, 2006), 299–310; and Douglas E. Noll and Linda Harvey, "Restorative Mediation: The Application of Restorative Justice Practice and Philosophy to Clergy Sexual Abuse Cases," in *Understanding the Impact of Clergy Sexual Abuse: Betrayal and Recovery*, ed. Robert A. McMackin, Terrence M. Keane, and Paul M. Kline (London: Routledge, 2009), 180–99.

6

The Fallout

Morally Injured Individuals and Communities

"[I experienced] extreme periods of low self-esteem for many years.... With a huge talent to cover it all up.... Mask it. I could wear any mask. I could present myself with a smile. Suit. Tie. Fresh haircut. And you would think that I had the world on a string ... **but I was a shell.**"
—Michael, survivor of clergy sexual abuse

"People are always telling me, 'Just move on.' And first and foremost, my question is how? Because **I literally don't know how to do that.**"
—Nathan, survivor of clergy sexual abuse

"You know, I always felt I was less than. That **I wasn't good enough**, but more importantly, it was because I didn't try hard enough."
—Deborah, survivor of clergy sexual abuse

In the previous chapters, we explored the history, causes, and the Catholic Church's responses to the clergy sexual abuse crisis. Now, we aim to enhance our understanding of the profound suffering this crisis has caused, alongside church leaders' and communities' inadequate responses, both on a personal and a communal level. This exploration is vital for the constructive discussions that will shape the latter part of this book. Without fully acknowledging and examining the extent of this pain, we cannot hope to grasp the true impact of the crisis or understand the crucifixion narrative in the context of clergy sexual abuse.

Up to this point, we've focused on the individual and deeply personal stories of survivors Nathan, Deborah, and Michael. I have treated each narrative separately to honor their unique journeys and insights. These stories have been crucial in shedding light on the personal dimensions of abuse and its repercussions.

However, as we seek to understand the broader implications of abuse on individuals and communities, I employ a different narrative technique to share survivors' experiences in this chapter. To capture the diversity of experiences and the common threads that bind them, I introduce two composite narratives. Through the fictional yet representative stories of James and Rebecca, I aim to illustrate the diverse yet common experiences of those affected by clergy sexual abuse. These "true fictions" are synthesized from the testimonies of several survivors I interviewed as part of the Taking Responsibility Research Grant. This approach allows us to honor the anonymity of those who shared their stories with us while investigating the widespread and varied impacts of the abuse on individuals and communities.

In this chapter, we begin with the impact of clergy sexual abuse on survivors as individuals through the stories of James and Rebecca. We then widen our scope to examine its effects on entire communities, particularly through the lens of moral injury. We will also explore the recovery needs for both individuals and communities affected by this crisis. In the next chapter, I will survey the Catholic Church's historical response to survivors and the broader community, beyond the handling of perpetrators outlined in the previous chapter. The shift in my way of presenting the survivor stories is designed to provide a fuller, more encompassing view of the crisis, acknowledging the myriad ways it has touched lives and communities.

James, a male survivor, grew up in a devout Catholic family, where attending Mass was a fundamental part of family life. He and his cousins served as altar servers, working closely with their parish priest. At the age of ten, both he and his cousin experienced sexual and spiritual abuse by their priest. By the time James reached high school, he quit attending Mass and the abuse stopped. After this he never returned to his church and now identifies as an atheist. The catalyst for James's healing journey was learning about the conviction of another priest, which prompted him to join a survivors' support group. Today, he is a vocal advocate for changing the statute of limitations on sexual abuse, working tirelessly with peer support and advocacy groups. James's decision to engage in public advocacy stems from his belief in the power of shared stories and community support in healing from clergy sexual abuse.

Rebecca's narrative presents a contrasting journey that is equally important. Raised in a Catholic, Mexican American household, she faced abuse by the priest who acted as the school counselor during her middle school years. It wasn't until her daughter was entering high school that Rebecca confronted her past trauma, marking the beginning of her healing process. Counseling has been a pivotal component of her recovery. Today, Rebecca remains a practicing Catholic, actively involved in her church. She is dedicated to working with other survivors and church leaders to establish safety protocols and response systems for clergy sexual abuse.

Victim Profiles

Clergy sexual abuse, much like the devastating ripple effects of a bomb's explosion, extends its impact far beyond the immediate pain and suffering of a single victim. At the heart of this catastrophe lies the victim, the epicenter of trauma, but the shockwaves do not stop there. In ever-widening circles, their family and friends surround them, bearing the brunt of secondary trauma; the adults who, through action or inaction, find themselves complicit; the parishioners of the abuser, grappling with betrayal; those entangled within church systems, and the broader community, all of whom are touched by the fallout of this crisis. But first, our journey begins at the core, with the survivors—James and Rebecca. Their stories illuminate both the depth of the tragedy and the far-reaching shadows it casts, inviting us to understand the full scope of harm and the urgent need for healing and change.

Clergy sexual abuse does not discriminate, touching the lives of many across different backgrounds. However, certain risk factors heighten one's vulnerability to exploitation by abusive clergy. Key among these is an individual's accessibility to clergy, often through roles within a church, such as employees, volunteers, altar servers (like James), or students (like Rebecca). This proximity increases their risk of encountering abuse. Furthermore, a lack of sexual abuse training and awareness compounds this vulnerability. Statistically, survivors frequently report previous instances of sexual abuse, substance dependencies, or mental health struggles. Predominantly, these survivors are under the age of twenty-four, female, and belong to minority groups, including racial, ethnic, disability, and sexual minorities.[1]

Impacts on Individual Survivors

The repercussions of clergy sexual abuse are severe and multifaceted, extending beyond the immediate physical and emotional toll, inflicting deep-seated psychological scars. Survivors, including James and Rebecca, exemplify the broad spectrum of post-traumatic stress symptoms common to sexual abuse survivors, including hyperarousal, constrictions, intrusion, and the trauma dialectic.[2] Such an event, marked by its malicious intent, thoroughly impacts a survivor's sense of safety, predictability, and benevolence in the world, negatively affecting their spiritual well-being.[3]

Survivors of clergy sexual abuse endure a complex array of post-traumatic stress symptoms, akin to those experienced by survivors of general sexual abuse. Both James and Rebecca, for instance, experienced symptoms of PTSD, depression, and anxiety, each manifest-

---

1. Nanette de Fuentes, "Hear Our Cries: Victims-Survivors of Clergy Sexual Misconduct," in *Bless Me Father for I Have Sinned: Perspectives on Sexual Abuse Committed by Roman Catholic Priests*, ed. Thomas G. Plante (Westport, CT: Praeger, 1999), 135–70.

2. Explored by Judith Lewis Herman, *Trauma and Recovery: The Aftermath of Violence—From Domestic Abuse to Political Terror* (London: Hachette, 2015).

3. See Kathryn A. Flynn, *The Sexual Abuse of Women by Members of the Clergy* (Jefferson, NC: McFarland & Company, 2003), 296; and Roger D. Fallot and Andrea K. Blanch, "Religious and Spiritual Dimensions of Traumatic Violence," in *APA Handbook of Psychology, Religion, and Spirituality, Volume 2: An Applied Psychology of Religion and Spirituality*, ed. Kenneth I. Pargament, Annette Mahoney, and Edward P. Shafranske (Washington, DC: American Psychological Association, 2013), 371–87.

ing uniquely throughout their lives. However, the specific identity of their abuser as a clergy person or spiritual leader introduced an additional layer of trauma—spiritual trauma—that distinguishes their experiences from others. This unique aspect of clergy sexual abuse alters a survivor's spirituality and can inflict significant wounds on their soul. Rebecca recounted her own despair after her abuse. She felt such deep shame and depression; she remembered feeling like nothing mattered. Everything—her family, her church, God—were all lies. And even doing good or acting morally in the world seemed pointless.

The complexity of clergy sexual abuse extends beyond physical, mental, and emotional dimensions, exacting spiritual wounds on the soul, making it uniquely devastating.[4] This multifaceted trauma is seen in James's own recounting of his abuse. He shared that his abuser framed the abuse as something special between him and the priest. He remembers thinking, "it can't be bad that a priest did it, ... priests, they don't do wrong. . . . I just knew that a priest couldn't sin."[5] This manipulation distorted James's perception of his abuse, falsely framing it as something good rather than the violation it was. It also extensively affected his self-image. He often wondered what was wrong with him that would cause this pain and suffering. Within his family and community, the priest's role was seen as sacrosanct, a direct emissary of God, beyond reproach or question. The profound betrayal felt when such a figure causes pain and suffering can shatter one's self-esteem and distort one's sense of agency. This narrative, shared by James, exemplifies the insidious impact of spiritual trauma, amplifying the traditional trauma response with layers of shame and guilt, fundamentally altering a survivor's self-worth and autonomy.

The unique aspects of the trauma experienced by clergy sexual abuse survivors goes beyond the immediate abuse. Survivors

---

4. See Elaine M. Bain, "The Abuse of Faith: The Effect of Clerical Child Sex Abuse on the Faith Life of Victims," in *The Dark Night of the Catholic Church: Examining the Child Sexual Abuse Scandal*, ed. Brendan Geary and Joanne Marie Greer (Stowmarket, Suffolk, England: Kevin Mayhew Publishers, 2011).

5. Quotes for James and Rebecca are all taken from interviews with clergy abuse survivors done in the winter and spring of 2021 through research completed at Xavier University and supported by the Taking Responsibility grant through Fordham University.

often experience a prolonged period of grooming, during which an intense psychological, emotional, and spiritual bond is fostered between the abuser and the survivor. This intricate bond, built on trust and reverence, magnifies the trauma when it is violated, collapsing the survivor's spiritual and existential frameworks. The dissonance between their image of the clergyperson and their lived experience of abuse causes many survivors to not label their experience as abuse at first.[6]

The complexity of this betrayal is further compounded by the reverence for the clergy displayed by the survivors' family and community. In some communities, any attention from a clergyperson is seen as an honor or blessing. This dynamic is poignantly captured in Rebecca's story. As a young girl within the Mexican American community, she was taught to view personal formation or guidance by a priest as a distinguished privilege, a sentiment echoed by her family and community. However, the honor associated with such attention clashed with the violation she endured, creating a mental conflict within her. This clash between her lived reality and the initial perceptions of the clergy's role shows the unique and devastating impact of clergy sexual abuse, complicating the journey toward understanding and healing.

The intersection of race and survivor experiences introduces additional layers of complexity. In communities where clergy are held in especially high esteem, such as in many Black and Hispanic congregations in the United States, while not monolithic, the betrayal cuts deeper.[7] Rebecca's experience is an example of this, where her family's involvement in and reverence toward the church complicated her inability to disclose the abuse to her father. Moreover, minority communities often grapple with nuanced relationships with law enforcement and the justice system, further complicated by internal and external pressures to uphold a positive community

---

6. See Flynn, *The Sexual Abuse of Women*; and Danielle M. McGraw, Marjan Ebadi, Constance Dalenberg, Vanessa Wu, Brandi Naish, and Lisa Nunez, "Consequences of Abuse by Religious Authorities: A Review," *Traumatology* (2019), https://doi.org/10.1037/trm0000183.

7. See Anne M. Pope, "A Response to Clergy Sexual Abuse: An African American Perspective," *Sexual Abuse in the Catholic Church: Trusting the Clergy?*, ed. Marie M. Fortune and W. Merle Longwood (Binghamton, NY: Haworth Pastoral Press, 2003), 79–85; and Ladan Alomar, "A Response to Clergy Sexual Abuse: A Latina Perspective," in Fortune and Longwood, *Sexual Abuse in the Catholic Church*, 75–77.

image.[8] This can lead to a perilous silence, where the protection of the perpetrator is unjustly prioritized over the welfare of the survivor. Addressing clergy abuse as merely a psychological issue, rather than a systemic and social one, neglects the intertwined challenges of racism and community dynamics, exacerbating the survivors' plight.

Gender also significantly influences the experiences of survivors of clergy abuse. While research predominantly focuses on male children and adolescents, the narratives of women and adults often remain in the shadows, leading to a skewed understanding of survivor experiences. In instances where women are abused by clergy, society often sees this through a lens of sexuality, misconstruing dynamics of coercion and power with mutual attraction. Similarly, male survivors grapple with societal ignorance and homophobia, complicating their ability to openly discuss and understand their experiences.[9]

This was poignantly illustrated by James, who found himself at a crossroads of confusion regarding his sexuality and the nature of his abuse. The prevailing silence in public discourse about sexuality and sexual abuse hampers male survivors' ability to articulate their experiences, often conflating them with issues of sexuality rather than recognizing them as manifestations of power and control. Additionally, the Catholic Church's historical stance on homosexuality further exacerbates the situation, layering same-sex abuse with stigma and shame.

The betrayal experienced by survivors of clergy sexual abuse extends beyond personal violation to include a breach of trust within the religious institution itself. This dual betrayal—by the individual abuser and by the religious system that fails to protect or

---

8. See Toinnette M. Eugene, "'Swing Low, Sweet Chariot!': A Womanist Response to Sexual Violence and Abuse," in *Violence against Women and Children: A Christian Theological Sourcebook*, ed. Carol J. Adams and Marie M. Fortune (New York: Continuum, 1995), 185–200; and Traci C. West, "The Fact of Race/Ethnicity in Clergy Sexual Abuse of Children," in *The Structural Betrayal of Trust*, ed. Regina Ammicht-Quinn, Hille Haker, and Maureen Junker-Kenny; Concilium 2004/3 (London: SCM, 2004), 40–50.

9. See Walter H. Bera, "Betrayal: Clergy Sexual Abuse and Male Survivors," in *Breach of Trust: Sexual Exploitation by Health Care Professionals and Clergy*, ed. John C. Gonsiorek (Thousand Oaks, CA: Sage Publications, 1995), 91–111.

believe them—exacerbates the trauma.[10] James's story starkly illustrates this phenomenon.

When he courageously reported his abuse to church officials, James was met with disbelief, denial, and accusations, further victimizing him and undermining his faith in the institution that was supposed to offer sanctuary. The diocese's response—dismissing his experience and accusing him of seeking financial gain—represents a devastating failure of moral and pastoral care, basic human empathy, and justice. James recounted that, at the time, he was even driven to suicidal thoughts, calling himself a "survivor of reporting to the church."

Driven by the Catholic Church's neglect and mistreatment of victims, James severed ties with the church community. Unfortunately, this is the outcome for many survivors. This systemic failure is an example of the urgent need for religious institutions to reevaluate their response to abuse allegations, ensuring that survivors are met with compassion, belief, and support rather than skepticism and hostility.

The disbelief and denial that survivors often face from family and friends further compound the trauma of clergy sexual abuse. This painful reality stems from the revered status of the abuser. Skepticism from loved ones deepens the sense of isolation and betrayal, exacerbating the symptoms of PTSD and complicating the path to healing.[11]

James was doubly betrayed when his cousin, also a victim, denied any involvement, distancing himself with a stark dismissal: "No, man. That was all you. You know. I [expletive] hated the church." This denial severed a once-close relationship, leaving James to grapple with loss and heartbreak. Mourning this loss, James told me, "We were so close and that breaks my heart because I love him so much."

Rebecca faced a different, yet equally painful, form of denial. Her mother discouraged her from revealing her abuse to her father,

---

10. See Carolyn Moore Newberger, "The Sexual Abuse Crisis: What Have We Learned? A Response to Archbishop Harry J. Flynn," in Fortune and Longwood, *Sexual Abuse in the Catholic Church*, 35–41; and Thomas P. Doyle, "The Spiritual Trauma Experienced by Victims of Sexual Abuse by Catholic Clergy," *Pastoral Psychology* 58, no. 3 (2009): 239–60.

11. See Flynn, *The Sexual Abuse of Women*.

fearing disbelief. This caution led Rebecca to choose silence over the risk of being disbelieved by her father, a decision underscored by her resolve: "I'm not gonna put myself through that. I'm not gonna—No way José. That is not gonna happen. 'Cause that would be too painful. Way too painful." In both cases, the anticipation or reality of disbelief by loved ones adds another layer of trauma to the survivors' experiences, illustrating the varied personal and communal responses to clergy sexual abuse. For both James's cousin and Rebecca's father, the truth was too painful, too beyond their normal experience to be believed.

The shattered trust in both individual and institutional relationships challenges survivors' faith, leading to intense introspection and, sometimes, transformation in their relationship with the Divine. Abusive clergy, often perceived as direct representatives of the Divine, wield spiritual coercion to intensify their bond with the survivor. This betrayal forces survivors to reassess their understanding of the Divine's nature and role, potentially causing a lifelong struggle with faith.[12] For some, like Rebecca, this journey leads to a radical reshaping of their God-image. Initially viewing God as a distant judge, her trauma transitioned her view of God to one of betrayal, before ultimately finding solace in conceiving God as a loving, paternal figure, describing him now as her "Daddy" and experiencing a relationship strength she never knew was possible.

This evolution shows the critical role of flexible theological language and imagery in healing from spiritual trauma. Whereas rigid God-concepts might fracture under the weight of such betrayal, adaptable faith perspectives can foster resilience, offering survivors new, comforting understandings of the Divine. As with James, whose understanding of God was authoritarian and inflexible, the trauma of clergy abuse can irreparably damage a survivor's relationship with the Divine.

During his abuse, James found himself questioning, "Why is God doing this to me?," as he grappled with the notion of being labeled an "evil child" by someone he was taught to see as a representative of God. This sense of injustice and betrayal by the Divine

---

12. Thomas P. Doyle, "Sexual Abuse by Catholic Clergy: The Spiritual Damage," in *Sexual Abuse in the Catholic Church: A Decade of Crisis, 2002–2012*, ed. Thomas G. Plante and Kathleen L. McChesney (New York: Bloomsbury Publishing, 2012), 171–82.

led to enduring anger toward God. James saw his abuse as an injustice that was never righted. Despite seeking solace and intervention during his darkest moments—"During the abuse, I remember multiple times [saying], 'Jesus help me.' Looking toward the Eucharist and asking for help, and it never came"—James's pleas for divine intervention went unanswered, cementing his disillusionment.

This led to a complete severance of faith, as James, citing the Gospel of Matthew, poignantly expressed his feelings of abandonment by God: "'I am mindful of the sparrow when it falls from the tree.' And I'm not as important as a stupid bird." James's journey shows the critical need for a malleable and evolving spiritual language within church communities. It serves as a cautionary tale of how a rigid, unchanging depiction of God can alienate those who have endured profound spiritual traumas, emphasizing why faith communities must foster environments where conceptions of the Divine can grow and adapt in response to congregants' life experiences.[13]

The relationship between a survivor's faith and their journey through the aftermath of clergy sexual abuse is complex, shaped by personal beliefs, spiritual flexibility, and the reactions of their faith community. The impact of faith on healing from such trauma is nuanced; it does not uniformly help or hinder recovery.[14] Stricter, more authoritarian religious frameworks can facilitate abuse, but the findings on how these strict religious views impact healing is mixed.

For Rebecca, her faith and identification with the Catholic tradition played critical roles in her healing, offering her a platform for advocacy and a sense of belonging that she deemed necessary despite its challenges. She admitted that "the easy part was to be a Christian," but that it wasn't always easy to remain Catholic.

Conversely, James found the very aspects of church and faith that once shaped his spiritual life to be sources of acute distress. From

---

13. Mary Gail Frawley-O'Dea, "God Images in Clinical Work with Sexual Abuse Survivors: A Relational Psychodynamic Paradigm," in *Spiritually Oriented Psychotherapy*, ed. Donald F. Walker, Christine A. Courtois, and Jamie D. Aten (Washington, DC: American Psychological Association, 2015), ebook.

14. Roger D. Fallot and Andrea K. Blanch, "Religious and Spiritual Dimensions of Traumatic Violence," in Pargament, Mahoney, and Shafranske, *APA Handbook of Psychology, Religion, and Spirituality*, 371–87.

the service and homily to the vestments, he finds many aspects of attending Mass triggering. He described one episode of panic attacks, physical pain, and nausea after being compelled to attend services with his family on the holidays.

This dichotomy is an example of the individualized nature of spiritual recovery paths. While some survivors, like Rebecca, draw strength and purpose from their faith, navigating its complexities to find healing and a voice within from her church experience, others, like James, experience religious environments as harmful, leading to a complete severance from their faith traditions. These divergent experiences show the essential role of supportive and understanding faith communities that can adapt to the varied needs of survivors. Through fostering environments where survivors can safely explore and express their spirituality, communities can offer crucial support on the path to healing.

The journey toward healing for survivors of clergy sexual abuse is influenced by the response of their religious community. In many cases, they are faced with disbelief or even adversarial responses, exacerbating their trauma.[15] As Rebecca's and James's experiences show, the church leaders and community's defensive posture and prioritization of its clergy over victims can magnify the wounds, leading survivors to feel alienated and even demonized. These stories emphasize the necessity for religious communities to adopt transparent, compassionate, and just approaches to dealing with abuse allegations, ensuring survivors do not face secondary victimization through institutional denial or neglect.

In a recent discussion over whether Rebecca's church community should continue to play the music of known sexual abuser David Haas, she took a firm stance against continuing to play his music. Her community began to isolate Rebecca for taking this stance and because of her public identity as a survivor. She began to attend a different church, farther away from her house, in order to avoid the community that she felt no longer wanted her. She hoped that one day she would be able to return to that parish and told me, "I just

---

15. See Marie Collins and Sheila Hollins, "Healing a Wound at the Heart of the Church and Society," in *Toward Healing and Renewal: The 2012 Symposium on the Sexual Abuse of Minors Held at the Pontifical Gregorian University*, ed. Charles J. Scicluna, Hans Zollner, and David John Ayotte (New York: Paulist Press, 2012), ebook.

hope that all of us can find a place in the church. . . . I hope that one day all of us can find our way back or find our way, whatever that is." Her resilience is exemplary of a desire for a church that embraces all, acknowledging the pain of those it has failed.

James's narrative, however, illustrates a severe breach of trust through both the abuse itself and church leaders' dismissive and defensive responses when he sought justice. His disillusionment is another example of the systemic failure to acknowledge and address the survivors' needs, pushing him away from his church community entirely. James felt the whole community has failed and continues to fail survivors. Exasperated, he told me, "They need to intervene, they need to participate." Like James, many survivors find that they receive much better support from outside their faith communities, through hospitals, social workers, and the justice system. In addition to a poor response from churches, survivors find there are few avenues for justice within current church structures. Many churches do not have clear or transparent ways of reporting abuse within the leadership. This can cause more trauma and stress by adding to a survivor's feelings of helplessness or hopelessness.[16]

While the devastating effects of clergy sexual abuse most significantly alter the lives of survivors, the ripple effects extend far beyond the individuals directly harmed. Those nearest to the survivors bear a significant burden in addition to the moral injury that is experienced by the broader community. Friends and family members, through their close connections with survivors, encounter secondary traumatic stress, mirroring the symptoms of PTSD.[17] This secondary trauma is further compounded by "faith-based dilemmas," as the very foundations of their spiritual lives are called into question.[18]

---

16. Deborah Sauvage and Patrick O'Leary, "Child Sexual Abuse in Faith-Based Institutions: Gender, Spiritual Trauma and Treatment Frameworks," in *The Sexual Abuse of Children: Recognition and Redress*, ed. Yorick Smaal, Andy Kaladelfos, and Mark Finnane (Clayton, Victoria, Australia: Monash University Publishing, 2016), 146–59.

17. Sauvage and O'Leary, "Child Sexual Abuse," in Smaal, Kaladelfos, and Finnane, *The Sexual Abuse of Children*, 146–59.

18. Leslie H. Wind, James M. Sullivan, and Daniel J. Levins, "Survivors' Perspectives on the Impact of Clergy Sexual Abuse on Families of Origin," *Journal of Child Sexual Abuse* 17, no. 3/4 (2008): 238–54.

These loved ones navigate a maze of conflicted feelings—toward their faith, trust in religious leaders, and their place within a religious community that may have failed to support their affected family member. Rebecca described her family as being "ripped apart" by the abuse. Her mother not only left her church in response, but she also felt her own sense of shame and guilt. Rebecca described how her mother was so ashamed on her deathbed that she had refused to see her. Rebecca told me, "She didn't know how I could forgive her."

These wider circles of fallout from the abuse include guilt, shame, and alienation that extends far beyond the immediate survivors. As we pivot toward understanding the experiences of secondary survivors, it is essential to keep in mind the interconnectedness of these traumas and the need for healing that spans individuals and communities alike.

Impact on Secondary Victims— the Catholic Community

The clergy sexual abuse crisis, compounded by institutional cover-ups within the Catholic Church, has traumatized the broader church community.[19] This trauma stems from the intimate relationship between priests, the Divine, and Jesus as the Christ, leading to a deep sense of betrayal that extends beyond direct victims to include their families, Catholic parents and children, and parish members formerly under the care of accused priests. Experts have recognized the entire church community's experience of secondary trauma, characterized by signs of moral injury, residual anger, and a significant decrease in participation due to a perceived lack of acknowledgment and accountability from church's leadership.[20]

Studies, including of both parishes directly affected by clergy sexual abuse and the general Catholic population, have shown that the laity has experienced trauma symptoms as a result of the clergy

---

19. See Brian F. Linnane, "The Sexual Abuse Scandal in the Catholic Church: Implications for Sexual Ethics," in *A Just and True Love: Feminism at the Frontiers of Theological Ethics. Essays in Honor of Margaret A. Farley*, ed. Maura A. Ryan and Brian F. Linnane (Notre Dame, IN: University of Notre Dame Press, 2007), 273–302.

20. Joseph P. Chinnici, *When Values Collide: The Catholic Church, Sexual Abuse, and the Challenge of Leadership* (Maryknoll, NY: Orbis Books, 2010).

abuse crisis and cover up. The closer the parish is to the incident, the more pronounced the symptoms. Poor responses from parish leaders also exacerbate these symptoms. A clear correlation exists between the absence of accountability and diminished congregational well-being. Studies have also documented a rising tide of hostility and anger toward church leadership, attributed to sluggish and inadequate institutional reactions.[21]

Revelations of abuse have reignited trauma among previously victimized parishioners and have plunged nonvictimized children into a maelstrom of anxiety, confusion, and questions regarding sexuality. Many studies describe feelings of betrayal, guilt, and embarrassment in both children and adult Catholic laity.[22] Theologian and ethicist Brian Linnane articulates the resulting "moral vacuum," where many now find church communities and their leaders lacking as a reliable "source of moral and spiritual insight."[23] This crisis has eroded the Catholic Church's public credibility in morality, holiness, and justice, marking a significant impact on the collective faith and trust of the Catholic faithful.[24] There remains a pervasive sense of betrayal, distrust of leadership, and moral disarray within church communities as a result of the crisis.[25]

---

21. See Deborah Pope-Lance, "Trauma Intervention: Planning Strategies for Recovery," in *When a Congregation Is Betrayed: Responding to Clergy Misconduct*, ed. Candace R. Benyei, E. Larraine Frampton, Nancy Myer Hopkins, Patricia L. Liberty, and Deborah J. Pope-Lance (Lanham, MD: Rowman & Littlefield, 2005), 46–50; and Nancy Nason-Clark, "The Impact of Abuses of Clergy Trust on Female Congregants' Faith and Practice," in *Wolves within the Fold: Religious Leadership and Abuses of Power*, ed. Anson Shupe (Piscataway, NJ: Rutgers University Press, 1998), 85–100.

22. See Nason-Clark, "The Impact of Abuses of Clergy," 85–100; Paul M. Kline, Robert A. McMackin, and Edna Lezotte, "The Impact of the Clergy Abuse Scandal on Parish Communities," in *Understanding the Impact of Clergy Sexual Abuse: Betrayal and Recovery*, ed. Robert A. McMackin, Terrence M. Keane, and Paul M. Kline (London: Routledge, 2009), 290–300; and Carroll Cradock and Jill R. Gardner, "Psychological Intervention for Parishes Following Accusations of Child Sexual Abuse," in *Slayer of the Soul: Child Sexual Abuse and the Catholic Church*, ed. Stephen J. Rossetti (Mystic, CT: Twenty-Third Publications, 1990), 123–42.

23. See Brian F. Linnane, "The Sexual Abuse Scandal," 273, 275.

24. Chinnici, *When Values Collide*.

25. See Kline, McMackin, and Lezotte, "The Impact of the Clergy Abuse Scandal," 290–300; Cradock and Gardner, "Psychological Intervention for Parishes," 123–42.

The Fallout

As the laity grapple with the repercussions of the abuse, a noticeable number have distanced themselves from their churches. Although precise statistics are elusive, there's a consensus among studies that the laity's connection with their churches has notably weakened in the wake of their awareness of the abuse crisis and subsequent cover-ups. This disillusionment has manifested in decreased attendance at Mass, reduced participation in confessions and volunteer activities, and a general withdrawal from church interactions. Remarkably, one study found that up to 50 percent of women reported less frequent attendance at Mass. Interestingly, despite this estrangement from their churches, many report that their personal relationship with God remains largely unaltered.[26] This divergence shows a critical distinction between faith in a higher power and trust in the institution that professes to represent it.

In our groundbreaking study, supported by the Taking Responsibility grant from Fordham University,[27] we explored the concept of moral injury—feelings of guilt and shame that arise when people witness, participate in, or fail to prevent actions that conflict with their fundamental beliefs—within the context of the Catholic Church's clergy sexual abuse crisis.[28] Our research spanned three distinct groups: adults who survived clergy sexual abuse, employees of Catholic dioceses, and students at a Jesuit university.

Unlike traditional studies on moral injury, which primarily focus on military personnel, our survey was designed to assess its presence among civilians who were affected by the crisis in the Catholic Church. We asked participants about their religious affiliations, beliefs, their awareness of the abuse, and how these experiences impacted their moral and spiritual lives.

Our findings confirmed what we had anticipated: both direct and indirect exposures to the abuse significantly heightened the incidence of moral injury. Remarkably, our study illuminated three key aspects of this injury: a significant breach of trust in religious and community leaders, a decrease in individuals' sense of personal and communal efficacy, and a troubling erosion of personal integrity and goodness.

---

26. See Nason-Clark, "The Impact of Abuses of Clergy," 85–100; Kline, McMackin, and Lezotte, "The Impact of the Clergy Abuse Scandal," 290–300.

27. https://takingresponsibility.ace.fordham.edu/final-report/.

28. https://takingresponsibility.ace.fordham.edu/measuring-moral-injury/.

Furthermore, our research investigated how moral injury varied among those directly abused by clergy compared to those less directly affected. By surveying survivors, diocesan employees, and Catholic university students, we discovered that, while those directly impacted showed higher levels of moral injury, this was a pervasive issue affecting all surveyed groups. This suggests a broader, more complex problem that warrants further investigation to understand how various levels of exposure influence the severity of moral injury in both religious and broader community contexts.

We also compared how much this moral injury affected the survivors of abuse versus those who might not have been directly harmed. All three groups we studied showed signs of moral injury. While it was especially pronounced in those who faced abuse directly, indirect exposure, such as that of college students at a Jesuit college, also increased symptoms. We found that many students indirectly exposed to the crisis experienced trauma-related symptoms, including negative emotions like sadness and grief, anger and shame, self-condemnation, confusion, and helplessness. Notably, 46 percent of students indicated that their comfort with their faith community had decreased because of the sexual abuse crisis.[29] This tells us that the impact of the scandal stretches far beyond the immediate victims. It suggests we need to dig deeper to understand how such experiences change people's trust in their religious communities and their own sense of right and wrong.

Conclusion

Through the narratives of survivors like Nathan, Deborah, Michael, James, and Rebecca, we have seen the complex and personal impacts of clergy sexual abuse. These stories are not just isolated incidents. They represent a broader crisis that has left a profound scar on individuals and church communities alike. The trauma extends beyond the immediate victims, reaching out to impact families, friends, and the larger faith community. This chapter has sought to illustrate the pervasive and complex nature of this harm, emphasizing the

---

29. Marcus Mescher, Kandi Stinson, Anne Fuller, and Ashley Theuring, *Measuring & Exploring Moral Injury Caused by Clergy Sexual Abuse*, Xavier University, 2022, https://www.xavier.edu/moral-injury-report/.

The Fallout

moral injury inflicted on the collective consciousness of the Catholic Church.

Our exploration of the "fallout" from clergy sexual abuse has highlighted the urgent need for systemic change and comprehensive support mechanisms. The stories of James and Rebecca represent the inadequacy of past responses from church leaders and communities. Survivors have faced disbelief, denial, and further victimization from the very institutions meant to offer solace and protection. This has compounded their trauma, fracturing the trust and faith of countless Catholics worldwide.

In the next chapter, our focus will shift toward the recovery needs of both individuals and communities. In addressing these needs, we will consider the psychological, emotional, spiritual, and communal dimensions of healing. The next chapter will also provide a comprehensive overview of strategies that can facilitate recovery and restore trust within the Catholic community. Additionally, we will critically examine the Catholic Church's response to the crisis, assessing the effectiveness of current measures and proposing pathways for meaningful reform. We will also explore how church leaders can move beyond mere damage control to adopt proactive and compassionate responses that prioritize the well-being of survivors and the integrity of the faith community.

7

Recovery Needs for Individuals and Communities

"I was set free. I can't tell you exactly the point, or that I felt any huge shattering experience, or a flash of blue light—as some people said they have experienced. . . . But I can tell you that something happened in my life. . . . There's a power greater than myself that helped me achieve that."
—Michael, survivor of clergy sexual abuse

Preliminary research indicates that the scope of the impact of the clergy sexual abuse crisis extends far beyond what the churches have previously recognized. Therefore, healing and justice initiatives must encompass not only survivors but the entire Catholic community. Below, we will first address the recovery needs of survivors. Then, we will consider the collective needs of the Catholic community to foster a path toward justice and healing.

Survivors' Recovery

The journey toward healing for survivors of clergy sexual abuse is multifaceted, encompassing psychological, social, and theological dimensions. Dr. Judith Herman identifies three major stages of recovery: safety, remembrance and mourning, and reconnection. These stages are not sequential but are interconnected, allowing survivors to navigate through them nonlinearly. Survivors may find themselves revisiting different stages at various points in their healing process.

The first critical stage is safety, which involves acknowledging the abuse, regaining control, and fostering a safe environment. This foundational step is essential for enabling further stages of healing. Achieving safety is particularly challenging for survivors of clergy sexual abuse because of the church's clericalism and the secrecy that supports it. The difficulty in finding safety for clergy abuse survivors is compounded by their young age. Many children find the experience of sexual abuse un-languagable. James's and Rebecca's stories show these difficulties. Despite feeling relatively safe today, both survivors had to navigate the complex process of naming their abuse and working toward creating safe spaces for themselves. Despite their long healing journeys, James and Rebecca both expressed persistent struggles with distrust, uneasiness with strangers, and concerns for their children's safety.

The process of healing from clergy sexual abuse necessitates that survivors name their abuse and create safe spaces for themselves and requires them to reexamine their spiritual or religious worldviews. Many of the traumatic impacts of such abuse stem from a survivor's internalized, shame-based beliefs, including detrimental perceptions of clergy and God. Thomas Doyle emphasizes the profound importance of this aspect of healing, suggesting that "perhaps the most fundamental and radical dimension of the healing process is re-imaging the notion or image of God."[1] Therefore, establishing a sense of safety for survivors includes creating safe religious environments and narratives that support their recovery. This path looks different for each individual. For some, like Rebecca, it means finding a congregation that affirms their identity and supports their journey toward healing. For others, like James, it might mean stepping away from their church entirely.

As the first stage of healing, safety requires survivors to accurately identify the abuse for what it truly was, separating their own feelings of guilt and shame from the realities of coercion and the absence of agency and consent. It's crucial for survivors to understand their abuse as an exercise of power and control rather than as a sexual act. This distinction can be particularly challenging for

---

1. See Thomas P. Doyle, "Sexual Abuse by Catholic Clergy: The Spiritual Damage," in *Sexual Abuse in the Catholic Church: A Decade of Crisis, 2002–2012*, ed. Thomas G. Plante and Kathleen L. McChesney (New York: Bloomsbury Publishing, 2012), 171–82, 179.

those who experienced sexual abuse in childhood, as their initial experiences of sexuality are entangled with their abuse, confusing their understanding of sex and sexuality with the trauma they endured. The healing journey for both male and female survivors often involves exploring and understanding their own sexuality and gender expressions. Research in psychology on post-traumatic growth indicates that, for male survivors of childhood sexual abuse, an important aspect of recovery includes developing a positive relationship with their gender roles and sexuality.[2]

The second stage of recovery, remembrance and mourning, focuses on a survivor's ability to articulate their experiences, comprehend the events that transpired, and grieve their losses. While similar to the initial stage of naming the abuse, remembrance goes further by allowing survivors to share their stories in a narrative form with others. This sharing might occur within formal contexts such as testimonies or in more personal settings like therapy sessions.

James, for instance, found peer support invaluable, participating in both Alcoholics Anonymous and a clergy abuse survivors' group. These groups provided a platform for him to discuss his abuse publicly and fostered a sense of solidarity and understanding among members. He observed how sharing in these settings enabled him to see his own experiences reflected in the stories of others, though it took several meetings before he felt ready to open up about his own story. Once he did, sharing became a crucial aspect of his advocacy, enhancing his confidence and ability to communicate his experiences.

For Rebecca, the path to healing and remembrance involved one-on-one counseling. She found an "amazing therapist" who listened attentively to her story, helping her recognize her own worth. Through therapy, Rebecca came to understand that she deserves a fulfilling life, affirming, "I'm worth having a good marriage. I'm worth somebody fighting for me." This personalized approach to recovery, compared to James's more community-based processing, shows us the diverse needs of survivors, as well as the importance

---

2. Hazel Lewis, Gundi Kiemle, Michelle Lowe, and Robert Balfour, "Men's Health across the Lifespan: Post Traumatic Growth and Gender Role in Male Survivors of Child Sexual Abuse," *International Journal of Men's Community and Social Health* 5, no. SP1 (2022): 50.

of finding a supportive environment that resonates with each individual's journey.

This stage also includes the importance of "mourning" for trauma healing. Survivors of abuse often grapple with profound losses that extend beyond the immediate impacts of their experiences. These losses can include their childhood, sense of safety, relationships, and mental health. James's journey exemplifies the deep sense of loss that can accompany the process of moving away from one's church. For James, his church had been a cornerstone of his identity and life. He described this departure as both a slow and painful process. "You know, [I] have kind of left the church. And that was just [a] very, very slow process. It was a very hurtful process.... Cuz this is—this was my life. It centered around it." Even as he identifies as an atheist, James expressed a poignant sense of longing for the community and rituals he left behind, admitting he did "miss being at church."

Another major factor of a positive healing journey is for survivors to feel that there was justice and accountability for what happened to them. Unfortunately, justice is rarely achieved in cases of sexual abuse. There is the added complication of church hierarchies ignoring or covering up clergy sexual abuse cases, so a sense of acknowledgment may never become a part of a survivor's healing.[3]

Though a critical aspect of this second stage of healing, the pursuit of justice and accountability is, tragically, seldom fully realized. Rebecca's experience with seeking justice illustrates the complexity of this journey. Though she encountered a moment of validation through the review board process and received an apology from the archdiocese's attorneys, the sense of justice it provided was fleeting. She reflected on the transient nature of this justice, acknowledging that, despite these acknowledgments, the emotional scars remain.

> I feel justice is a funny word, because I felt civic justice by going through the review board process, and I met with the arch-

---

3. See Marie Collins and Sheila Hollins, "Healing a Wound at the Heart of the Church and Society," in *Toward Healing and Renewal: The 2012 Symposium on the Sexual Abuse of Minors Held at the Pontifical Gregorian University*, ed. Charles J. Scicluna, Hans Zollner, and David John Ayotte (New York: Paulist Press, 2012), ebook.

diocese's attorneys, and they apologized to me; they admitted and apologized. And I felt that justice for about a day, right? . . . But you're still left with a broken heart. . . . You have a broken heart until you die.

These narratives show the complex interplay between mourning, justice, and a survivor's ongoing journey toward healing.

The third and final stage of recovery, as outlined by Herman, is reconnection. During this stage, survivors work toward reconciling with both themselves and others. This often involves reestablishing connections with trustworthy family members and friends and reframing their identity around being a survivor and advocate. Engaging in social action and finding a mission can also be part of this transformative process. James and Rebecca, for instance, have embraced roles as public advocates for survivors to some degree.

James has actively participated in peer support and advocacy groups, aiming to assist other survivors and advocate for legislative reforms. He views his involvement in these groups as his chosen method of confronting his past abuse. The importance of peer support in the healing journey of survivors of clergy sexual abuse cannot be overstated. Given that survivors frequently face exclusion from their religious communities after the abuse, finding or creating new communities that are safe, understanding, and inclusive is vital for fostering a sense of belonging.[4] Support-group facilitators have noted the benefits of operating outside the traditional structures of the Catholic Church. This independence allows for greater flexibility and enables laypeople to contribute more effectively to church reform efforts. Furthermore, when these secular survivor groups manage to incorporate elements of spirituality, their impact on the healing process of clergy abuse survivors is significantly enhanced.[5]

---

4. See Robert A. McMackin, Terrence M. Keane, and Paul M. Kline, eds., *Understanding the Impact of Clergy Sexual Abuse: Betrayal and Recovery* (London: Routledge, 2009); Michaela Mendelsohn, Judith Lewis Herman, Emily Schatzow, Melissa Coco, Diya Kallivayalil, and Jocelyn Levitan, *The Trauma Recovery Group: A Guide for Practitioners* (New York: Guilford Press, 2011).

5. See Elizabeth Pullen, "An Advocacy Group for Victims of Clerical Sexual Abuse," in *Wolves within the Fold: Religious Leadership and Abuses of Power*, ed. Anson Shupe (Piscataway, NJ: Rutgers University Press, 1998), 85–100; Mendelsohn et al., *The Trauma Recovery Group*.

Rebecca discovered that her path to healing didn't necessarily involve adopting a prominent public role. Instead, she found solace in rekindling connections with her church community, friends, and family, alongside her therapeutic relationship. However, navigating the healing process within a religious community brought its challenges, notably the expectation to forgive her abuser. This expectation can be distressing for survivors, especially when it precedes the attainment of justice and accountability at both the individual and community levels.[6] For Rebecca, the emphasis on forgiveness within her church has been a source of anxiety. Despite grappling with the notion of forgiving her abuser through prayer and reflection, she is hindered by the persistent lack of accountability. This unresolved issue leads her to believe that forgiveness, in this case, may be unattainable.

Marie Fortune has written extensively on the concept of forgiveness in the context of sexual abuse, emphasizing that several conditions must be met before forgiveness can even be considered. She critiques the notion of "cheap forgiveness"—forgiveness offered without accountability—as harmful, perpetuating the cycle of abuse. Fortune asserts that "authentic forgiveness" requires empowerment and vindication of the survivor, and ultimately depends on the survivor's choice to release their pain and anger. Additionally, this process necessitates a religious community that embraces openness and transparency, acknowledges the wrongdoing, and fosters truth-telling, instead of minimizing or concealing the abuse. Forgiveness should not be mandated for survivors to participate in their faith community. However, it is often used by survivors to circumvent conflict within their religious environment.[7]

---

6. See Doyle, "Sexual Abuse by Catholic Clergy: The Spiritual Damage," 171–82; Marie M. Fortune, "Forgiveness: The Last Step," in *Violence against Women and Children: A Christian Theological Sourcebook*, ed. Carol J. Adams and Marie M. Fortune (New York: Continuum, 1995), 201; Katharina von Kellenbach, "Guilt and Its Purification: The Church and Sexual Abuse," *CrossCurrents* 69, no. 3 (September 2019): 238–51.

7. See Marie M. Fortune, "What about Forgiveness?," in *Sexual Violence: The Unmentionable Sin* (New York: Pilgrim Press, 1983), 162–70; Marie M. Fortune, "Forgiveness the Last Step," in *Abuse and Religion: When Praying Isn't Enough*, ed. Anne L. Horton and Judith A. Williamson (Lexington, MA: Lexington Books, 1988), 215–20; Joretta L. Marshall, ed., *Forgiveness and Abuse: Jewish and Christian Reflections* (Binghamton, NY: Haworth Pastoral Press, 2002).

Healing from clergy sexual abuse involves a critical component that differs from addressing general PTSD: the need to confront moral injury. Within psychology, this aspect is referred to as "moral repair." The common shortfall of many mental health treatments is their lack of focus on moral and spiritual exploration, crucial elements in the process of moral repair.[8] This gap exists because therapists and clinicians generally receive no training in the nuances of moral identity. Consequently, many experts suggest faith communities could serve as venues for the moral repair journey.[9]

However, turning to a faith community for help with moral repair is challenging for survivors who have distanced themselves from their churches, like James, or those who perceive their faith community as triggering, unresponsive, or even harmful. Despite these challenges, Rebecca has engaged in constructive work within her church to organize healing circles that unite survivors, clergy, and lay members. These circles have played a vital role in helping her, and others, reevaluate and strengthen their moral identity, sense of agency, and interpersonal connections. The path forward for the moral repair process remains uncertain, emphasizing the need for approaches that are attuned to the diverse needs of survivors, clinicians, and the wider community.

Caring for the Community after Abuse

In alignment with the general best practices for preventing and responding to clergy sexual abuse discussed in chapter 5, there are specific measures that should be adopted to reduce the trauma and

---

8. Although several therapies, such as Cognitive Processing Therapy, Exposure-Response Therapy, and Eye Movement Desensitization and Reprocessing, are traditionally recommended for those dealing with moral injury, "Adaptive Disclosure" stands out as the only therapy specifically tailored to address moral injury. See Brian J. Griffin, Nicole Purcell, Kimberly Burkman, Brett T. Litz, Craig J. Bryan, Mark Schmitz, Carlos Villierme, Jenna Walsh, and Shira Maguen, "Moral Injury: An Integrative Review," *Journal of Traumatic Stress* 32, no. 3 (2019): 350–62.

9. See Warren Kinghorn, "Combat Trauma and Moral Fragmentation: A Theological Account of Moral Injury," *Journal of the Society of Christian Ethics* 32, no. 2 (2012): 57–74; Chris J. Antal and Kimberly Winings, "Moral Injury, Soul Repair, and Creating a Place for Grace," *Religious Education* 110, no. 4 (2015): 382–94; Rita Nakashima Brock and Rebecca Ann Parker, *Saving Paradise: How Christianity Traded Love of This World for Crucifixion and Empire* (Boston: Beacon, 2008).

moral injury experienced by the wider Catholic community. First, it's crucial to establish immediate and transparent communication channels between church leadership and the parishioners. The approach should be one of openness and inclusivity, moving away from defensiveness and secrecy. The laity should be kept informed, consulted, and involved in the processes of justice and healing.[10] James and Rebecca both advocate for greater involvement, accountability, and awareness among the lay members. Historical evidence suggests that transparency and directness from churches lead to more effective healing for all parties involved.[11]

Second, churches must recognize and acknowledge the pain they have caused. This involves not only apologies from church leadership but also providing opportunities for parishioners to voice their grievances and share their experiences. Through such acknowledgments and listening sessions, churches can aim to rebuild the laity's trust in their community. Remarkably, this restoration can occur independently of formal reparations through the justice system or from the perpetrators. Instead, it requires initiative from the community itself, given the leadership's past failures in accountability. Encouragingly, examples from the past demonstrate the effectiveness of proactive and restorative community engagement in healing both individuals and churches as whole communities.[12] It's essential to confront and openly address the collective moral injury suffered by church communities.

---

10. See Carroll Cradock and Jill R. Gardner, "Psychological Intervention for Parishes Following Accusations of Child Sexual Abuse," in *Slayer of the Soul: Child Sexual Abuse and the Catholic Church*, ed. Stephen J. Rossetti (Mystic, CT: Twenty-Third Publications, 1990), 123–42; Beth Ann Gaede, ed., *When a Congregation Is Betrayed: Responding to Clergy Misconduct* (Herndon, VA: Alban Institute, 2005).

11. See Murdock Smith, "Women Priests and Clergy Sexual Misconduct," in *Predatory Priests, Silenced Victims: The Sexual Abuse Crisis and the Catholic Church*, ed. Mary Gail Frawley-O'Dea and Virginia Goldner (Mahwah, NJ: Analytic Press, 2007), 35–57.

12. See Paul M. Kline, Robert McMackin, and Edna Lezotte, "The Impact of the Clergy Abuse Scandal on Parish Communities," in *Understanding the Impact of Clergy Sexual Abuse: Betrayal and Recovery*, ed. Robert A. McMackin, Terrence M. Keane, and Paul M. Kline (London: Routledge, 2009), 290–300; Cradock and Gardner, "Psychological Intervention"; Nancy Meyer Hopkins, *The Congregation Is Also a Victim: Sexual Abuse and the Violation of Pastoral Trust*, Special Papers and Research Reports series, no. OD88 (Bethesda, MD: Alban Institute, 1992); Gaede, *When a Congregation Is Betrayed*.

The Needed Church Response

Up to this point in history, the Catholic Church has largely overlooked the urgent needs of survivors and the community for accountability, public disclosure, and a moral reimagining. The extensive and devastating impact of the clergy sexual abuse crisis is undeniable, as encapsulated by the remark from the survivor from chapter 1, Michael: "I think the Protestant Reformation was a walk in the park compared to what [the Catholic Church is] facing now." How, then, should the Catholic Church address this crisis? What measures are necessary to guide survivors, the laity, and church structures toward healing? To explore these questions, we will first examine the actions that have been undertaken historically, before considering what further steps are required.

Historical Response of the Church

Extensive research and personal accounts have thoroughly documented the Catholic Church's inadequate response to the clergy sexual abuse crisis, exacerbating the trauma for victims and affecting the broader church community. Churches have prioritized their institutional interests over the well-being of victims. The Catholic Church has adopted an adversarial position toward those whom it perceives as external to its hierarchy, including victims, the general public, the media, and even the lay community.

As we see in the experience of James, the church leadership's and community's failure to support survivors has deep and troubling consequences. His struggles with mental health and suicidal thoughts were profoundly impacted by his church's disbelief and negligence. This glaring inability to recognize the extent of harm inflicted on survivors, coupled with aligning itself with perpetrators, has led to dangerous outcomes and a significant lack of public accountability. Furthermore, the pressure on survivors to forgive and "move on" serves to deflect criticism and protect church structures, an approach that demands scrutiny and calls for a more compassionate and accountable response.[13] Like James, many have felt abandoned by their church.

---

13. See James Martin, S.J., "How Could It Happen? An Analysis of the Catholic Sexual Abuse Scandal," in *Predatory Priests, Silenced Victims: The Sexual Abuse Crisis and the Catholic Church,* ed. Mary Gail Frawley-O'Dea and Virginia Goldner

Church leaders have used silencing tactics—including ignoring, denying, threatening, or financially compensating victims who attempt to report abuse—to protect churches' reputations at the expense of truth and justice. This practice, as shared by survivors like James and detailed in conversations with advocate Marie Collins—an Irish survivor of abuse who has worked in the Vatican to promote change—names a systemic issue: church leaders have not only failed to address abuse but have actively covered it up. Echoing James's own experience and showing the betrayal felt by many, Collins quotes a survivor as telling her, "I am still struggling to regain the trust and respect I once had for the Catholic Church. . . . My religion was not taken from me by my abuser but the church itself."[14]

This pervasive culture of denial and silence has fostered deep mistrust among the laity, the general public, and the media, effectively isolating the church community from potential allies and crucial support. A significant consequence of sidelining the laity is the exclusion of women. Despite constituting over half of church congregations, women find themselves barred from the clergy and, thus, from pivotal roles in addressing the crisis.[15] In her own healing work as a survivor, Rebecca initiated healing circles in her church that brought together survivors, laity, and clergy. Her efforts to facilitate these inclusive discussions offer a promising model for how churches might engage all their members in meaningful conversation and mutual healing.

Despite the rarity of such initiatives, Rebecca's experience gives us a glimpse of the potential for progress when diverse voices are heard. As stated in the 2002 Charter for the Protection of Children and Young People, adopted by the U.S. Conference of Catholic Bishops, "the overwhelming weight of opinion is that the bishops did

---

(Mahwah, NJ: Analytic Press, 2007), 35–57; Stephen J. Rossetti, "Learning from Our Mistakes: Responding Effectively to Child Sexual Abusers," in *Toward Healing and Renewal: The 2012 Symposium on the Sexual Abuse of Minors Held at the Pontifical Gregorian University* (New York: Paulist Press, 2012), ebook.

14. See Marie L. Collins, "Breaking the Silence: The Victims," in *The Structural Betrayal of Trust*, ed. Regina Ammicht-Quinn, Hille Haker, and Maureen Junker-Kenny; Concilium 2004/3 (London: SCM, 2004), 19.

15. Donald B. Cozzens, *Sacred Silence: Denial and the Crisis in the Church* (Collegeville, MN: Liturgical Press, 2002), 49.

little to repair the lost trust of the laity."[16] The absence of lay church community voices has impoverished responses to the crisis.

Strategic decisions by the Catholic Church to silence or mislead the laity and public are driven by a desire to protect the institution, often prioritizing the Catholic Church's image over pastoral care, ethical considerations, and demands for justice.[17] Church leaders, caught in a response crisis, have adopted a leadership style marked by control, competence, and unwavering certainty. This method, investigative reporter Jason Berry points out, morphs church structures into "monarchies" without true accountability or justice.[18] Such leadership is at stark odds with the transparency and accountability needed to tackle the sexual abuse crisis's roots, including entrenched clericalism and secrecy.

However, there is some hope. Church leaders who embody transparency, directly engage with survivors, and push for substantial reforms are emerging. These individuals and groups, though few, shine as beacons of hope. They suggest that a shift toward real accountability and the dismantling of destructive power structures is within reach. By adopting and nurturing these models of leadership, churches can initiate healing and rebuild trust both internally and with the broader public. In her local church and community work, Rebecca holds hope for her church to adopt a new leadership approach in addressing the clergy sexual abuse crisis. She sees potential in the bishops to guide the church community toward truth and vulnerability. Rebecca believes that, through "truth and reconciliation" efforts, the Catholic Church "could be a place of hope and healing for everyone." This vision mirrors a wider call for leadership that values the community's well-being and voices.

Unfortunately, survivors seeking involvement in the justice pro-

---

16. Terrence A. Carroll, "The Failure of the Dallas Charter and Canon Law: A Blessing in Disguise," in Plante and McChesney, *Sexual Abuse in the Catholic Church*, 56.

17. Martin, "How Could It Happen?," 35–57.

18. Jason Berry, *Render unto Rome: The Secret Life of Money in the Catholic Church* (New York: Broadway Paperbacks, 2011); see also Kimberly D. Elsbach, "Looking Good vs. Being Good: Pitfalls of Maintaining Perceptions of Strong Leadership Following Organizational Scandals," in *Church Ethics and Its Organizational Context: Learning from the Sex Abuse Scandal in the Catholic Church*, ed. Jean M. Bartunek, Mary Ann Hinsdale, and James F. Keenan (Lanham, MD: Rowman & Littlefield, 2005), 69–80.

cess often find themselves marginalized by church leaders, who prefer legal defenses to open dialogue. This strategy, sidestepping public accountability, compels many survivors to seek justice through criminal and civil courts. There, they confront a church hierarchy resistant to legal challenges and quick to label justice-seekers as adversaries. James's ordeal exemplifies this, as he navigated a maze of legal obstacles and encountered church attorneys as its primary front. Time and again, church leaders have prioritized the protection of the clergy, the institution's image, and its wealth, rather than address the needs and rights of abuse survivors.[19]

In the previous chapters, we explored the institutional roots of the clergy sexual abuse crisis, focusing on how a lack of sexual abuse education and the entrenched practices of clericalism have fueled this tragedy. A devastating outcome of these deficiencies is the church leadership's widespread ignorance regarding the nature and impact of clergy sexual abuse, including its prevalence and the profound harm it causes. The leadership's discomfort with discussing sexuality has led to a lack of the critical training and understanding necessary for recognizing and addressing abuse. Consequently, many church leaders are ill-equipped to identify the warning signs of abuse, often underestimating, ignoring, or minimizing cases brought to their attention.[20]

Clericalism and bureaucratic procedures have led to a response system that is both cumbersome and resistant to change.[21] This system, marked by a reluctance to adapt, has effectively shielded church leaders from external scrutiny, the concerns of the laity, and even insights from their peers. This creates a "feedback loop," where the momentum to maintain the status quo makes acknowledging issues like sexual abuse more difficult. As we've discussed, the intertwining of clericalism with church operations often blurs the line between what benefits the community and what serves the institution's image, fostering an environment where constructive criticism is dismissed rather than welcomed.[22] Instead of hearing

---

19. Martin, "How Could It Happen?," 35–57.
20. See Martin, "How Could It Happen?," 35–57; Charles J. Scicluna, Hans Zollner, and David John Ayotte, eds., "Learning from Our Mistakes," in Scicluna et al., *Toward Healing and Renewal*.
21. Martin, "How Could It Happen?," 35–57.
22. See John Beal, "'As Idle as a Painted Ship upon a Painted Ocean': A People

or seeking critical advice, church leaders often relied too heavily on institutionally friendly psychiatrists, psychologists, and lawyers.[23] These advisors often echoed the belief that clergy abuse could be resolved within the church hierarchy alone.

The U.S. Catholic Church has historically faced limited support from the global Catholic community and the Vatican in addressing the clergy abuse crisis. Initially, the Vatican characterized the crisis as an "American problem," attributing it to factors unique to the United States. Among these were the propensity for civil litigation in America, seen as a catalyst for the multitude of allegations. Moreover, the societal climate in the United States, perceived as hostile toward Catholicism, led some to view the allegations as manifestations of "anti-Catholicism." Additionally, the U.S. Catholic Church's challenges with bipartisanship were thought to exacerbate the crisis, with political divisions believed to manipulate and intensify the crisis.[24]

These perceptions of the U.S. Catholic Church have a basis in reality and have influenced the handling of the crisis. The media, often critical of the Catholic Church, has played a significant role in shaping public perception, at times stereotyping and demonizing the church leadership and communities, including their responses to the clergy abuse crisis.[25] The U.S. Catholic Church's stonewalling tactics can be seen as defensive responses born from decades of mistrust of the media.[26] Nevertheless, media exposure is crucial for public accountability and oversight.[27] The *Boston Globe*'s exposé

Adrift in the Ecclesiological Doldrums," in *The Structural Betrayal of Trust*, ed. Regina Ammicht-Quinn, Hille Haker, and Maureen Junker-Kenny; Concilium 2004/3 (London: SCM, 2004), 87–97.

23. Martin, "How Could It Happen?," 35–57.

24. John Allen, "Clergy Sexual Abuse in the American Catholic Church: The View from the Vatican," in *Sin against the Innocents: Sexual Abuse by Priests and the Role of the Catholic Church*, ed. Thomas G. Plante (Westport, CT: Praeger, 2004), 13–24.

25. Philip Jenkins, "'The Perp Walk of Sacramental Perverts': The Pedophile Priest Crisis," in *The New Anti-Catholicism: The Last Acceptable Prejudice* (New York: Oxford University Press, 2003), 137.

26. Martin, "How Could It Happen?," 35–57.

27. Philip Jenkins, "Creating a Culture of Clergy Deviance," in *Wolves within the Fold: Religious Leadership and Abuses of Power*, ed. Anson Shupe (Piscataway, NJ: Rutgers University Press, 1998), 85–100.

on sexual abuse within the Boston Archdiocese exemplifies how media scrutiny can bring justice to situations of clerical corruption. The widespread coverage of the abuse crisis has also enhanced public awareness, providing victims, such as James and Rebecca, with the language to articulate their experiences and seek healing and justice.[28]

In recent years, as awareness of clergy sexual abuse has expanded to other countries like Canada, Ireland, and Australia, the Vatican and the global Catholic Church have begun to address the issue more earnestly. However, this delayed acknowledgment has significantly eroded public trust in the Catholic Church in the United States. The complex history between the United States and the Catholic Church continues to fuel the hierarchy's defensive posture and the laity's skepticism toward its leadership.

Future Response of the Church

Time and time again, experts and faithful alike have urged churches to truly embody the compassion and care that Jesus demonstrated, especially toward the most vulnerable.[29] Jennifer Beste, a Catholic feminist theologian, specifically urges the Catholic Church to prioritize survivors of abuse and protecting children, reflecting the church's stated "preferential option for the poor."[30] Despite a tradition rich in ethical and moral teachings, the reality is that church leaders have often fallen short of these ideals. Many, including survivors like James, argue that the failure of the Catholic Church to safeguard children disqualifies it from any future role in their care.[31] Yet, there's a pressing question for those who still hold hope for reform: how can the church acknowledge these criticisms and

---

28. Flora A. Keshgegian, "'And Then I Remembered.' Childhood Sexual Abuse," in *Redeeming Memories: A Theology of Healing and Transformation* (New York/Nashville, TN: 2000), 36–56.

29. Thomas G. Plante, "Conclusion," in Plante, *Sin against the Innocents*, 183–92; Alan J. Placa, "Legal Aspects of the Sexual Abuse of Children," in Rossetti, *Slayer of the Soul*, 149–73.

30. Jennifer Beste, "Envisioning a Just Response to the Catholic Clergy Sexual Abuse Crisis," *Theological Studies* 82, no. 1 (2021): 29–54, 30.

31. See John C. Gonsiorek, Claire M. Renzetti, and Sandra Yocum, "The Interplay of Psychological and Institutional Factors in the Sexual Abuse by Roman Catholic Clergy," in *Clergy Sexual Abuse: Social Science Perspectives*, ed. Claire M. Renzetti and Sandra Yocum (Boston: Northeastern University Press, 2013), 37–59.

fears, and what steps can we take to make amends and ensure real change?

Educating every member of the church is crucial for creating effective and compassionate responses to the clergy abuse crisis in the future. Leaders within churches, along with experts, have emphasized the need for prevention and response strategies that take into account the diverse cultures within the Catholic Church.[32] Such strategies must support ongoing and transparent research into clergy sexual abuse and the broader challenges facing those in pastoral and advocacy roles.[33] Currently, there's a significant gap in our understanding of the factors that have allowed clergy sexual abuse to persist within churches and other organizations worldwide.[34] A comprehensive examination is necessary, one that considers both the systemic and personal contributors to the crisis, including the impact of priesthood on mental health.[35] The more we understand, the better equipped we will be to prevent abuse and support those affected.

Another key step toward a constructive future for the Catholic Church involves educating its leaders, congregations, and the wider community about understanding and responding to trauma more generally. It's essential for faith communities to embrace prevention and intervention strategies that are grounded in the core principles of trauma-informed care: ensuring safety, building trust, offering choice, fostering collaboration, and empowering individuals.[36] Looking ahead, prioritizing the well-being of survivors above

---

32. See Stephen J. Rossetti et al., "Learning from Our Mistakes," in Scicluna et al., *Toward Healing and Renewal*.

33. See Plante, "Conclusion"; Gonsiorek, Renzetti, and Yocum, "The Interplay of Psychological."

34. Kirk O. Hanson, "What the Bishops Failed to Learn from Corporate Ethics Disasters," in Plante, *Sin against the Innocents*, 169–82.

35. See Donald B. Cozzens, "Keynote: The Sexual Abuse Crisis: What Issues Do We Still Have to Face?," *Journal of Religion and Abuse: Advocacy, Pastoral Care and Prevention* 5, no. 3 (2003): 43–52; Marie M. Fortune and W. Merle Longwood, eds., *Sexual Abuse in the Catholic Church: Trusting the Clergy?* (Binghamton, NY: Haworth Pastoral Press, 2003).

36. See Roger D. Fallot and Andrea K. Blanch, "Religious and Spiritual Dimensions of Traumatic Violence," in *APA Handbook of Psychology, Religion, and Spirituality, Volume 2: An Applied Psychology of Religion and Spirituality*, ed. Kenneth I. Pargament, Annette Mahoney, and Edward P. Shafranske (Washington, DC: American Psychological Association, 2013), 371–87.

the institution's reputation or the perpetrator's interests is crucial. Churches need to lead the way in safeguarding against further harm to survivors and their families, actively working to prevent additional trauma, especially during the legal proceedings of both criminal and civil cases.[37] Moreover, churches should champion efforts to eliminate bias among public officials, ensuring they hold church authorities accountable for their actions.[38]

In addressing misconduct, churches must also be proactive and pastoral. Anyone accused of abuse should be promptly removed from their ministry duties, while pending investigation.[39] Unfortunately, as the current *Charter for the Protection of Children and Young People* states, accused priests are presumed innocent, remaining in all of their duties, until there is sufficient evidence that sexual abuse of a minor has occurred.[40] This policy lacks the immediacy and support needed to deal with child abuse. It also currently overlooks cases of nonsexual abuse among adults or between coworkers, revealing a gap that needs addressing.

Moreover, accountability must extend to those who have shielded abusers, including the higher echelons of church leadership. Ethicist William Spohn has argued that any bishop who has moved abusers to new assignments, allowing them to harm again, should step down.[41] This accountability should also cover those in leadership before their ascension to bishopric if they played a role in such reassignments. There's a consensus among experts that investigations into allegations should not just focus on the perpetrators but also scrutinize those in supervisory positions to prevent future

---

37. See Hanson, "What the Bishops Failed to Learn," 169–82; Placa, "Legal Aspects of the Sexual Abuse of Children"; John F. Kinney and Bishops' Ad Hoc Committee on Sexual Abuse, *Restoring Trust: A Pastoral Response to Sexual Abuse*, Vol. 1 (Washington, DC: National Conference of Catholic Bishops, 1994); Plante, *Sin against the Innocents*.

38. Gonsiorek, Renzetti, and Yocum, "The Interplay of Psychological."

39. Hanson, "What the Bishops Failed to Learn"; Carol Stanton, "Officially Responding to an Accusation of Sexual Abuse: Reflections of a Diocesan Communications Director," in Rossetti, *Slayer of the Soul*, 143–48.

40. United States Conference of Catholic Bishops, *Charter for the Protection of Children and Young People*, 2018, https://www.https://www.usccb.org/offices/child-and-youth-protection/charter-protection-children-and-young-people.

41. See William C. Spohn, "Episcopal Responsibility for the Sexual Abuse Crisis," in Plante, *Sin against the Innocents*, 155–68.

incidents.[42] The harm and continued abuse caused by shuffling abusive priests between dioceses was tremendous and common. This was the case for both James and Rebecca, who later found that their abusers had been relocated to their dioceses because of previous allegations of child abuse.

To forge a future in which they respond positively to the clergy sexual abuse crisis, churches must prioritize transparent and honest communication with the public. This commitment should manifest in public apologies, detailed reporting on the causes and potential solutions of the crisis, clarity on what is known versus unknown, and updates on any policy changes and developments. Many experts advocate for the establishment of a media team, led by a designated spokesperson, to ensure open and continuous public access. The Catholic Church's stance should move away from defensiveness, embracing a posture of responsibility and proactive truth-seeking instead.

Another vital step toward a constructive church response involves fostering shared governance and reducing hierarchical structures. Best practices in shared governance suggest keeping all stakeholders informed about proceedings, inviting the laity to participate in leadership roles and vision-setting, exploring methods to involve the laity and the public in the healing process, and decentralizing leadership appointments to reinforce the significance of the local church community. This approach both democratizes church structures and reinvigorates its foundational mission by embodying a more inclusive and collaborative spirit.[43]

Conclusion

In undertaking this journey of healing, more than just policy and governance need to be reimagined in churches. There is a side to the work ahead that is deeply theological, intertwined with the

---

42. Gonsiorek, Renzetti, and Yocum, "The Interplay of Psychological."

43. For more on best practices, see Cozzens, *Sacred Silence*; Hanson, "What the Bishops Failed to Learn"; Jeremy M. Bergen, "Sexual Abuse, Violence, Injustice," in *Ecclesial Repentance: The Churches Confront Their Sinful Pasts* (London: T. & T. Clark International, 2011), 87–114; Kinney and Bishops' Ad Hoc Committee, *Restoring Trust*; Plante, "Conclusion"; Gonsiorek, Renzetti, and Yocum, "The Interplay of Psychological"; Stanton, "Officially Responding to an Accusation"; Spohn, "Episcopal Responsibility for the Sexual Abuse Crisis."

Recovery Needs for Individuals and Communities

very fabric of our faith narratives, as explored in the initial chapters. The stories of Michael, Nathan, Deborah, James, and Rebecca lay bare the profound suffering inflicted by clergy sexual abuse. Their stories have revealed a complex problem of spiritual and moral magnitude that resonates through both the individual and the collective church body. In reexamining our atonement theologies and narratives, we begin to see their dual potential for healing or further harm. We can see the crucial role that these narratives can play in personal recovery and in the communal reclaiming of faith and trust.

The crisis of clergy sexual abuse presents a particular kind of suffering that is layered with spiritual and moral questions. Responding well necessitates a narrative transformation that acknowledges the crucifixion experienced by survivors and looks toward a resurrection of hope and renewal for the church at large. As we transition into the next chapters, our focus shifts toward cultivating narratives that do justice to the suffering endured while fostering a path to resurrection that is inclusive of survivors and, ultimately, healing for the entire church community.

Part III

Salvation Reimagined

*The Cross and Resurrection
of Survivors*

8

The Power of Trauma-Sensitive Passion Narratives

Purpose and Themes

"Jesus was fighting institutions. Jesus was crucified by a powerful institution. So how is [my experience] any different than what Jesus went through?"
—Nathan, survivor of clergy sexual abuse

In the previous chapters, we observed how religious and spiritual narratives profoundly shape survivors' experiences of their trauma. This influence can be positive, as illustrated by Nathan's and Rebecca's experiences. They found solace in understanding Jesus as a fellow trauma survivor, which provided them with a sense of solidarity, meaning, and purpose. Nathan saw his advocacy for justice within his church community for survivors of clergy sexual abuse as aligned with Jesus's opposition to the Roman Empire and its injustices. Similarly, Rebecca connected her own initiative to establish healing circles in her church with the sense of community and love that Jesus embodied in his mission and life.

However, these religious narratives can also exacerbate trauma, as seen in Deborah's, Michael's, and James's stories. Their childhood religious narratives clashed dramatically with their abuse experiences. Deborah was told she was evil and that her abuse was necessary for salvation, a manipulation of the narrative about sin and evil. Michael's abuser twisted the sacrament of confession into a tool for abuse, leading Michael to doubt God's goodness and blame God for his suffering. James felt utterly forsaken by God, his prayers to the crucifix to end his abuse unanswered. These distortions of religious concepts of sin, suffering, and atonement deepened their trauma, illustrating how religious narratives, when manipulated, can inflict additional pain rather than offer solace.

Much of the Christian tradition centers on the life, death, and resurrection of Jesus of Nazareth, narratives that form the bedrock of its theological and religious discourse. These stories, as we've explored in this book's first part, profoundly influence our understanding of suffering, sin, healing, and atonement. This, in turn, molds our moral compass—shaping notions of right and wrong, our self-perception of virtue, and our overall well-being across mental, physical, and spiritual dimensions. The portrayal of the crucifixion and resurrection, therefore, plays a pivotal role in our lives, for better or worse. The significant influences of these narratives on individual and collective consciousness point us to a possible theological response to the clergy sexual abuse crisis.

The second part of the book incorporated the specific circumstances and suffering defined as the clergy sexual abuse crisis, illustrating its ongoing repercussions on survivors, bystanders, perpetrators, and the whole church community. This crisis remains unresolved, leaving deep, unhealed wounds for all. Beyond the immediate suffering and trauma resulting from the abuse and its concealment, prevalent theological interpretations of the crucifixion and resurrection have contributed to further distress through moral injury. Given this ongoing suffering and the significant influence of prevailing theological narratives, the final section of this book is pivotal, offering crucial insights and potential pathways forward.

Here, we begin reimagining the narratives of crucifixion and resurrection. Our goal is to forge stories that serve as healing frameworks for both survivors of clergy sexual abuse and the church at large. In this chapter, we begin with a deep dive into the passion narrative of Mark's Gospel. This narrative illuminates the profound truth of communal suffering and charts a course toward healing. Through the lens of Mark's Gospel, we engage with the perspectives of feminist, liberation, and nonviolent theologians, whose insights shine lights of hope for survivors. This exploration ultimately identifies key themes for our renewed narrative: the symbolism of the cross, a critical view of self-sacrifice, God's solidarity with the suffering, naming and resisting evil, and the indispensable role of community in the healing process.

Mark's Passion Narrative Overview

The Gospel of Mark is often described as a passion narrative—a story of suffering and sacrifice—preceded by an expanded introduction. It is recognized as the earliest written Gospel in the Christian canon, and its depiction of Jesus's arrest, trial, and crucifixion has sometimes been interpreted by scholars and believers alike as a straightforward historical report. Biblical scholar Arthur Dewey refers to this assumption as the "Markan default,"[1] suggesting a common tendency to read these ancient texts as direct historical accounts. However, there's scant historical evidence outside these texts to detail Jesus's crucifixion. The symbol of the cross, central to Christianity today, doesn't appear in physical artifacts until the fifth century.[2]

Instead, Mark's narrative might be understood as an exercise in ancient memory-keeping, blending storytelling and interpretive tradition in a process known as midrash. Unlike today's emphasis on distinguishing fact from fiction, the people of the ancient world used storytelling primarily for its ability to be remembered and to strengthen communal bonds. In an era where few could read or write, oral storytelling played a crucial role in preserving a community's narrative and identity.[3]

Beyond serving as a narrative framework for the ancient memory, the Gospel of Mark's midrash technique weaves together insights from Jewish Scriptures, enriching the story of Jesus with deep connections to the ancient Jewish traditions. Midrash operates on the premise that Jewish traditions are dynamic, ever-evolving narratives rather than static texts. By intertwining various, seemingly disconnected episodes from the past, midrash breathes new life into these stories, offering fresh interpretations for contemporary contexts.[4]

---

1. Arthur J. Dewey, *Inventing the Passion: How the Death of Jesus Was Remembered* (Salem, OR: Polebridge Press, 2017), 3.
2. Dewey, *Inventing the Passion*, 2.
3. Dewey, 67–68.
4. Dewey, 70.

This creative approach to Scripture is not just limited to Judaism; the sacramental worldview of the Christian tradition grounds a similar practice. Christianity, with its focus on the ongoing revelation through the Holy Spirit, invites followers to view the world and their traditions as open to new interpretations. However, modern inclinations toward rigid historical accuracy often deter contemporary Christian thinkers from exploring Scripture with the same level of creativity. While historical events and religious traditions significantly influence today's theological thinking, the relevance of our current experiences in interpreting the past is frequently overlooked. A persistent gap exists between the past and the present in theological reflection—a gap the next chapter aims to bridge.

Jewish midrash is practiced by scholars and communities seeking to infuse ancient texts with new significance, especially during times of change or crisis. The Gospel of Mark was born out of such a period, during the tumultuous Roman-Judean War from 66 to 70 CE. This historical backdrop helps explain why scholars commonly date Mark's Gospel to the years 70–75 CE, aligning it with the catastrophic fall of the Second Jewish Temple in Jerusalem. An analysis of the Gospel's narrative style and themes reveals an undercurrent of urgency, as if the text itself is responding to the immediate crises of its time.[5]

Through its apocalyptic tone and prophetic warnings of the "last days," the Gospel reflects a community grappling with war, persecution, and the seeming absence of divine intervention. This context transforms Mark's retelling of the Jesus story, casting it against a backdrop of national trauma and loss. It's a narrative deeply influenced by its historical moment, one in which the Jewish community faced persecution without clear signs of God's presence.[6]

The origins and sources behind the Gospel of Mark are less straightforward than those of the other synoptic Gospels, reinforcing the "Markan default," especially of the passion narrative. Scholars believe that Mark creatively interpreted Jewish Scriptures by drawing from the oral traditions and liturgical practices of the early Christian community. This approach allowed Mark to explore

---

5. Daryl D. Schmidt, *The Gospel of Mark with Introduction, Notes, and Original Text*, The Scholars Bible (Sonoma, CA: Polebridge Press, 1990), 3.

6. See Schmidt, *The Gospel of Mark*, 4; Michael White, *From Jesus to Christianity* (New York: HarperOne, 2004), 231.

and reinterpret the significance of Jesus's teachings and his role as the Messiah, especially in the aftermath of the failed Jewish rebellion against Rome and the devastating destruction of the Second Temple.[7]

The Destruction of the Temple in Mark

A community who is grappling with intense questions sits at the heart of Mark's narrative. For example, how could they reconcile Jesus's teachings with the recent events that seemed to contradict the arrival of God's kingdom they had hoped for? Through the disciples' consistent failure to fully grasp Jesus's mission and teachings, Mark's text reflects a community feeling abandoned by God. The community's sense of abandonment reaches its climax with the destruction of the temple, a symbol of their perceived forsakenness by God. Through this Gospel, Mark challenges the interpretation of these events as divine desertion, instead inviting readers into a deeper understanding of Jesus's message and the nature of God's presence amidst suffering.

Mark's portrayal of Jesus's relationship with the temple is central to the apocalyptic message in the Gospel. The conflict and subsequent Roman destruction of the Second Jewish Temple was a transformative event for the early Christian community, signaling a shift away from the temple's central role in religious and community life. Jesus talked about cleansing the temple in an "apocalyptic discourse," the phrase scholars use to identify Jesus's prophetic teachings about the temple's destruction as the dawn of a new era. Mark, through Jesus's teaching, interprets these events as "birth pangs" rather than the end of times. Through these narratives, Mark's Jesus challenges the existing temple-centered religious practices, suggesting they no longer fulfill their intended purpose.[8]

This critique of the temple serves multiple functions within Mark's Gospel. Primarily, it addresses the community's existential question: If Jesus is the Messiah, why do we continue to experience suffering, such as the trauma of the temple's destruction? Where

---

7. See Schmidt, *The Gospel of Mark*, 6; John R. Donahue, "Introduction: From Passion Traditions to Passion Narrative," in John R. Donahue, *The Passion in Mark: Studies on Mark 14–16* (Minneapolis: Fortress Press, 1976), 1–20; White, *From Jesus to Christianity*, 233.

8. White, *From Jesus to Christianity*, 238.

was God when this happened? By reimagining the temple not as the heart of the community but as an institution that had lost its way, Mark's Jesus shifts the focus from a physical structure to a more spiritual community centered on the disciples.[9] This transition implies that the devastation of the temple was not the cataclysmic end many feared but a necessary step toward a new understanding of the Kin-dom of God. According to Mark, the early Christians misunderstood the speed at which the community would experience the end of suffering. They still suffered because the Kin-dom of God was not yet complete; there was work still to do.[10]

Furthermore, Mark's portrayal of Jesus's opposition to the temple practices provides a rationale for the Jewish priests to bring him to trial. Again, Mark is not portraying a factual recounting but a theological statement on Jesus's mission and identity.[11] The trial scene, laden with irony and false accusations, emphasizes the disconnect between the religious leaders' charges and the community's understanding of Jesus's true message and mission. Many aspects of Jesus's trial in Mark's portrayal are meant to reinforce Jesus as the Messiah, connecting him to King David through both action and lineage.[12] Mark's portrayal of Jesus as the Messiah is also contradictory, for Jesus wields power differently, emphasizing a kingship that contrasts with contemporary understandings of power and authority. Through these layered narratives, Mark communicates a central theological vision: the redefinition of community, suffering, and messianic hope in the wake of profound societal upheaval. This vision challenges the early Christians to reconsider their expectations of the Messiah and the nature of God's unfolding kingdom.

Jesus's Death in Mark

In addition to making sense of the temple's destruction, Mark's Gospel probes the meaning of Jesus's death. At its heart, the Gospel weaves together various traditions into a passion narrative, help-

---

9. John R. Donahue, "Temple, Trial, and Royal Christology (Mark 14:53–65)," in Donahue, *The Passion in Mark*, 70.
10. White, *From Jesus to Christianity*.
11. Donahue, "Temple, Trial, and Royal Christology," 63.
12. See Donahue, "Temple, Trial, and Royal Christology," 61–79; Stephen P. Ahearne-Kroll, *The Psalms of Lament in Mark's Passion: Jesus' Davidic Suffering* (Cambridge, UK: Cambridge University Press, 2007).

ing the Markan community understand Jesus's death as part of a larger, meaningful story. This narrative reinterprets both Jesus's death and the sacred texts it echoes, offering renewed significance to both. As we follow sources that shape this narrative, we uncover a rich tapestry of influences: the trials and sacrifices of early Jewish and Christian martyrs, the poetic agony of Isaiah's Suffering Servant (Isaiah 52:13–53:12), and even threads of Hellenistic culture.[13]

To relate the audience to Jesus's death, the Markan Gospel draws from the tragic legacies of Jewish and early Christian martyrs. Jesus's crucifixion is portrayed as the ultimate act of obliteration by those in power. Crucifixion, a Roman method of execution, aimed to erase the victim from memory, a practice known as *damnatio memoriae* (condemnation of memory).[14] Yet, the stories of martyrs, while highlighting the stark reality of evil and suffering, celebrate the enduring legacies of those who faced such injustices. Martyrs are immortalized as symbols of righteousness and divine recognition. They are honored not for their defeat but for their unwavering commitment to justice, transcending their violent ends.

The tradition of martyrdom elevates the dead above the systems that punished them. Dewey points out that reimagining Jesus's death within this noble tradition was a deliberate choice, countering Rome's narrative of suppression. In this context, sacrifice is more than a ritual; it's a statement of value, suggesting that what is offered to the Divine is of the utmost worth. By framing Jesus's ordeal as a story of martyrdom and sacrifice, the Gospel elevates his legacy to that of a faultless hero, whose memory and significance endure far beyond his death.[15]

Alongside the frame of martyrdom, Mark draws from Isaiah's Suffering Innocent One (52:13–53:12) to shape the passion. Using the term *paradidomi*—"to turn someone in," "turn someone over to someone"—to emphasize betrayal and sacrifice, Mark connects Jesus's death to Isaiah 53's portrayal of an innocent person suffering for others' sins.[16] This alignment with the Suffering Innocent One frames Jesus's passion within a broader context of enduring

---

13. Donahue, "Introduction: From Passion Traditions to Passion Narrative," 15.

14. Dewey, *Inventing the Passion*, 39.

15. Dewey, 54.

16. Schmidt, *The Gospel of Mark*, 23.

innocence amidst affliction. Mark does not merely recount Jesus's trial. This Gospel weaves a larger tapestry of righteous suffering that resonates with the community's experiences, particularly during the fall of Jerusalem. In doing so, Jesus is depicted not just as a singular victim of injustice but as a part of a long tradition of suffering innocents whose ultimate vindication lies in being claimed by God, thus becoming enduring symbols of justice.[17]

In Mark's portrayal, Jesus embodies the essence of suffering discipleship, standing with those who are marginalized and facing the wrath of the powerful for his advocacy. This concept, identified by Elisabeth Schüssler Fiorenza as "suffering discipleship," highlights that the path Jesus walks is one of solidarity with the oppressed, not of seeking suffering.[18] His journey to the cross emerges from his commitment to justice, rather than being a prerequisite of his faith. This distinction critically influences how we understand the nature of sacrifice within the narrative of Jesus's passion.

Framing Jesus's experience through the lens of "suffering servanthood" reflects a devotion to uplifting others through self-giving love, which paradoxically leads to one's own fulfillment by enabling the flourishing of others. Importantly, Mark's account steers clear of depicting Jesus's passion as a mandate for the oppressed to embrace self-sacrifice. Instead, it presents Jesus's actions as a model for engaging with the world in a way that challenges unjust systems without glorifying suffering itself.

While some scholars reject the hypothesis that Mark was directly referencing Isaiah's prophecy of the Suffering Innocent One, it is widely agreed upon that the Gospel connects Jesus's ministry to the forgiveness of sins. Mark 10:45 is a pivotal verse that is often discussed for its reference to Jesus serving as a ransom for many. However, Mark clarifies that this ransom is directed not toward God as a payment for human transgressions but against the earthly powers that oppress and dominate. In this light, Jesus's ultimate sacrifice is portrayed not as an atonement required by divine decree but as a profound act of liberation from worldly tyrants. Jesus's role is one of challenging the status quo and demonstrating the cost of true dis-

---

17. Dewey, *Inventing the Passion*, 80 and 93.
18. Elisabeth Schüssler Fiorenza, *In Memory of Her: A Feminist Theological Reconstruction of Christian Origins* (New York: Crossroad, 1983), 310–30.

cipleship and liberation.[19] In this case, Jesus's death is emblematic of God's unwavering nearness and the inevitable outcome of genuine discipleship.

Purpose of the Passion in Mark

None of these interpretations of Mark's passion—the final decentering of the temple for the community, a midrashic reinterpretation highlighting the Suffering Innocent One, a direct outcome of discipleship, or a metaphor for ransom from oppression—lend support to an atonement theory solely based on Jesus's self-sacrifice. The Anselmian reading of the crucifixion—Jesus's death as sacrifice to God for humanity's salvation—struggles to find relevance within the Markan Gospel's context, just as our contemporary interpretations diverge from both the Markan and Anselmian perspectives.

If the passion narratives are understood not as historical accounts but as narratives crafted to derive meaning from Jesus's death within a specific context, then we, too, are invited to engage in a similarly imaginative, narrative process today. This is especially true for our context marked by clergy sexual abuse. The inadequacy of modern atonement theories to address the suffering of sexual abuse survivors suggests that we might consider Dewey's provocative suggestion: perhaps in the cross "there is no meaning whatsoever."[20]

In their depictions and reimaginings of Jesus's crucifixion, artists throughout history have known intuitively that the death of Jesus isn't just a "factoid memory" but a "true fiction."[21] The Gospel of Mark has several of these "true fictions" as part of the passion narrative; one of the more well-known is Pontius Pilate's choice presented to the crowd, a tradition without historical foundation. The narrative implies a tradition in which a prisoner could be released and Pilate gives the crowd the choice between Jesus and Barabbas. Despite the lack of evidence for such a tradition, this story reveals a profound truth about the community's feelings of powerlessness and oppression under Roman rule. The illusion of choice that is

---

19. See Sharyn Dowd and Elizabeth Struthers Malbon, "The Significance of Jesus's Death in Mark: Narrative Context and Authorial Audience," *Journal of Biblical Literature* 125, no. 2. (2006): 271–97.

20. Dewey, *Inventing the Passion*, 6.

21. Dewey, 7.

presented is not about freedom but is a declaration of Rome's power. This isn't a literal historical account but a "true fiction."[22]

The passion narrative of Mark doesn't offer a single narrative for direct correlation between the suffering of Jesus and that of abuse survivors. Instead, it provides a methodology for making meaning after trauma. The postdeath experience of the Jesus community and the experiences of the Markan community during the Roman-Judean War were "so provocative that [they] called for a ransacking of the religious memories."[23] This approach aligns with psychological literature on narratives of healing that we explored in the introduction. Humans intuitively use metaphors and narratives to understand their experiences post-trauma. Meaning-making through narratives is contextual, speaking directly to the survivors' experiences and their communities. This process requires survivors to draw from a diverse set of resources, including their own history, tradition, and communal imagination, to construct their narratives.[24]

In Mark, the passion narrative serves a dual purpose. It names the evil, warning against systemic oppression, and it uplifts the audience by pointing toward hope and a path forward.[25] When an event shatters our world and old narratives of understanding, engaging in midrashic activity, as found in Mark, becomes necessary. We are at a similar crossroads today. How do we reinterpret the story of the cross to both caution and uplift survivors and the churches grappling with the reality of clergy sexual abuse?

Crucifixion Today: Contemporary Feminist, Liberation, and Nonviolent Traditions

In chapter 3, we explored the enduring popularity of crucifixion narratives that center on Jesus's self-sacrifice and a grand divine plan, portraying his suffering as ultimately "good" or "worth it." These narratives persistently shape our understanding of personal

---

22. Dewey, 88.
23. Dewey, 62.
24. Flavius D. Raslau, "Updated Christus Victor: A Neurotheological Perspective," *Journal of Psychology and Christianity* 40, no. 4 (2021): 329–43, 333; J. Llewellyn-Beardsley et al., "Characteristics of Mental Health Recovery Narratives: Systematic Review and Narrative Synthesis," *PLoS ONE* 14, no. 3 (2019): e0214678, https://doi.org/10.1371/journal.pone.0214678.
25. Dewey, *Inventing the Passion*, 81.

suffering, teaching us to accept our pain as part of a larger, divine scheme, mirroring Jesus's sacrifice. Yet, this interpretation isn't the only way to view the cross.

Scholars of feminist, liberation, and nonviolent theologies have been reevaluating this narrative for decades, seeking alternatives that resonate with our experiences without glorifying suffering. By examining key contributions from these fields, we can start to reimagine the cross in ways that speak to the complexity of human pain and the quest for justice, especially in light of the devastating impact of clergy sexual abuse. This journey through alternative theological perspectives aims to open new pathways for talking about salvation and healing.

A Nonviolent Christus Victor Theory

Many modern scholarly approaches to atonement and the significance of the cross draw inspiration from engaging with the *Christus Victor* theory. As we explored in chapter 1, this early construct of salvation emerged in the patristic era, deeply rooted in scriptural analysis. Often termed the "classical model" or "patristic model," it portrays the divine act of Jesus as the Christ as a heroic liberation of humanity from the clutches of sin, death, and the devil.

Darby Kathleen Ray presents a notable feminist critique of the *Christus Victor* narrative in her 1998 work, *Deceiving the Devil: Atonement, Abuse, and Ransom*. In the concluding chapters, Ray offers a compelling reinterpretation of atonement that challenges the notions of power (power-as-control) that are found in some post-patristic atonement narratives. Advocating for a vision of power centered on justice, community, and the common good, she invites us to reconsider our understanding of evil and salvation.

Ray's redefinition of power as a commitment to compassion rather than control reshapes our perception of evil, as well as salvation. By illuminating evil's roots in greed and entitlement, Ray gives us a fresh perspective through which to view issues like domestic violence, poverty, and environmental degradation. In this light, the cross transcends its traditional symbolism of victory over evil, embodying instead a profound resistance to oppression, through love.[26]

---

26. Darby Kathleen Ray, "A Praxis of Atonement: Confounding Evil Through Cunning and Compassion," *Religious Studies and Theology* 18, no. 1 (1999): 34–46.

This contemporary take on the *Christus Victor* model does not see the struggle between God and evil as a destructive confrontation but rather as an act of divine resistance. Influential theologians such as Walter Wink, Cynthia Crysdale, and J. Denny Weaver all articulate a vision of atonement that emphasizes this nonviolent narrative, focusing on the transformative power of love over the forces of domination and injustice.

While each of these theologians offers a nuanced perspective on atonement, they converge on key convictions. Central to their thought is the idea that Jesus was martyred by the world's malevolent forces for his radical defiance. By advocating for a divine vision of justice and peace, Jesus exposed the prevailing societal structures as fundamentally flawed. In response, these powers unleashed their wrath through violence, mockery, and, ultimately, execution, aiming to quash his revolutionary message. However, these scholars unanimously assert, Jesus's martyrdom was not futile. Instead, it served to further unveil the deceit and corruption at the heart of these systems.[27]

In this revision of *Christus Victor*, God does not resort to violence to reconcile humanity. Instead, the cross becomes a testament to the violent backlash against Jesus's revolutionary teachings. Jesus's mission was not to seek out martyrdom but to embody divine love amidst "our warring madness,"[28] fully embracing the risk of rejection. René Girard's theory of scapegoating delves further into this, identifying scapegoating as a fundamental human sin.

The ancient practice of scapegoating paradoxically brings communities together through the exclusion and suffering of an innocent party. In this version of the cross, God, by becoming incarnate in Christ, intentionally immerses in the human condition, only to be met with rejection. This act of divine solidarity exposes and

---

27. "Jesus died just like all the others who challenge the Powers that dominate the world." Walter Wink, "Breaking the Spiral of Violence: The Power of the Cross," in *Engaging the Powers: Discernment and Resistance in a World of Domination, Vol. 3 of The Powers* (Minneapolis: Fortress, 1992), 149.

28. Martha Schull Gilliss, "Resurrecting the Atonement," in *Feminist and Womanist Essays in Reformed Dogmatics*, ed. Amy Plantinga Pauw and Serene Jones, Columbia Series in Reformed Theology (Louisville, KY: Westminster John Knox, 2006), 125–38, 135.

challenges the very foundations of scapegoating, spotlighting the plight of all who suffer unjustly. According to Girard, the crucifixion's violence is not a divine decree but a manifestation of human failings. Jesus's life and death propose an alternative model for community—one built on inclusivity and mutual understanding rather than division and exclusion.[29]

These contemporary interpretations of the *Christus Victor* atonement theory have not escaped criticism. Hans Boersma, in his work *Violence, Hospitality, and the Cross: Reappropriating the Atonement Tradition*, argues that a nonviolent approach might inadvertently endorse violence by failing to hold it accountable. He argues that, without confronting evil directly, there's no safeguard for victims nor a path to justice—a point we'll look at more closely during our later discussions on justice. For Boersma, the true defeat of evil is a prerequisite for the hope of salvation. Moreover, he contends that portraying God as inherently nonviolent is a misreading of Scripture, creating a disconnect between the Gospels and the Hebrew Bible.[30]

While some scholars suggest that these nonviolent interpretations of *Christus Victor* stray from biblical foundations, our exploration of Mark's passion narrative above reveals that Scripture offers a diverse array of perspectives on salvation and atonement.[31] Scripture does not hold a singular understanding of salvation. The nonviolent theologians explored here all engage with Scripture in different ways, challenging the notion that their approaches lack scriptural legitimacy. Instead, the variety of these theories illuminates the breadth of biblical narratives on these profound theological concepts.

---

29. See René Girard, *I See Satan Fall Like Lightning*, trans. James G. Williams (New York: Orbis Books, 2001); S. Mark Heim, "Saved by What Shouldn't Happen: Anti-Sacrificial Meaning of the Cross," in *Cross Examinations: Readings on the Meaning of the Cross Today*, ed. Marit Trelstad (Minneapolis: Fortress Press, 2006), 211–24; Anthony W. Bartlett, *Cross Purposes: The Violent Grammar of Christian Atonement* (Harrisburg, PA: Trinity Press International, 2001).

30. See Hans Boersma, *Violence, Hospitality, and the Cross: Reappropriating the Atonement Tradition* (Grand Rapids: Baker Academic, 2004), 150.

31. See Stephen Finlan, *Problems with Atonement: The Origins of, and Controversy about, the Atonement Doctrine* (Collegeville, MN: Liturgical Press, 2005).

A Modern Moral Influence Theory

While some modern feminists find the concept of atonement through the triumph of the cross and resurrection compelling, others argue that our salvation is rooted primarily in Jesus as a moral exemplar. This idea, briefly introduced in chapter 1, came to prominence through the moral influence theory of Abelard, which emerged in contrast to Anselm's satisfaction atonement theory. Abelard shifted focus from Christ's sacrifice and reconciliation with God to Jesus's life and his resistance to evil, emphasizing the moral example that Jesus set.

These modern atonement theories, including *Christus Victor* and moral influence, often intersect one another rather than exist in isolation. For instance, Girard's scapegoat theory, while primarily framed within *Christus Victor*, incorporates elements of moral influence theory. It highlights how Jesus's compassionate act not only unveils worldly powers as illusory but also prompts humanity toward transformation.[32]

A key strength of the moral influence theory is its emphasis on human agency and freedom. It posits that salvation is rooted in our dynamic relationship with God, imitating Jesus's way of life, rather than in a divine intervention overriding human freedom. This perspective is notably supported by feminist theologian Pamela Dickey Young, who articulates that God offers an ongoing salvific relationship, embodied in Jesus. This modern moral influence theory encourages us to reject emulating suffering as a path to salvation. Instead, Jesus's example of resisting evil demonstrates a rejection of death's glorification and a solidarity with human suffering, highlighting our potential for change and resistance.[33]

Significant modern reinterpretations of the moral influence theory are most evident in the writings of womanist theologians. Delores Williams, in her monumental work *Sisters in the Wilderness*, draws from the experiences of Black women in America to critique traditional atonement theories that portray Jesus as the ultimate

---

32. See Bartlett, *Cross Purposes*.
33. See Pamela Dickey Young, "Beyond Moral Influence to an Atoning Life," *Theology Today* 52, no. 3 (1995): 344–55, 353; James N. Poling, "The Cross and Male Violence," in *Cross Examinations: Readings on the Meaning of the Cross Today*, ed. Marit Trelstad (Minneapolis: Fortress Press, 2006), 50–62, 61.

scapegoat or surrogate.[34] She argues that such theories perpetuate the harmful practice of surrogacy, as seen in the historical exploitation of Black women. Williams rejects interpreting Jesus's death as either voluntary or coerced forms of surrogacy. She, instead, advocates for a model of atonement that sees Jesus's resistance in the wilderness as the true act of salvation that we should emulate, rather than his sacrifice.[35]

In her analysis of the cross as a symbol of suffering and sacrifice, JoAnne Marie Terrell, a fellow womanist theologian, critiques Williams's outright dismissal of the cross as a site of salvation. Through the poignant narrative of her mother's brief and tragic life, Terrell posits "that anyone's death has salvific significance if we learn continuously from the life that preceded it."[36] Her concern extends to the erasure of a tradition deeply resonant with Black women's experiences, fearing that, by sidelining the cross and its redemptive power, Williams inadvertently neglects a rich tradition. Terrell's critique suggests that the cross, in embodying both suffering and salvation, holds a dual significance that should not be overlooked by a purely moral influence approach.

A Modern Crucified God

Terrell passionately argues that Jesus's crucifixion reveals God as a "divine co-sufferer," an insight critical to our understanding of salvation.[37] This perspective emphasizes God's intimate involvement in human suffering and has roots in the influential work of Jürgen Moltmann. In *The Crucified God*, Moltmann engages a theology of the cross in the post-Auschwitz era, proposing that God's capacity for love inherently means that God can suffer.[38]

Moltmann challenges the classical Christian view influenced by Greco-Roman thought, which sees God as unchangeable, proposing instead a vision of God drawn from the dynamic, relational nature of the Trinity. This concept allows for a God who undergoes

---

34. Delores S. Williams, *Sisters in the Wilderness: The Challenge of Womanist God-Talk* (Maryknoll, NY: Orbis Books, 2013).

35. Williams, *Sisters in the Wilderness*.

36. JoAnne Marie Terrell, *Power in the Blood? The Cross in the African-American Experience* (Maryknoll, NY: Orbis Books, 1998), 127.

37. Terrell, *Power in the Blood?*

38. Jürgen Moltmann, *The Crucified God* (London: SCM Press, 1972).

suffering and love, illustrating through the Trinity how suffering is uniquely experienced by the Father and the Son—the Son in the abandonment by the Father, and the Father in the loss of the Son. For Moltmann, the cross is a pivotal moment of godforsakenness, essential for completing the Incarnation and ensuring our salvation.

Despite its innovative approach, Moltmann's theology has been met with skepticism. Critics of this approach include Karl Rahner and Johannes Metz from the Catholic tradition, who maintain that God is beyond suffering. They argue that the mutable, evolving aspects of the Incarnation are confined to Jesus's humanity, not his divinity. This is possible only through the incarnational act of kenosis, the self-emptying of God.[39] Feminist theologians, including Dorothee Soelle, liken the depiction of the Father's abandonment of the Son to portraying God as an abusive or absent father.

Wonhee Anne Joh, in her work *Heart of the Cross*, puts forth a particularly interesting postmodern engagement with and expansion of Moltmann's crucified God.[40] Utilizing a postcolonial perspective informed by the Korean American experience, Joh challenges the traditional dichotomies of *han* (sin/suffering) and *jeong* (love/salvation). Joh builds upon Soelle's critique of Moltmann's trinitarian interpretation of the cross, arguing that, while Moltmann seeks to portray God's solidarity with the oppressed through Jesus's suffering, this inadvertently upholds a hierarchical view of the Trinity. Joh then introduces a postmodern reimagining of the trinitarian dynamic, critiquing its conventional boundaries and the patriarchal distinction between Father and Son. She finds promise in Moltmann's approach for its portrayal of the cross as a symbol of solidarity in suffering but calls for a dismantling of the rigid separation between the Father's and the Son's suffering. Rather than the separation between the suffering of Father (a suffering of solidarity love, *jeong*) and Son (the suffering of abjection and abandonment, *han*), Joh proposes a complex understanding of the cross, in which suffering and salvation are intertwined, transforming the cross into a symbol of the lengths love will go. This reimagined Christology of *jeong* depicts a relational, salvific power, shifting from the idea of

---

39. Karl Rahner, *Foundations of Christian Faith: An Introduction to the Idea of Christianity*, trans. William V. Dych (New York: Crossroad, 1982).

40. Wonhee Anne Joh, *Heart of the Cross: A Postcolonial Christology* (Louisville, KY: Westminster John Knox Press, 2006).

sacrificial suffering to a model where love and relationality are at the heart of salvation.

Atonement through the Incarnation

In exploring a theology of salvation that eschews the notion of sacrificial suffering, several feminist theologians have shifted their focus toward alternative aspects of Jesus's nature and experiences. This move away from traditional interpretations of the cross develops theological thought that predates the conventional "classical theories." Throughout Christian history, the Incarnation and the communal life of Jesus have been vital for understanding salvation.

Theologians such as Kathryn Tanner, Sally Alsford, and Rita Nakashima Brock look to the theology of the Incarnation and Jesus's earthly experiences to explore reconciliation between God and humanity in the person of Jesus Christ. The doctrine of hypostatic union, which envisions Jesus as both fully divine and fully human, serves as a metaphor for bridging the divine–human divide. This contemporary engagement with the Incarnation echoes the systematic theology of Karl Rahner, who posited that theology is fundamentally anthropology.[41]

Rahner, in his contemplation of the Incarnation, sees the hypostatic union as intrinsic to humanity's relationship to God through grace.[42] Incarnation-centered atonement theories view the resurrection as God's ultimate affirmation of the Incarnation, overcoming rejection and death. Like Rahner, Tanner and Alsford emphasize the resurrection as the key salvation narrative, validating human history and experience—a process initiated at the Incarnation, manifested throughout Jesus's life, and culminated in the resurrection. For feminists like Tanner and Alsford, the crucifixion is not the catalyst of salvation but rather a poignant reflection of God's alignment with the marginalized.[43]

Incarnation-focused salvation theories, especially those which understand the Incarnation as deepening over the life of Jesus, are

---

41. Sally Alsford, "Sin and Atonement in Feminist Perspective," in *Atonement Today*, ed. John Goldingay (London: SPCK, 1995), 148–65.

42. Rahner, *Foundations of Christian Faith*.

43. Kathryn Tanner, "Incarnation, Cross, and Sacrifice: A Feminist-Inspired Reappraisal," *Anglican Theological Review* 86, no. 1 (2004): 35–56, 39; Alsford, "Sin and Atonement," 148–65.

important and powerful in showing that historical circumstances and our communities shape us. Rita Nakashima Brock argues that, if Christ was liberated, he was formed in a community of liberation. The Incarnation includes and looks beyond Jesus's life to include his community in the work of salvation. Referring to this expanded salvific work as the Christa-community, Brock corrects the overemphasis on the individual in the salvation conversation.[44]

Expanding Atonement Strengths

In the beginning of this chapter, we explored midrash as it was practiced in the Gospel of Mark, referred to as a "ransacking of the religious memories."[45] This method is successful in crafting a narrative that acknowledges the evil its readers face while outlining pathways toward practices of hope. This approach intricately ties Jesus and his community's ordeal of death and trauma to the broader Jewish narrative of the Suffering Innocent One. This book aims to create a similar fusion, juxtaposing the experiences of clergy sexual abuse survivors with modern atonement theories, all while engaging in dialogue with the Gospel of Mark and its methodologies.

Robert Sherman, in his work on trinitarian theology of atonement, champions a diverse approach to understanding salvation—a theme that has echoed through the annals of theological history. The absence of a singular, dogmatic view of atonement within the church, in addition to the intricate dynamics of the human–divine relationship, all point to this truth of a more open understanding on salvation.[46]

Feminist perspectives on atonement, as exemplified by the ones surveyed above, are significant components of our current "religious memory," yet their theological depth is frequently overlooked. Several key themes for our current understanding of atonement and crucifixion, especially in the context of clergy sexual abuse and its concealment, emerge from this study. These themes—emphasizing

---

44. See Rita Nakashima Brock, *Journeys by Heart: A Christology of Erotic Power* (New York: Crossroad, 1988).

45. Dewey, *Inventing the Passion*, 62.

46. Robert J. Sherman, *King, Priest, and Prophet: A Trinitarian Theology of Atonement* (New York: T. & T. Clark, 2004), 9.

the cross as a symbol, critiquing the notion of self-sacrifice, affirming God's solidarity with the suffering, recognizing and resisting evil, and acknowledging the role of community—interweave with and add depth to the major motifs identified in Mark's Gospel.

Importance of the Cross as a Symbol

The Gospel of Mark made a purposeful narrative choice in using the cross, given its profound resonance with the intended audience. The crucifixion of Jesus, a narrative woven from the threads of Jewish tradition and the tribulations of early martyrs, employs the cross as a deliberate symbol. This choice illuminates the full extent of Rome's annihilative power, the obliteration of those oppressed by the empire, and Jesus's solidarity with all who have endured suffering.[47] The Markan author includes the cross not merely to shock but to forge a connection between Jesus and countless other victims. Similarly, the theologians discussed earlier incorporate the cross in their atonement theories, recognizing its enduring presence in our Christian imagination and its ability to resonate with contemporary experiences of suffering.

In contemporary discussions of atonement, the crucifixion and the cross are decisive symbols in the discourse on salvation. While some feminist and womanist theologians argue against making meaning out of suffering by using the symbol of the cross, others, like JoAnne Marie Terrell, insist that, because the cross has been an important symbol of solidarity and liberation, it cannot be ignored. Terrell points to the experience of Black women and other survivors of violence and how these women have turned to the crucifixion as the primary example of "God's with-us-ness (that is, of God's decision to be at-one with us; or, better said, of the fact that we are already at-one). The empty cross is a symbol of God's continuous empowerment." Terrell makes the point that Black Christians identify with Jesus's cross and the death of the martyrs because they suffer unjustly.[48] Echoing the Suffering Servant theme of the Markan Gospel, Terrell argues that there is power in the blood of the cross because it elevates unjust, unnecessary Black suffering. Terrell writes, "Seen in this light, Jesus's sacrificial act was not the

---

47. Dewey, *Inventing the Passion*, 39.
48. Terrell, *Power in the Blood?*, 125.

objective. Rather, it was the tragic, if foreseeable, result of his confrontation with evil. This bespeaks a view of Jesus and the martyrs as empowered, *sacramental*, witnesses, not as victims who passively acquiesced to evil."[49]

Nathan's own experience of the cross, discussed in chapter 1, resonates with this view, understanding the cross as an empowering symbol for his own survivor mission and healing. When I asked about whether his experience of clergy sexual abuse challenged his moral actions, Nathan revealed a paradoxical empowerment. He disclosed that, although it wasn't always the case, he has, over time, become a more committed moral activist. "I actually feel closer to Jesus Christ now than I ever have," he shared, "because I feel like I've endured what he's enduring."

Critique of Self-Sacrifice

In Mark's Gospel, the narrative of Jesus's death is framed as the natural outcome of a life committed to "suffering discipleship." Rather than stemming from the notion of self-sacrifice, Jesus's demise is depicted as arising from his steadfast opposition to suffering, oppression, and the dominion of imperial powers. Mark's Jesus beckons his followers toward a form of discipleship distinguished from the traditional concept of self-sacrifice—a distinction that becomes somewhat blurred in subsequent interpretations.

This nuanced understanding of the cross—as a symbol of solidarity, as opposed to a symbol of self-sacrifice—is also prevalent in contemporary feminist discussions of atonement. These discussions advocate for a critical stance on self-sacrifice. If Jesus's crucifixion is to embody sacrifice, it must reflect a decision made freely. The notion of self-sacrifice, when deprived of voluntariness by societal, political, or economic constraints, loses its redemptive potential. Instead, Jesus's sacrifice is underscored by his autonomy, highlighting the element of choice in his actions.[50]

Wonhee Anne Joh introduces the Korean concept of *jeong* to interpret Jesus's love and sacrifice on the cross, showing that such sacrificial love is grounded in Jesus's unmitigated exercise of power

---

49. Terrell, *Power in the Blood?*, 142.
50. See Alsford, "Sin and Atonement."

and agency.[51] Furthermore, the divine act of self-emptying, or kenosis, that is observed in the Incarnation and crucifixion may be reenvisioned not merely as sacrifice but as an embrace of risk. Cynthia Crysdale draws upon Sharon Welch's notion of an ethic of risk, which acknowledges the protracted nature of battles against oppression. This ethic resonates through the life, death, and resurrection of Jesus, who confronts evil with nonviolence, thereby breaking the cycle of violence. Most provocatively, the Incarnation itself emerges as an expression of this ethic, with God adopting the perilous and nonviolent course of assuming human form.[52]

Role of God: Solidarity and Compassion of God

While Mark's Gospel indeed employs "ransom" terminology when referring to Jesus's crucifixion (Mark 10:45), we must clarify that this isn't a ransom paid to God, as Anselm's atonement theory might suggest. Instead, Mark's metaphor likens Jesus's sacrifice to a payment made to free captives from the grasp of worldly powers.[53] By viewing Jesus's death through the lens of the Suffering Servant, it becomes evident that his crucifixion shows God's unwavering solidarity and presence with those who innocently suffer. This notion of divine empathy resonates deeply with many feminist theologians, who regard God's alignment with our suffering as a focal aspect of atonement. Whether envisioning God as an intimately involved co-sufferer or as a more removed observer of our pain, the concept of an actively compassionate Divine is indispensable for a meaningful interpretation of the cross.

Engagement with Evil

A profound confrontation with the nature of evil lies at the heart of Mark's Gospel. Through the agony of the crucifixion, the disciples' despair, and the foretold destruction of the temple, the Gospel portrays evil as a formidable force that afflicts humanity. All of this echoes the tribulations and trauma faced by Mark's contempo-

---

51. See Joh, *Heart of the Cross*.

52. See Cynthia Crysdale, "Jesus Died for Our Sins: Redemption as an Ethic of Risk," in *From Logos to Christos*, ed. Ellen Leonard (Waterloo, ON: Wilfrid Laurier University Press, 2010), 209–28, 225.

53. Dowd and Malbon, "The Significance of Jesus," 281.

rary community. This enduring presence of suffering within the Markan community appears to cast doubt on the fulfillment of the messianic promise. However, the Gospel meticulously acknowledges and renounces the tangible evil and anguish within the community's midst, affirming their reality rather than denying it. In doing so, the Markan Jesus heralds the gradual realization of the Kin-dom, embodying the resistance against evil until the promise comes to fruition.

Feminist theological interpretations of the cross have taken up this fundamental engagement with the concept of evil. Understanding, identifying, and repudiating evil is essential in atonement theology. Darby Ray looks to the patristic model's capability to confront evil—even when stripped of its mythological elements, such as the Devil or demonic forces. These models, whether framing evil as personified in the Devil or as an abstract adversarial force, effectively assert victory over evil. Ray argues for an atonement theory that acknowledges evil as a significant adversary to God that is ultimately subordinate to God. Her feminist perspective, which recognizes the profound impact of violence and oppression, leans toward salvation theories that confront these forces that are antagonistic to God.[54]

Naming and opposing evil is both a critical part of Mark's Gospel and any atonement theology aiming to resonate with contemporary audiences. The Gospel narrative distinctly identifies the injustices of the cross and Roman systemic oppressions as manifestations of evil. Contemporary theologians, discussed above, endeavor to name the specific evils plaguing their communities—be it racism, sexism, economic inequality, or clergy sexual abuse—by drawing parallels with the Gospel message. By acknowledging these modern-day evils, they also firmly reject any notion of God's approval of such systems.[55]

In addition to naming and rejecting evil, the contemporary atonement theologies explored above show that evil can be resisted. The core principle of nonviolent theologies is that evil can be countered and transformed through love, a force that transcends death.[56]

---

54. See Ray, "A Praxis of Atonement," 34–46.
55. Terrell, *Power in the Blood?*, 121.
56. See Crysdale, "Jesus Died for Our Sins," 217; Walter Wink, *Engaging the Powers: Discernment and Resistance in a World of Domination*, The Powers 3 (Minneapolis: Fortress Press, 1992).

Walter Wink eloquently captures this sentiment, describing the attempt to extinguish Jesus's message through his death as "trying to destroy a dandelion seed-head by blowing on it. It was like shattering a sun into a million fragments of light."[57] Jesus's life and death pave the way for alternative realities, culminating in the resurrection.

The ongoing prevalence of clergy sexual abuse starkly illustrates that and how evil persists in our midst, with the practice of power-as-control still prevalent. As Darby Ray posits, Jesus's defiance against evil should not be viewed merely as a conclusive triumph but as an ongoing redemptive practice. This perspective regards Jesus's actions as fundamentally resistant to evil, urging us to cultivate a similar resistance in our lives. It positions salvation as an earthly endeavor, actively involving us. Jesus's resistance throughout his life, though not eradicating evil entirely, inaugurates a tradition of opposition that we continue to navigate.[58]

Community's Role in Salvation

Jesus's fellowship serves as a mirror for the Markan community and their challenges. The women at the empty tomb embody hope, symbolizing the pivotal role of the community in the processes of healing and salvation—a motif echoed within feminist atonement theories.[59] Rita Nakashima Brock emphasizes that Christ's essence transcends the individuality of Jesus, encompassing the collective efforts and support of the community that enabled his mission. This concept of a Christa-community parallels the broader church's identity as the body of Christ. Rosemary Radford Ruether elaborates, "Christ, as redemptive person and Word of God, is not to be encapsulated 'once-for-all' in the historical Jesus. The Chris-

---

57. Wink, *Engaging the Powers*, 154.

58. "Such satisfaction is always piecemeal and transitory, and the liberations are inevitably partial; but they are the best of the possible, and they may just be enough to sustain and enrich us in the daily work of cultivating meaning and making love." See Darby Kathleen Ray, "A Praxis of Atonement: Confounding Evil through Cunning and Compassion," *Religious Studies and Theology* 18, no. 1 (1999): 34–46.

59. Ashley E. Theuring, "Women's Suffering, Salvation, and the Empty Tomb," in *Fragile Resurrection: Practicing Hope after Domestic Violence* (Eugene, OR: Wipf & Stock, 2021), 93–119.

tian community continues Christ's identity. As vine and branches Christic personhood continues in our sisters and brothers."[60] This interpretation envisions the Christa-community as spanning the time both before and after Jesus's earthly life: from the formation of the nurturing community that would rear and support him to the ongoing salvific endeavors of the church.

Moral Injury's Impact on Crucifixion Narratives

In the preceding chapter, we explored the concept of moral injury, distinguishing it from other trauma responses like PTSD by its hallmark features of guilt and shame. Unlike other traumatic experiences, those who endure morally injurious events grapple with a profound moral dissonance in which their foundational beliefs about the world and justice are starkly contradicted. This dissonance, coupled with a struggle to articulate their turmoil, leads to diminished moral agency and a tarnished moral self-perception. Healing from moral injury thus involves embracing new vocabularies and beliefs to restore moral clarity, agency, and self-worth.

Understanding moral injury can enrich our exploration of the cross and atonement within the Markan Gospel and the insights of contemporary feminist theologians. The narrative of unjust suffering that is a key theme in Mark's account of the crucifixion is also a quintessential story of moral injury. The premise is clear: innocence should negate suffering and punishment. Yet, the reality that Mark portrays—the crucifixion of the innocent Jesus—reveals a profound moral crisis, possibly reflecting the Markan community's own confrontation with unjust persecution, oppression by the Roman Empire, and the devastating loss of their temple.

Likewise, contemporary feminist and nonviolent theologians address communities affected by sexism, racism, and economic injustice. These injustices carry a moral weight, challenging societal ideals of equality, freedom, and goodness. Like Mark's Gospel, these theologians grapple with moral injury's critical questions: Why do the innocent suffer? How can healing occur in a world rife with injustice?

Reconsidering the crucifixion narratives through the lens of

---

60. Rosemary Radford Ruether, *To Change the World: Christology and Cultural Criticism* (Eugene, OR: Wipf & Stock, 2001).

moral injury sheds new light on their significance. The cross symbolizes the paradox of unjust suffering and divine solidarity, embodying the contradiction faced by those enduring moral injury. It represents the limitation of moral agency, challenging the notion of self-sacrifice without true freedom to choose. For survivors of moral injury, understanding and making peace with their experiences are vital steps toward recovery. Here, we find a mirror in the resurrection, where God affirms solidarity with the suffering.

Conclusion

God's presence in the crucifixion narrative offers a powerful antidote to the shame and guilt that often accompany moral injury, affirming a God who stands against our self-condemnation. The narrative of Jesus's death and resurrection provides a framework for recognizing and naming evil, offering a vocabulary for acknowledging and resisting unjust suffering. Finally, these theological perspectives show the crucial role of community in both the genesis of suffering and the path to healing, emphasizing the importance of a positive sense of self and community connection in overcoming moral injury.

In the following chapters, we will turn our attention to the stories of clergy sexual abuse survivors themselves, exploring how their experiences can further inform a theology of the cross that draws on the Markan Gospel's midrashic approach and contemporary feminist atonement theories.

9

A Narrative of the Crucifixion of Clergy Sexual Abuse

Mary Ann's childhood was filled with joy.[1] She loved school, her family, her friends, and her faith. By the time she was eleven and in the sixth grade, however, her life took a dramatic turn. Enrolled in a Catholic grade school, Mary Ann was immersed in an environment where religious practices were an integral part of the daily routine. This suited her just fine—she had a genuine love for her church. For Mary Ann, attending Mass was not merely an escape from the classroom; it was a dive into a mystical experience she treasured but couldn't quite name. The rituals, the harmonies, the scent of incense, the taste of the Eucharist, and the sip of slightly warm, sweet wine transformed the hour into a sanctuary of comfort.

She held in high esteem the sisters who dedicated themselves to teaching and managing the school, as well as Father Robert, the priest who led their weekly Mass and served as the students' confessor. Contrary to what one might expect, Mary Ann welcomed confession, having been raised to view it as a crucial component of a virtuous life and ensuring her salvation.

Mary Ann's deepest desire was to be seen as a good girl by her parents and God, having been raised to believe that obedience and faithfulness would secure divine love and protection. She clung to the promise that God wouldn't let an innocent child suffer or

---

1. Mary Ann's narrative in this chapter is a "true fiction." I've constructed this story using Jesus's crucifixion; the feminist, liberation, and nonviolent atonement theologies in the previous chapters; and the personal stories of fifteen survivors who took part in the Taking Responsibility moral injury interviews.

burden anyone beyond their capacity to bear. Each personal loss—her grandmother's death, the euthanizing of her dog—she interpreted as trials for a greater divine purpose. This was all for the glory of God, for something good would come out of her suffering.

There was a tragic irony in her unawareness that God's love for her was unconditional, not contingent on her goodness or faith. God did not will her suffering; rather, God's heart broke with hers, especially when she endured abuse by Fr. Robert. In these moments of deep betrayal, it became painfully clear: God was not a distant observer but a compassionate presence, mourning, suffering, and raging alongside her.

In Mary Ann's school, confession was a semi-annual ritual, observed once during Advent and again in Lent. This tradition stirred a mix of anxiety and anticipation within her, especially during the Advent season of her fifth grade. Mary Ann entered the small room where Fr. Robert waited for her. After they had been talking for a few minutes, Fr. Robert laid his hands on her, and, from that point on, she was trapped. Mary Ann was frozen in fear and confusion. His authority over her was absolute, reinforced by his adulthood, his role as a school authority, and, most significantly, his position as a priest—a direct emissary of God, deemed holy and beyond reproach by Mary Ann and the entire community. He was someone whom she had been told to trust and knew him as a holy and good person.

He struck her head, spat upon her, and knelt down to threaten her from telling anyone. Afterward, he cloaked her in a purple prayer shawl, an act that should have symbolized comfort but instead felt like a binding, as he escorted her back to her classroom. Throughout the silent, bewildering walk back, a haunting question echoed in Mary Ann's mind: "My God, why have you forsaken me?"

Mary Ann's suffering served no purpose. It was the direct result of Fr. Robert's disturbing abuse of power within the framework of religious authority. Fr. Robert, himself a victim of past disempowerment, misused his position not for spiritual guidance or empowerment but for asserting dominance over Mary Ann. Mary Ann's ordeal did not bring her closer to God, nor did it test or strengthen her spirit. Instead, it was a manifestation of evil—purposeless and deeply entrenched in larger mechanisms of power and oppression.

These mechanisms shielded Fr. Robert, a figure revered by the school's community, under layers of institutional protection. First, clericalism enveloped him, with peers aware of allegations of inappropriate behavior yet remaining silent. Some of his fellow priests and mentors knew of his own experiences of being abused as a child and young seminarian. He had chosen to enter the seminary precisely because he had sought religious clarity and power. He also held a place of privilege within the diocese, having been assigned to the school by the local bishop. Second, Fr. Robert benefited from patriarchal structures that inherently valued men's needs over women's, enabling his actions without question. Lastly, his adult agency and understanding of consent became tools for exploitation, taking advantage of those who could not fully assert their own rights due to their developmental stage.

Mary Ann had no agency. Even if she had been able to speak, no consent could have been given, for she was stripped of her agency through the same systems of oppression that emboldened Fr. Robert: clericalism and patriarchy. Similarly, these mechanisms of oppression curtailed the influence of the Divine. The traditional avenues through which God interacts with the world and influences human lives were obstructed by the structures themselves and by the decisions of numerous individuals in Mary Ann's circle, most critically those made by Fr. Robert.

Struggling to find the words for her ordeal, Mary Ann moved through her days engulfed in shock. The seasons changed from Christmas to Lent without her being able to share the weight of her pain with her parents. The anticipation of school confessions loomed large, especially since Mary Ann had steered clear of the confessional after Fr. Robert had acted so strangely during Advent.

Wracked with guilt, she confided in her mother about her reluctance to attend confession, though Mary Ann did not have the language to tell her mom that Fr. Robert had sexually and spiritually abused her. She could only say, "I felt sad." Her mother asked her why. But Mary Ann was silent and did not answer. Again her mother asked her why and then exclaimed, "Have you no answer?" Then her mom, remembering her own experience in confession as a younger person, tried to be sympathetic and loving. She explained, "I know it's uncomfortable and sad to think about the bad things you've done, but it is important to confess your sins so God can forgive you and you can go to heaven." When dropping Mary Ann off at school, her mother kissed her.

In the midst of a religion class, an announcement broke the routine, urging those who hadn't confessed during Lent to do so. Obliged to adhere to the school's directives, Mary Ann's teacher handed her over to attend confession. There, Mary Ann silently pleaded, "Father, for you all things are possible; you could stop this if you wanted," even as she endured the abuse from Fr. Robert. Mary Ann experienced a great betrayal in her confrontation with evil. She was helpless and blameless. Transitioning to high school brought Mary Ann under the care of a new priest, and, with that change, the abuse ceased. However, the fog of confusion and silence remained for two decades.

At thirty-one years old, a seemingly innocuous email from her mother shattered the silence that had long enveloped Mary Ann's past. Attached was a report listing priests credibly accused of sexual abuse within her state; Fr. Robert's name was plainly there. Accompanied by her mother's simple query—"Wasn't Fr. Robert your priest in elementary school?"—the document named Mary Ann's suffering in a stark reality: abuse. On reading the report and email, Mary Ann gave a loud cry and breathed out the last of her silence.

Bringing All the Pieces Together

In this chapter, we explore the deep connections between the stories of those who have experienced clergy sexual abuse and the story of Jesus's crucifixion. At the heart of our discussion is Mary Ann's story, which mirrors Jesus's crucifixion, enriched not only by a strong tradition of feminist, liberation, and nonviolent atonement theologies but also by the personal stories of fifteen individuals who have bravely shared their experiences of clergy abuse.

We've explored how the story of Jesus's suffering and sacrifice helps shape our moral imaginations, influencing our perceptions of evil, suffering, sacrifice, and our ethical responsibilities. The Gospel of Mark is an early engagement with these themes, aligning the community's experiences of oppression with the motif of the Suffering Innocent One. In a similar way, by sharing the stories of modern-day survivors as reflections of Jesus's story, we listen to and prioritize their experiences in the church today while bringing fresh perspectives to the story of Jesus's crucifixion. This doesn't lessen the importance of Jesus's story. Instead, it shows how powerful it can be in addressing the pain and injustice that people face now.

To prepare our constructive theological reflection, this chapter first explores how the stories of those who've survived clergy abuse reveal the deep moral wounds that such abuse can cause to individuals, their families, and the wider community. Following, we revisit the five major themes of atonement narratives, showing how these ideas appear in the experiences of those who have faced clergy abuse. Carefully and deliberately, I demonstrate how Jesus's crucifixion continues to be relevant as an offer of hope and healing to those who have been hurt. By weaving together these personal stories into a renewed crucifixion narrative, we can gain a deeper understanding of pain, healing, and redemption in today's world.

Listening to Survivors' Voices: Moral Injury and Crucifixion

Mary Ann's narrative emerges from an in-depth exploration of the profound, often concealed traumas of clergy sexual abuse. It draws from common themes and experiences in fifteen individual interviews with survivors that were conducted as part of the Taking Responsibility research project at Fordham University.[2] These stories deepen our understanding of the personal costs of abuse and introduce six overarching themes of moral injury. Through their accounts, we witness the intricate interplay of faith, betrayal, and the challenging journey toward healing.

---

2. "Taking Responsibility: Jesuit Educational Institutions Confront the Causes and Legacy of Clergy Sexual Abuse" (2024), https://takingresponsibility.ace.fordham.edu/. The fifteen survivors interviewed included five women and ten men, all of whom identified as having been raised Catholic. Six of the survivors remained Catholic, while five identified as spiritual, and four identified as nonreligious/nonspiritual. The age at the time of abuse ranged from six to sixteen years old, with an average age of 10.8 years. The length of time over which the abuse took place also varied, with a range of four months to ten years, averaging an abuse time frame of 3.06 years. The interviews took place over one to two hours and were crafted to focus on questions of moral injury in clergy sexual abuse. Afterward, the interviews were transcribed, anonymized, and thematically coded.

The first theme, "Moral Confusion," captures the dissonance that survivors experience when their trusted spiritual leaders betray them, fundamentally challenging their understanding of morality and faith. The second theme, "Moral Agency," discusses how the lack of language to describe their experiences strips survivors of the ability to process and articulate their trauma, leading to diminished personal control. The third, "Moral Identity," explores the deep-seated guilt and shame that erode survivors' self-worth and alter their self-perception. The fourth theme, "Damage to Relationships with Others," shifts focus to the external impacts of abuse, revealing how trauma disrupts familial and social bonds, often resulting in isolation. The fifth theme, "Damage to Faith," reflects on the spiritual crisis precipitated by abuse, with many survivors grappling with a fractured relationship with God and a loss of spiritual community. Lastly, "Damage to Relationship with Church" examines the broader institutional betrayal, focusing on the survivors' disillusionment with a church community that failed to protect them, challenging their trust in and connection to the institution. Collectively, these themes present a complex portrait of the enduring personal and communal consequences of clergy sexual abuse.

Moral Confusion—The Contradiction of Moral Beliefs

"Who would believe that the hands of . . .—that were raised over us in blessing—would ever harm a child of God."
—Michael, survivor of clergy sexual abuse

For the survivors of clergy sexual abuse whom I interviewed, their experiences sharply contradicted their previous perceptions of priests, the world, the church, their Catholic community, and the concepts of sex and abuse. We termed this dissonance "moral confusion." One survivor described this confusion as "a mess, a deep, muddy mess in my head." This confusion primarily stemmed from their Catholic upbringing and the exalted status that was attributed to priests.

Many survivors recalled believing as children that priests were almost divine or at least sinless. They described growing up with the belief that priests were sacrosanct and infallible, positioned next to God. Following the abuse, because they believed priests incapable of evil, they rationalized the abuse as somehow being good. One survivor said, "I remember at first thinking well it can't be bad that a priest did it . . . they don't do wrong . . . I just knew that a priest couldn't sin." Another recalled being taught that "the priest was God's representative on Earth. That he was not a human being anymore because he was ordained and became this exalted being." This belief, while not actually a part of doctrinal belief, was reinforced again and again for these survivors as children in the actions, practices, and sacraments attributed to the role of the priest.

In addition to their exalted status, attention and favor from a priest were perceived positively. Many survivors recounted early grooming experiences as special, saying "it made me kind of special" or "singled me out." This notion of favoritism was common, with one describing a competition among altar servers to be the favored one; "we were all wanting to be in his favor." The attention they received reinforced their internalization of clericalism, connecting their own self-worth to their relationship with their abuser. One survivor explained, "to have this representative of God paying this attention, telling me I'm special, and that he wants to help me get closer to God, was like, 'Wow!'" For some, the belief in priests' infallibility persisted into adulthood, complicating their ability to confront or report the abuse. One survivor told me, "Even as an adult, I was like, I don't want to get Father [name] in trouble. I don't want to get him in trouble."

The authority of priests was heavily underpinned by a message of obedience, a theme prevalent in Christian teachings. As seen in previous chapters, the concepts of self-sacrifice and obedience have been exploited to justify abuse. Many survivors shared that, during their childhoods, the church seemed to demand unwavering obedience. One survivor depicted their view of God as a stern judge: "God will judge you on everything, and you can't say no. You must always obey." This requirement extended beyond divine judgment to include all church authority figures. Another survivor noted, "You do whatever the priest tells you to do."

This emphasis on obedience was so ingrained that any deviation was met with harsh penalties. A survivor recounted, "If the priest or the nuns tell you to do something, you do it without question. . . . If we find out that you have disobeyed the nuns or the priest or you've talked back to them, you'll be beaten on the bare butt with a belt." The legacy of such strict obedience persists into adulthood for many survivors, complicating their ability to say no or disappoint others. One explained, "You know I have the whole Catholic guilt or whatever . . . and I won't say no to some things."

Beyond the immediate circle of church authority, survivors also navigated a landscape of moral expectations set by their parents and reinforced by their Catholic upbringing. Important tenets included attending Mass, practicing forgiveness, understanding the role of sacrifice, and the significance of prayer. Many felt tremendous pressure not to let their parents down. "I felt I was a failure, and I had to honor what Mom and Dad wanted me to do. What Mom and Dad expected of me. These were the rules. You don't mess with the rules," one survivor shared. Missing Mass was considered sinful, adding to the confusion for those who felt unsafe in what should have been a sanctuary.

As illustrated in Rebecca's narrative from chapter 6, the enforced religious importance of forgiveness added to the turmoil, as survivors wrestled with the notion of forgiving their abusers, alongside their parents and church community. The pervasive theme of sacrifice often loomed large in their minds as they endured abuse, influenced by a church that emphasized the transformative power of suffering. This belief was sometimes encapsulated in the misleading reassurance offered during prayer, with survivors, like Deborah from chapter 3, being told, "If you pray to God with a pure heart, nothing can hurt you because God would never let an innocent child suffer." Unfortunately, such statements, though meant to comfort, only served to deepen the feelings of guilt, responsibility, and shame among the survivors.

Moreover, silence around topics of sex and abuse, fueled by misconceptions that these were shameful or should be kept secret, exacerbated the survivors' moral confusion. They described a lack of differentiation between consensual sexual acts and abuse, with one survivor bluntly stating, "I took it all. It was my fault in every situation. Including the abuse." This culture of silence trapped survivors, leaving them without anyone with whom to discuss their confusion or to question whether their experiences were good or bad. Exemplifying this confusion, Michael, the survivor from the introduction, shared with me: "Who am I going to talk to? And who am I going to ask? Whether this is good or is this bad? What's the difference?"

On the other hand, some survivors talked about how the abuse was normalized and even acknowledged, but taboo to talk about. In these situations, silence was expected by all involved. One survivor reflected that, in her high school, even after these survivors grew up, many believed their experience to be rare or should be a secret.

A common belief among survivors is that abuse is rare. Many described feeling isolated, believing they were the only ones suffering, or that only a few others were affected. The misconception that clergy sexual abuse involves just a "few bad apples" only intensifies survivors' feelings of isolation and confusion. For instance, one survivor, abused within her Catholic school, recalled thinking as a child, "I'm the only evil person in the school that he wants to do that to."

Conversely, other survivors noted that, while the abuse was normalized and even acknowledged within their community, it remained a taboo subject. Silence was expected and maintained by everyone involved. Reflecting on her high school experience, one survivor shared, "Everyone knew that somebody was probably being abused somewhere, it was just kind of how we grew up.... And so, you would never ever tell anyone. You would never mention this." This silence persisted into adulthood, with many still believing their experiences were rare and should remain secret. In the words of Michael, "That's what they taught. They taught me how to be silent about the bad things that were happening in my life."

Survivors often recount a contradiction in their experiences after disclosing their abuse. Initially, many maintained a belief in church structures' inherent goodness, convinced that their abuse was not knowingly permitted. In seeking support from churches, responses varied significantly. While some found compassion and assistance, others were met with denial, rejection, or disbelief, deepening their moral confusion and pain. As Nathan, the survivor from chapter 1, heartbreakingly shared, "I spent seven or eight years waiting for them to help me. And to a degree the eleven-year-old still thinks—slash hopes—that they're going to help me."

Moral Agency—Loss of Language and Understanding

"I was writing a note to my wife and just all it said was, 'I'm sorry but Father . . . , you know this priest, was a real mean

The Crucifixion of Clergy Sexual Abuse

person to me when I was growing up.' And that's all I kind of looked at it as. . . . You know? Like what he did was really mean. . . . I never really heard or thought or ever really considered abuse growing up. I had never really heard that word used."

—Transcript 6, survivor of clergy sexual abuse

The harsh reality of clergy sexual abuse shattered many moral narratives that survivors held before their abuse, leaving them without the language or framework to process their experiences in healthy ways. Instead, they grappled with misconceptions, silence, or toxic theologies. Many survivors expressed that they couldn't articulate their experiences, leading to feelings of powerlessness, guilt, and shame. This lack of language is partly due to the pervasive silence about sex in both churches and families. Time and again, survivors confessed to their confusion during the abuse, with thoughts like, "Is this what guys do? Is this normal?," or "We all thought we were in trouble. Because we did always get in trouble." One survivor frankly admitted, "I didn't know anything about sex to tell anyone."

The core narratives—that clergy are inherently good, that adults should be respected, and that God protects good children—were completely contradicted by survivors' experiences of abuse. In addition, the moral narratives and frameworks they possessed before the abuse limited survivors' responses. Commonly, they felt trapped, unable to alter their situations, or they concluded that, if priests are good, the abuse must be either acceptable or their own fault. One survivor recalled, "I remember at first thinking, 'Well, it can't be bad that a priest did it . . . they don't do wrong. . . . And while I was still naïve back then, I just knew that a priest couldn't sin, but it didn't seem right.'" This confusion was prevalent among many survivors, with another noting, "There's something wrong with me that he wants to do these painful, awful things to me. There must be something wrong with me that I have caused a priest to want to do these things."

Another survivor shared the insight that the emotional capacity to deal with and express this type of abuse and trauma is not yet developed in children. He reflected, "I had kept all this inside, uh, because any kind of youth doesn't have the emotional capacity to express my own needs. . . . Those types of scenarios are literally impossible for a young person to overcome." The absence of appropriate language left many survivors unable to discuss their experiences, seek help, or express their needs. One explained the paralyzing effect of this silence, "I knew at some point, this wasn't right, but I couldn't articulate, and there's no ability in my family to expose that." To cope, another survivor said they minimized the abuse, "I would say I self-minimized a lot. Like, I definitely made it less than it was, as an adult. And now." One linked their silence to lack of "confidence in what I say has value."

Due to their inability to verbalize their experiences or understand what was happening, many survivors remained silent for decades. Research indicates that childhood trauma often resurfaces later in life. While survivors didn't necessarily forget their trauma, they lacked the framework to recognize it as abuse until much later. When survivors eventually found the language to describe their experiences, the passage of time made it even harder to disclose. "It was one of those things, I wanted to tell somebody, but you've been living this lie for ten, fifteen years, and you—it's like, how do you break through? . . . How do you, how do you tell someone?"

This enduring silence exacerbated their feelings of powerlessness, a sentiment echoed by many survivors. They described their responses to the abuse and its aftermath with words like, "I just kind of froze, and I didn't react," "I feel ineffective," "[I] just withdraw in myself and don't do anything," "[I'm] malleable to everything," or "[I feel] like I was not making my own decisions." Michael, the survivor from the introduction, humorously remarked that he still requires "adult supervision" to make decisions.

The impact of this powerlessness often extended into their adolescence and young adulthood, marked by risky behaviors like drug use or unsafe sex. One described it as if another "person was running my life. . . . And really poorly." Despite their extensive volunteer efforts in various organizations, one survivor still believed, "[I] have no impact or very little impact. And, y'know, this despite being told repeatedly that [my] actions do. I just think everybody's wrong." Feeling similarly ineffective, many others chose to isolate themselves from the world.

Moral Identity—Damage to Self

"I didn't have a voice. I didn't matter. I was a failure."
—Survivor of clergy sexual abuse

Ultimately, these feelings of powerlessness and inexpressibility lead to damage in a survivor's sense of self and moral identity. Here the term "moral injury" becomes crucial to understanding the type of trauma experienced by survivors of clergy sexual abuse. Survivors frequently reported feelings of guilt, shame, worthlessness, and disgust.

Many survivors believed they should have been able to stop the abuse, or felt guilt about their perceived inaction. Some expressed regret for "letting the abuse continue" and wondered why they "didn't say something." Others felt they "didn't try hard enough." Some survivors even harbored guilt about causing the abuse in some way. One survivor reflected, "I'm flawed because something I did caused, was a cause of this, I am to blame for some reason. . . . It's a recurring theme, there's gotta be something about me, a flaw, something I did, even though my therapist says 'no, it wasn't your fault.'" Many framed the abuse they suffered in childhood and young adulthood as a grave personal failing. Others expressed guilt over the belief that, if they had come forward immediately, they could have stopped their abuser from hurting others.

Shame was another pervasive theme in the interviews. Often interwoven with feelings of guilt but distinct, shame manifested as a deep-seated belief of being broken, wrong, or irreparable. Nathan explained the difference, "I do feel a fair amount of shame; I don't feel any guilt. I was just, I was in the wrong place at the wrong time, and I wasn't protected by the adults at [church]." Shame is less about self-blame and more about a perceived inherent brokenness, a sense of worthlessness. "I have never felt that I am worth a whole lot. I have always felt that there was something bad about me that I couldn't get rid of, that I was different from other people, and not in a good way. . . . That there's something intrinsically bad, that kind of poisons everything," another survivor shared. This deep sense of shame seeped into the way many survivors saw themselves. One survivor told me that they didn't think they "deserve anything good" and would self-sabotage to avoid the good things in their life.

The sexual aspects of the abuse were particularly tied to the survivors' sense of shame. For many male survivors, like Nathan, questions of gender and sexuality exacerbated their feelings of sexual shame. Another male survivor recounted talking with other survivors, asking, "Are we men? Does this make us gay?" He also worried about how his hobby, painting, was perceived as a reflection of his masculinity.

Survivors of both genders experienced shame related to their bodies, particularly concerning sexuality or attraction, leading them to see their bodies as sources of shame and nonagency. One survivor recalled, "I had to hide from my own body; it was really a weird situation like looking back. . . . I would like wear a lot of baggy clothing." This survivor also struggled with body image and eating disorders. When sexual agency was felt by survivors, it was often framed negatively, as causing others to sin or as a last resort for connection. "I'm not good for anything else," one survivor lamented about her sexual relationships.

Many survivors described their guilt and shame as feeling "dirty." One stated, "I couldn't live with myself. . . . It felt like I had a disease on me, and I didn't know what to do with it." Another described her emotional state as "the disease of shame," with multiple survivors using the metaphor of feeling "dirty" to describe their post-abuse selves. Reflecting on this pervasive sense of shame, one survivor confessed, "I was a dirty rag and it's like no amount of bleach could ever get me clean after what he did."

Damage to Relationships with Others

> "I'm also grateful that [my parents] aren't alive to hear what I have to say about the Catholic Church, the church hierarchy, and the people that they trusted so much."
> —Michael, survivor of clergy sexual abuse

The experience of sexual abuse profoundly alters how survivors view themselves, erasing their language for understanding and damaging their moral self, which in turn deeply affects their relationships. For some survivors, this trauma has shattered their ability to form close bonds. Others find their familial relationships most significantly impacted. Many survivors I spoke with shared that stepping forward and beginning their healing journey strained their relationships as they integrated the new identity of "survivor" into their lives. One survivor summarized the dual impact, noting, "In some ways it's made some relationships really good but other ones it's kind of destroyed."

A pervasive sense of shame and guilt led many survivors to veil their personal lives in secrecy, concealing even from their closest friends and family the truth of their abuse. Time and again, survivors disclosed that they had kept their abuse secret for decades. This shroud of secrecy not only isolates survivors but also severely impairs their ability to trust, particularly authority figures. This enduring mistrust stems from the abuse itself and from the inadequate responses and support they received afterward. As one survivor expressed, "I just don't think I'll ever be able to trust the way I did when I was younger after what I went through." For many, this distrust persists, shaping their interactions and relationships long after the abuse has ended.

One of the most profoundly affected relationships for many survivors was with their parents. Some feared the disappointment they might cause by revealing the abuse. Others worried that their parents would not believe them or would even punish them. A sense of deep betrayal was common, particularly among those who felt their parents should have protected them. Many survivors never disclosed the abuse to their parents, finding the courage to begin healing only after their parents had passed away.

Reflecting on this delicate dynamic, one survivor shared a poignant moment with her mother, who, overwhelmed by guilt upon learning of the abuse, felt unworthy of her daughter's presence. Even during her final days in hospice, her mother refused to see her. The survivor explained to me: "She didn't know how I could forgive her."

This feeling of betrayal extended beyond parental figures, including other trusted adults in survivors' lives. Many survivors felt that those around them—parents, teachers, ministers, and other adults—should have noticed the signs of abuse. Expressing frustration, Deborah, the survivor from chapter 3, pointed out the apparent obliviousness of multiple adults to the inappropriate situations in which she found herself, exclaiming, "I mean, that rectory had a housekeeper, a cook, a secretary, other priests. What did they think he was doing with a seven-year-old in his bedroom?"

Some survivors identified adults who were complicit in the abuse, whether knowingly or through ignorance. For many, especially those abused over several years, the abuse became a normalized part of their childhood. "There was no physical trauma, no panic. My parents had to drive me to get abused and then had to go pick me up, after the abuse. I mean this was just normalized," one survivor recounted, focusing on the disturbing normalization of their experiences.

Survivors often find that their experiences of abuse, as well as their healing journeys, strain their relationships for various reasons, including others minimizing, misunderstanding, and even denying or disbelieving their accounts. Many survivors feel unwelcome to discuss their experiences meaningfully, as people frequently don't know how to respond and might even change the subject abruptly. One survivor noted the indifference of some reactions: "Oh that's too bad. Hey, what'd you think about the baseball game?"

This reflects a broader sentiment, particularly among those identifying as Catholic, who seem to wish survivors will just "get over it." Even in supportive relationships, the shadows of abuse linger. One survivor described how his activism within the survivor community placed a strain on his otherwise healthy marriage: "[My wife] hasn't always, uh, understood every time I've wanted to speak out publicly, or speak at a Mass. In her view, she would rather I stop talking about it."

The most destructive reaction that survivors encounter is outright denial of their experiences. One explained the irreparable damage caused by disbelief: "If somebody said, 'I don't believe you,' you're never going to repair that relationship." Another survivor recounted the painful loss of his relationship with his cousin, also a victim of the same abuser. When he disclosed his abuse, his cousin became uncomfortable and ultimately denied the events, severing their close bond. The survivor expressed his heartbreak: "He was done with me after that. We were so close and that breaks my heart, because I love him so much."

Survivors often expressed feelings of stigmatization and isolation, stemming from their status as victims of clergy sexual abuse. Alongside the common sentiment that they should "just get over it," many felt unwelcome and ostracized. They described feeling shunned, blamed, ignored, and invisible. Victim-blaming reactions were frequent, with accusations such as, "Didn't you know better?," or "Why didn't you speak up? Why didn't you stop that?" Those who took on public advocacy roles experienced particularly severe isolation during events. Nathan recounted a vigil during which "none of the priests would even look at me."

Male survivors also reported experiencing a dual layer of stigmatization, including homophobia, that silenced many for decades. One described the survivor stigma as a "big red mark on my chest. You know. A scarlet letter kind of thing. Everybody would see it. Everybody would know what happened to me."

This pervasive sense of alienation often led survivors to isolate themselves, intentionally distancing from family, community, and religious congregations. Others felt expelled from these circles. Whether isolation was self-imposed or enforced, it compounded the trauma, moral injury, shame, and guilt that they endured. As we will explore further, relationships and community are irreplaceable in the healing process. Unfortunately, the silence and isolation that shroud survivors' experiences are significant parts of the ongoing harm inflicted by clergy abuse.

Damage to Faith-Relationship with God

> "I don't believe in God. Because he said, 'I am mindful of the sparrow when it falls from the tree.' And I'm not as important as a stupid bird. So, no. . . . No thank you."
> —James, survivor of clergy sexual abuse

Many survivors experienced a profound loss of faith, which paralleled the complications in their relationships with friends and family. The abuse, its subsequent cover-up, and the healing process deeply affected their relationship with God. For some, enduring these trials ultimately strengthened their faith. They continue to participate in church activities or choose to raise their children within the Catholic faith. However, for others, the experience severely shook their faith, leading to a complete rupture in their relationship with God.

Survivors often recounted moments during the abuse when they reached out to God, asking, "Why is God doing this to me?," or expressing anger toward God for punishing them unjustly. In Mary Ann's story above, she prays to Jesus on the cross, looking to a crucifix for salvation. This image was directly taken from a discussion with one survivor, who shared a poignant memory from their childhood: "During the abuse I remember multiple times being like you know they say, 'Jesus help me.' Looking toward the Eucharist and asking for help, and it never came." For these individuals, their experiences of abuse became inextricably linked with their perceptions of God and the church. Another survivor expressed, "I totally associated this violent, cruel . . . I associated that with faith and God and whatever. It's like . . . why is [God] doing this to me?"

As adults, many survivors continue to harbor anger toward God or have abandoned their belief entirely. Others grieve the loss of their faith and the community that was once a cornerstone of their lives. Reflecting on what was lost, Deborah lamented, "We've lost like the magic of midnight Mass. And you know baptisms and all of these things are lost, which I think were good things. But they're lost now. . . . The beautiful music. All these things are gone."

Damage to Relationship with Church

> "If we're one body—and let's say the survivors are a part of that body—I feel like the church just wants to amputate that part. Just say, 'Forget about it. It's ugly. It's gross. And we don't want to talk about it. Pretend it never happened.'"
> —Transcript 6, survivor of clergy sexual abuse

In addition to affecting their personal relationships and their faith in God, all fifteen survivors noted a significant shift in their relationship with the Catholic Church as an institution. For some, the church leadership's and community's lack of response or justice after they reported their abuse felt as traumatic as the abuse itself. One survivor revealed, "I thought that the rape earlier was enough of a trauma, but it felt like I was violated and raped again when I reported to the church." Nathan wryly noted, "The reason why I say 'and then things got really bad,' is what the experience of trying to get help from the church did to me, and how hard, and how badly that shook me."

Many survivors, including those who still identified as Catholic, felt church structures were morally compromised by the abuse and its cover-up. They pointed to church communities' failure to protect survivors and their adherence to clericalism as evidence of betrayal. Michael disclosed,

> In my parish, both of my abusers were already known to the archdiocese as having abused children before they were transferred to [the survivor's church]. . . . They were transferred multiple times after they left [the survivor's church]. They let it happen. They knew and they let it happen. . . . No one knew more. No one did less than the church officials themselves.

The church leaders and communities not only failed to protect these survivors from abusive priests, but their responses were often slow, absent, or even outright denial. One survivor expressed, "If you're not willing to protect kids, if you're more interested in your prestige, power, and profits over kids, no. No, thank you. Not gonna have any part of it." Time and again, survivors recounted instances of deep-seated corruption in church systems of governance, appearing to work harder to protect itself and its power structures than the survivors themselves. Deborah told me that the review board handling her case included an abusive priest. Reflecting on the systems of protection and collusion within the Catholic Church, Nathan said, "Everybody is enabling and protecting the archdiocese, and trying to protect [city]." One survivor, who had been actively working with a survivor group to extend the statute of limitations for sexual abuse in their state, shared their frustration, noting, "The only opposition to it is the Catholic Church. . . . It's the only group that opposes it."

A disturbing number of survivors recounted instances where church officials minimized or outright denied their experiences of abuse. Nathan recalled how a bishop dismissed their claims because the accused priest was a personal friend of his, asserting, "I know he could never do anything to hurt a child." Another survivor was told by a confessor that the sexually abusive priest was merely "trying to educate you on yourself." Highlighting the extent of such dismissals, Deborah shared her experience of reporting abuse, during which the bishop insensitively remarked, "Well, you must have been sexually developed very early." To this, she responded, "I was six. I didn't have front teeth. I don't think I was, you know, . . . a wild and crazy woman."

Although a few survivors did encounter positive reactions from church officials, even they felt that the church leadership and communities' efforts were inadequate, merely offering support or directing them to resources without genuine engagement. As Nathan pointed out, "If you are a survivor, and you don't already have the name of a therapist, they will give you the name of a therapist. That's the only thing they do. That's all that they do." Many described their church's response as overly transactional, feeling as though they were being "paid off." One survivor shared a particularly distressing interaction, "I couldn't believe it, I couldn't believe the disrespect, because here I tell them the gut-wrenching story about my mother and what I had to go through . . . and you, they're lookin', they're not listening, and so they came back and told me, 'We'll take it to $35,000.'"

Another survivor revealed a shocking discovery—a chart used by the diocese to determine restitution amounts based on the nature of the abuse, describing it as "totally disgusting." The chart stipulated amounts ranging from $10,000 for being molested over clothes to significantly more for more severe abuses. Another survivor felt utterly abandoned by their church after his case was concluded, likening his treatment to a bureaucratic process: "Get it over with. Just, on to the next number. O.K. number 27. Just like the B.M.V. [Bureau of Motor Vehicles] is the way they made me feel."

All of the survivors I spoke with felt that their relationship with their church had been severely impacted by their experiences of clergy sexual abuse, the subsequent cover-up, and the process of coming forward. The church response often exacerbated their feelings of guilt, shame, invisibility, stigmatization, isolation, and abandonment. Many survivors grieved the loss or fracture of their relationship with their church community. Michael, the survivor from the book's introduction, reflected on his diminished faith, saying, "A faith that I loved. And there's still parts that really, really struggled. I can walk into a church for a funeral or wedding, and I can go through those motions. I can't do Sunday Mass. I can't do any of those things that I once enjoyed. Um, but I loved the foundation of my faith." Another described the ordeal as "a very hurtful process. . . . 'Cause this is—this was—my life. It centered around [the church]." Later he sighed, "I will say, I miss, um, being at church."

One survivor, who grew up admiring Catholics devoted to teaching and social justice, lamented, "It's a shame that, to me that, this other thing has just . . . overshadowed that completely." Another survivor articulated the profound impact of the abuse on his faith, "I believe [my abuser] deprived me of my faith. I really do. I don't have that opportunity for healing and consolation. I've internalized that. I understand it, but it's made me angry."

While a few still viewed the Catholic Church as a moral center of their lives, many no longer saw it as a credible moral authority due to the clergy sexual abuse and the cover-up. Their experiences had led them to question, "Why would I listen to anything the church had to say?" Nathan expressed his disillusionment in stark terms, "I really do believe that Satan is inside the Catholic Church."

Crucified Self—Mental Health Impacts

Survivors of clergy sexual abuse have experienced profound trauma and moral injury, both from the abuse itself and the subsequent cover-up, deeply affecting their lives thereafter. The interviews exhibited common symptoms of post-traumatic stress, including anxiety, depression, and pervasive fear. Nearly every survivor reported experiencing one or several of these symptoms, which have significantly impacted every aspect of their lives.

They described living in a constant state of fear—fear of the abuse and the abuser, fear of sharing their story, fear of discovery, fear of disbelief, fear of retaliation, fear for their current stability, fear related to their symptoms of PTSD, and fear of being around others. Physical symptoms were also common, including disruptions in sleep and eating patterns, nightmares, insomnia, confusion, sexual dysfunction, and physical pain. Additionally, many survivors have adopted negative coping mechanisms such as dissociation, denial, numbness, substance abuse, suicidality, and general avoidance of social interactions, leading to isolation.

Another prevalent emotional response among the survivors is grief, with many reporting uncontrollable tears as a common—if not daily—experience. One male survivor shared, "I cry virtually every day. I have tears every day. I manage it, and then you, you go on." He described his enduring grief as having a "broken heart," telling me, "You have a broken heart until you die. . . . And it's not a small thing. It's a big wound." These survivors mourn the loss of their childhood, family relationships, friendships, mental and physical health, faith, and community. One even expressed feeling as though the experience "stole their soul."

Moreover, anger is a persistent emotion in their lives—anger at the abuse and the abuser, at themselves, at the inadequate response of their community and church leadership, and at the laity's ongoing indifference to the reality of clergy abuse. One survivor noted that she worked with many survivors whose "anger is like a sparkler. It just goes everywhere. . . . Their anger so consumes them that they cannot basically function." For some, this anger motivates their involvement in volunteer and advocacy efforts, pushing for societal outrage and change similar to the civil rights movement. "It's a war against children," one survivor declared, emphasizing the need for public outcry.

One survivor summed up his experience, saying, "There's a model for rage and anger. And we know what rage and anger look like. There is no vocabulary for healing." Reflecting on his long-term struggle with PTSD and moral injury, he added, "It isn't normal, but it was my normal."

Major Theological Themes of a Modern Crucifixion

These stories shared by survivors, marked with profound betrayal and moral injury, call the church to action and prompt critical theological reflection. Their honesty compels us to reconsider the symbols and narratives that are foundational to our faith communities. As we transition from these impactful survivor narratives to a theological inquiry into suffering and redemption, we delve into five critical themes that have surfaced from our previous discussions.

These themes include a reevaluation of the cross as a symbol, a critical view of self-sacrifice, an affirmation of God's solidarity with those who suffer, the naming and resistance of evil, and an appreciation of the community's role in healing and transformation. Drawn from both the scriptural insights and theological examination of chapter 8, these themes represent lived realities—particularly true for survivors of clergy abuse. This exploration does not merely aim to honor the theological insights and truth of survivors' experiences, but also deepens our understanding of the cross, challenging us to reenvision our most sacred symbols and stories in a way that resonates with contemporary suffering and God-forsakenness.

First, the symbol of the cross occupies a prominent place in the Christian imagination and psyche. Exploring the narrative of clergy sexual abuse as a form of crucifixion requires us to confront the powerful symbolism of the cross. Beyond the trauma of abuse, survivors often suffer moral injury when their experiences of sexual violence clash with their understanding of the world, particularly their perceptions of priests, the church, and their own autonomy. For Christians, the figure of Jesus and his crucifixion significantly shapes these worldviews. In Mary Ann's story above, her experience of abuse clashed significantly with her images of God and Christ. She believed that if she were "good enough" at imitating Jesus, God would protect her from suffering. Therefore, when she suffered the abuse, she was left confused, feeling betrayed, and shameful.

Today's popular religious and cultural portrayals often fail to capture the radical essence of the cross as understood by the original audience of the Gospel of Mark. For them, the cross was not just a religious symbol but a stark emblem of the oppressive and corrupt power of the Roman Empire. Jesus's crucifixion, therefore, was more than a personal sacrifice. It was a profound alignment with all those who suffered unjustly under imperial dominance, weaving his story into the broader narrative of Jewish suffering.

In a similar vein, Mary Ann's experience of abuse at the hands of a priest should serve as a potent contemporary symbol, much like the crucifixion did for the Markan community. In this retelling, the entrenched systems of clericalism and hierarchical power within church structures mirror the corrupt systems of the Roman Empire. Just as Mark's narrative of Jesus confronts the evils, suffering, and losses inflicted by the Romans, Mary Ann's outcry against the injustices and abuses of clericalism calls for a radical acknowledgment and action. This framing not only draws parallels between the sufferings of Jesus and those of abuse survivors. It moves us toward divine solidarity and the potential for communal liberation.

The cross's enduring impact in Christian thought is undeniable. While many abuse survivors choose to leave their church or distance themselves from triggering doctrines of atonement, this usually takes place after moral injury has already occurred. The harm from toxic narratives about the cross has often already been done. For instance, the call to imitate Jesus can be problematic if it's misunderstood as endorsing passivity in the face of abuse. However, if we reinterpret Jesus's death on the cross to explicitly denounce the evils of abuse, differentiating between agency and coercion, it can foster a healthier moral imagination. Mary Ann's narrative attempts to articulate even more clearly the distinctions between agency and passivity, consent and coercion, and healthy versus unhealthy forms of trust, contributing to moral clarity around the sexual abuse crisis.

Second, a contemporary narrative of clergy sexual abuse framed as crucifixion challenges the ideals of self-sacrifice and scrutinizes the spiritual, emotional, and physical coercion embedded within. The survivor testimonies reveal that as children, these individuals lacked the vocabulary to express concepts of consent, personal freedom, or bodily autonomy. Instead, they internalized moral narratives centered on obedience, self-sacrifice, and personal sinfulness, which fostered moral identities steeped in shame and guilt. These survivors were manipulated by perpetrators who exploited these toxic narratives to assert control, further embedding feelings of guilt and shame.

The reimagined narrative of Mary Ann illuminates and affirms survivors' agency and consent, redefining the suffering of discipleship as a form of resistance against oppressive structures. This resistant "suffering disciple" emerges not as a passive victim but as an active advocate against evil, rooted in the inherent goodness of humanity and our creation in the image of God. Here, moral identities are transformed into those of justice advocates and resisters of evil, reclaiming the narrative power for healing and change. This part of the narrative will be further explored in the next chapter.

Third, the narrative of clergy sexual abuse framed as crucifixion portrays God's role as a co-sufferer and companion to the victims. Interviews reveal that many survivors grapple with God's role or presence during their abuse. They struggle with the contradiction of a worldview that believes a benevolent God would prevent the suffering of innocent children, leaving many to question their relationship with the Divine—sometimes irreparably. For others, healing involved reimagining God's interaction with the world. Often, the existing frameworks and language available to these survivors were insufficient to sustain their mental, emotional, spiritual, and moral well-being.

The reimagined crucifixion narrative through Mary Ann offers a theology that acknowledges survivors' deep theodicy questions and feelings of abandonment without resorting to victim-blaming or depicting God as the architect of their suffering. It illustrates God as a co-sufferer and companion, emphasizing that the Divine, while not the author of evil, is intimately involved with and stands in solidarity with those who suffer.

Fourth, in reimagining the narrative of clergy sexual abuse as crucifixion, it is crucial to explicitly name the evils of clericalism, abuse, and the undermining of agency. Renewed narratives also chart a path toward practices of resistance and the possibility of a fragile resurrection, which we will further explore in the next chapter. Interviews with survivors exposed a significant gap: the lack of language and public discourse within the church about child and clergy sexual abuse, which obscured their ability to identify and comprehend their experiences. Confusion over why the abuse occurred further compounded the issue. Providing clear explanations about the nature and causes of abuse is essential, as it empowers victims to recognize abusive situations, seek help, and resist effectively.

This understanding fosters a sense of self-worth by acknowledging a survivor's agency, offering them avenues for healing and active resistance. It wasn't until the language of abuse was given to Mary Ann that she was able to begin her healing process. Like many child abuse survivors, survivors of clergy sexual abuse are not able to process their trauma until they are given language and a framework for understanding that experience as abuse. In the next chapter, we will see how Mary Ann continues to develop language around the evils of clericalism and abuse as part of her healing process, imagining an alternative past in which she and her entire community had the language and frameworks needed to resist abuse in the first place.

Fifth, the narrative of clergy sexual abuse framed as crucifixion emphasizes the community's role in both perpetuating and healing the suffering. Clergy sexual abuse is a systemic issue, fueled by both individuals and networks of power, and it requires a communal response for resolution. In the interviews, survivors shared how their relationships with family, friends, and church communities were severely damaged by the trauma of abuse and the ensuing moral injury. This disruption often isolates survivors from their support systems, compounding their trauma and hindering recovery.

The modern interpretation of the crucifixion in Mary Ann's narrative illustrates the communal dimensions of moral injury and the collective responsibility in the healing process, highlighting both the community's complicity in the abuse and its crucial role in forging a path toward recovery. There were several adults in Mary Ann's life who were implicated in or missed the warning signs of her abuse. The larger societal silence around sexual education, safety, and consent, in addition to church structures and school systems of clericalism, created a context in which abuse could flourish. In the next chapter, we will see how the community also plays a large role in shaping the possible paths of healing for survivors.

Conclusion: From Crucifixion to Resurrection

In conversation with Scripture, tradition, and the lived experiences of clergy sexual abuse survivors, we have embarked on the imaginative task of reconstructing a crucifixion narrative that resonates with our present context. This reimagined narrative foregrounds the voices and experiences of clergy abuse survivors. This focus extends beyond mere theoretical comparisons between survivors and Jesus—it influences practices and church and community structures. The final chapter will detail practical implications of this focus and propose steps forward. This narrative revision goes beyond the crucifixion, reaching through the resurrection of Christ as well.

In the next chapter, we will explore themes of healing and resurrection following clergy sexual abuse. Just as centering survivors' experiences has enriched our understanding of theological concepts like suffering and crucifixion, reinterpreting Christ's death and resurrection through survivors' stories will transform our understanding of resurrection and healing post-abuse. The next chapter aims to provide comfort while actively co-creating a future where churches acknowledge their failings and rejuvenate through the resilient spirit of those they have failed.

10

A Vision of Hope, Justice, and Resurrection

After reading the email from her mother and a report on local priests accused of abuse, Mary Ann sank into a deep depression, her PTSD symptoms intensifying. When it came time to report to the bishop, her mother and sister flanked her for support, one on her right and one on her left. As they approached, bystanders shook their heads, muttering, "She's just seeking attention." Inside, the bishop and his secretary dismissed her claims with a scoff, mocking her among themselves, "We know Fr. Robert would never do such a thing. These reports are false."

The police response mirrored this disbelief. "Why didn't you leave then?," the police officer questioned her sharply. "Fr. Robert touched you before your confession? And you stayed after? And you went back the next time?" Mary Ann, drained, could only reply, "You say so." As the officer's questions grew more accusatory—"Why did it take so long to report this? Have you no answer?"— Mary Ann remained silent, leaving the officer visibly frustrated. Back in her community, especially within her parish, many continued to testify falsely against her, claiming, "She's just seeking attention. She was always like that."

Eventually, a local reporter reached out to Mary Ann. He was writing about clergy members accused of abuse, including Fr. Robert. Encouraged by her family, Mary Ann agreed to speak with him and scheduled a meeting at his office. The reporter was a young man, dressed in a white collared shirt, sitting on the right side of the room. Mary Ann was alarmed. "Don't be alarmed," the reporter told her. "You are one of the survivors of Fr. Robert's abuse. But he can no longer hurt you, and because of your testimony, others will seek healing." During the interview, Mary Ann responded to his questions but, worried about potential backlash, chose to remain anonymous in the publication.

The initial days, weeks, and months of Mary Ann's journey toward healing were fraught with difficulty. She started seeing a therapist, funded by the diocese. Grappling with the reality of her past was challenging enough, compounded by the judgment and retraumatization she endured from reporting to the diocese and the police. Despite the hardships, she felt there was no turning back.

After a year of individual therapy, Mary Ann's therapist recommended that she join a support group. Ready to take this step, she was picked up by her mother and sister very early on the first day of the week, when the sun had risen, to attend her first survivors' meeting. That initial gathering was overwhelming, a whirl of faces, names, and stories, each painfully reminiscent of her own experiences.

As the meeting concluded, the leader encouraged them, "Go and tell other survivors, we are here and doing this healing work." After the meeting, Mary Ann left in terror and amazement, overwhelmed by the sheer number of fellow survivors. She did not speak to anyone while she processed her own feelings and trauma. She was afraid. But that fear began to fade.

Alongside joining the support group, Mary Ann started to reexamine her relationship with God. Prompted by a friend from her group, she attended a retreat tailored for survivors of sexual abuse. It was there that she began the delicate process of healing her bond with God, initially by seeking divine recognition of her suffering.

During the retreat, the companionship of fellow survivors and the guidance of a spiritual director helped her to reshape her perception of God's role during her abuse. Instead of the absence she had felt for two decades, she started to perceive God as a source of love, as protection, and as a co-sufferer. To her surprise, this shift in perspective also transformed her view of the cross. It no longer symbolized Jesus's silent burden. It became a mark of solidarity and, eventually, a symbol of the fight for liberation alongside her.

Having finally found the language to articulate her experiences, Mary Ann could identify and make sense of her own past, beginning to discard the false narratives she had internalized over the previous twenty years. She was not evil. The actions of Fr. Robert, and the systems that enabled him, were truly malevolent. As Mary Ann healed, she also grappled with anger—anger for her younger, unprotected self and for others who remained disenfranchised and oppressed, those who similarly suffered from nonagency and the inability to consent.

Over time, encouraged by her family, friends, and fellow survivors, Mary Ann felt empowered to share her story more widely and advocate for others. Unlike during her childhood, marked by vulnerability and victimization, she now embraced the power of choice, consent, and resistance against the evils of clericalism and patriarchy. She cast aside the narrative of self-sacrifice and silence—carrying her cross—that she had long believed she must endure. Now, she understood that, as a child, such choices were never hers to make. Through her own growth, empowerment, and reclaimed agency, she could now make these decisions.

As Mary Ann began to openly confront the evils that had facilitated her abuse, namely clericalism and patriarchy, she started seeing these oppressive structures reflected elsewhere. This awareness transformed her perspective. She no longer saw herself as a victim but as a survivor, an advocate, and a champion for justice.

Her resistance against these larger structures grew stronger, particularly in her work with children. Mary Ann advocated for more thorough discussions about sexual consent and abuse, inspired by her own childhood experiences of struggling to articulate the abuse to her mother. She hoped that, by equipping children and vulnerable adults with the necessary language, they might recognize and disclose abuse more readily.

Mary Ann also became actively involved in public events addressing clergy sexual abuse, which she found both exhilarating and nerve-wracking. At these events, individuals often approached her to share their own stories as survivors or as witnesses. Many expressed their shame and guilt for not having recognized the abuse occurring within their communities. Some even apologized for their previous ignorance of the abuse that had been taking place under the aegis of their trusted church community.

Mary Ann found both empowerment and challenges in her role as an advocate for abuse survivors. At times, she doubted whether change was possible, feeling lost, alone, and questioning the worth of her efforts as she knew abuse still occurred. There were moments when she feared she might not have the strength to continue, fearing her happiness was sacrificed for a seemingly lost cause.

Even within survivor groups, doubts would surface; they would say to one another, "Who will continue this work? We are not strong enough." Yet, these periods of despair were transient, as Mary Ann would soon be reminded of the divine presence manifest in those who supported her healing, listened to her story, and affirmed her experiences.

Mary Ann often reflected on the pivotal role her family played in her journey toward recovery. She believed that, had her mother not acted upon learning about Fr. Robert from a report on local abusive priests, she might still be grappling with a lack of language and undiagnosed depression, anxiety, and trauma. The support from her father and sister was crucial, but the survivor community was paramount in her healing process. Simply being among people who understood her background and daily challenges made a significant difference. After a decade of dedicated healing work, Mary Ann was beginning to embrace a "new normal." It was different from the normalcy of her pre-abuse childhood, but it was her own, reshaped and resilient normal.

* * * * *

One night, Mary Ann had a dream. In this dream, she moved backward through time, pausing briefly at significant events in her life—moments that defined her healing and her trauma. In her real, lived experience, these episodes each had a fatal gravity, pushing her toward trauma, disintegration, and crucifixion. But in her dream, each moment transformed into a resurrection, a renewal of life. As she revisited these events, they branched into new, reimagined timelines, creating a fractal effect throughout her entire life.

In one reimagined timeline, she stood with her survivor group in the halls of Congress. Everywhere she looked, congressmen and women thanked her and the other survivors for their efforts to change the statute of limitations law for sexual assault. Catholic clergy and laity were also there, holding signs that called for accountability, stated apologies, and supported the survivors in their advocacy. Mary Ann saw her own bishop and parish members among the crowd, all sacrificing their time and energy to walk in solidarity with her and the other survivors.

A Vision of Hope, Justice, and Resurrection

And then, she was suddenly back to the first night of sitting in the survivor support group. She could see all the other faces welcoming her, understanding her, imbuing her with their own healing energy. She felt the awakening of being acknowledged and affirmed.

In another timeline, she sat with the reporter, absorbing his kind words of affirmation and hope like a healing salve.

In yet another timeline, she sat with the police officers. This time, the officer sitting across from her listened, did not question, and patiently waited for her to gather her thoughts and recount her story. A survivor advocate was present, helping her understand the procedures, making her feel empowered.

In another timeline, she was sitting in front of the bishop. He was contrite, kneeling on the ground with tears in his eyes, praying. There were no lawyers present.

In a different timeline, she was sitting with her mother, father, and sister. The report of local priests accused of sexual abuse was in Mary Ann's hand. They all listened, nodding and crying, believing her story immediately and offering comments of sympathy, affirmation, and apology.

In another reimagined version of her life, she was back in sixth grade, sitting at her desk with tears in her eyes. Her teacher had approached to send her to confession. Upon seeing Mary Ann's distress, the teacher stopped and instead walked her directly to the counselor. There, the teacher and counselor talked with her about her anxiety and fear, recognizing the signs and planning to intervene immediately, saying, "He will be gone today." And unlike before, she believed them.

Still a sixth grader, she found herself at the kitchen table talking to her mom. This time, she had the words and the precise language to describe what had happened in the confessional. Although she still felt the fear and confusion in her body, the moment her mom heard and believed her, hope began to take root.

In the final moments of the dream, before she woke, Mary Ann was even younger, maybe five or six years old. And in this timeline, there was no mandatory confession, no Fr. Robert. Her mother ate breakfast with her and dropped her off at school with a kiss. At school, she learned about consent along with her classmates, and the teachers encouraged them to role-play situations where they could practice their own agency in establishing healthy boundaries. She felt empowered, knowledgeable about her own body, and safe.

Surprisingly, in this new reality, Mary Ann felt the presence of God more strongly throughout these experiences. The absence of the patriarchy, the clericalism, and the authoritatively certain clergy that had marked her lived experiences did not diminish the Divine. Rather, it highlighted an overabundance of divine presence in herself and the people who cared for her, loved her, and taught her how to love.

A Way Forward: Listening to Survivors' Voices on Healing and Resurrection

Before we delve into major themes of resurrection, hope, healing, and justice as part of our constructive reinterpretation, it is essential to revisit the transcripts from interviews with clergy sexual abuse survivors in the Taking Responsibility study. The healing experiences of the survivors whom we interviewed varied significantly. There is no uniform vision of what successful healing from sexual abuse looks like. While some survivors were at the early stages of their healing journey, others felt that they had largely moved through their recovery, forever changed yet adapting to a "new normal."

Despite the diversity in their experiences, several key themes emerged that suggest specific components are critical for healing from this type of moral injury. Notably, survivors experienced a sense of moral clarity, achieved by articulating and fully understanding their experiences as abuse. This clarity enabled them to reclaim their agency and identity. As they healed, relationships, particularly with fellow survivors, became pivotal in shaping their self-perception and future outlook.

Importantly, none of the survivors considered their healing journey complete. The impacts of their experiences will last a lifetime. Although they did not choose to become victims of clergy sexual abuse, their path to recovery requires a daily commitment to pursue a different future. These interviews uncovered a traumatic wound that is far from healed, affecting not only the survivors but the Catholic Church as a whole.

Addressing community-wide trauma requires the Catholic

A Vision of Hope, Justice, and Resurrection

Church to publicly and transparently acknowledge the abuse and cover-ups, apologize, and accept accountability. Even if the safety plans and strategies implemented since 2002 succeed in preventing future abuses, the damage to survivors, parishioners, and public trust still requires healing. A healing church demands justice.

Moral Clarity: A New Language and Understanding

Healing from moral injury encompasses more than conventional trauma recovery methods. It demands moral clarity, a reaffirmed moral self-identity, and supportive relationships with allies. These steps require survivors to clearly articulate and understand their experiences. For many survivors I interviewed, being able to use the specific language of abuse was a crucial step in their healing journey.

The media coverage of the clergy sexual abuse crisis often played a crucial role in helping them name their experiences. Like Mary Ann, several survivors cited reading an article or seeing their abuser's name in the news as significant moments of recognition. Many did not have access to the language of abuse until adulthood. In their childhoods, a pervasive silence around abuse, sex, and sexuality prevented them from even recognizing, let alone naming, their experiences within the context of sexual abuse.

As survivors began to adopt the framework of child sexual abuse to reflect on their past, their perception and the language they used to describe these events transformed. Previously, as noted in the prior chapter, many survivors believed the abuse was their fault. However, once they started using specific abuse-related terminology, their understanding changed; they realized the abuse was not their fault. One survivor explained, "And any kind of faults or difficulty we had, were not the, not because we were faulty, or we were bad, but because we were affected by a really bad man."

For some, this realization occurred as an epiphany, a sudden, clear insight into their innocence. Another survivor recounted an instance of awakening from a nap with a jolt of clarity, thinking, "Ah, that was terrible. Oh, that was not my fault. That was his." These moments of realization enabled many survivors to begin distancing themselves from the decades of guilt they had carried.

Many survivors also explained how adopting this new language and reframing their experiences altered their perception of God's role in their experience. Those who maintained their faith generally did not hold God responsible for the abuse. Instead, some attributed the blame to the individual actions of the priests, others to a corrupt system and flawed priestly formation, and a few even cited external malevolent forces like Satan. As Nathan, from chapter 1 expressed, "Everybody is vulnerable to Satan, I don't care who you are, I don't care where you are. I'm vulnerable to Satan, you're vulnerable to Satan, everybody is vulnerable to Satan. The pope is vulnerable to Satan. Satan is everywhere."

Another survivor stated decisively, "I don't think [God] did this to me; I think a really bad man did this to me." This survivor noted that his experience of abuse had lacked spiritual or theological manipulation, unlike the experiences of others. Conversely, a survivor who suffered severe spiritual abuse saw God not as the perpetrator but as a source of grace throughout her ordeal. She shared, "For me, God's grace was present all through—because I shouldn't be alive right now. You know of all the crazy things I did. I should not be alive. . . . If it were not for God's grace."

As survivors progressed in their healing, many reported gaining a refined moral clarity about good and evil that was influenced by their harrowing experiences. This clarity motivated them to make intentional choices toward goodness in their daily lives. One survivor explained, "I have a very good understanding of what's right and wrong because of the things that happened to me. And I choose to live in the light, I choose, y'know, healthy over harmful." Several survivors noted that their sense of moral clarity felt unusually pronounced. For instance, one survivor humorously dismissed others' opinions, saying, "I don't care. I just do what I think's right."

However, not all felt able to act on their convictions. One survivor struggled with the fact that he had never reported his abuse to authorities like church leadership or the police. He shared, "I think that reporting the abuse to the church, or to somebody, would be the right thing to do," yet he admitted that taking such a step was beyond his current comfort level.

Moral clarity often provided survivors with the necessary language and frameworks to identify their unhealthy coping mechanisms. Many engaged in substance abuse or struggled with anger management, viewing these issues as part of their healing journey. One individual recounted a pivotal counseling session during which he confronted his own abusive behavior. He explained, "I kind of discovered a conscience or something you know? . . . Yeah. You know my counselor uses the term—hurt people hurt people. You know, I was definitely doing that a lot." After acknowledging his experience with abuse in that moment, he began to heal and transform his behavior.

Moral clarity played an important role in the healing journeys of many survivors, providing them with a trusted sense of right and wrong. It empowered them to rely on their own judgment rather than "defer to anybody else," enhancing their self-confidence and agency. For some, this deepened sense of morality, encompassing values like compassion and generosity, became a cornerstone of their spirituality. One survivor expressed, "I feel like, if I have a spiritual side, it's the attachment to these values that I consider to be greater than any of us." Naming the importance of empathy, another survivor emphasized the golden rule as a vital moral principle she imparted to her grandchildren: "Treat others as you would want to be treated. . . . And that's the one big message I keep giving my grandkids. . . . Be kind. Kindness is free. And it's the best thing you can give anybody."

Agency: Enabled by Moral Clarity

This moral clarity empowered many survivors to take control over their own lives, healing, and futures—a significant shift from their experiences of abuse and life before confronting their trauma. They viewed their journey to healing as an active choice. Though not an easy or straightforward one, this choice toward healing was lifesaving. As one survivor shared, "I choose, y'know, healthy things in the light. I choose to live in hope because I don't want to live in the darkness. . . . And I've been through four years of counseling, and the muddy mess is still there. But you have to cope and you find ways to make good decisions." Michael, the survivor from this book's introduction, emphasized the daily commitment to their healing process and their effort to positively impact the world, reflecting, "99.9 percent of the time when I lay my head down at night, I can say that I left the day a little bit better than I found it."

The decision to remain a member of the Catholic Church itself became an expression of personal agency for many survivors. One survivor described this choice as a daily act of commitment: "It's one of the hardest things. It's a daily choice to be Catholic. That's a hard part. The hard part is to be a Catholic. The easy part is to be a Christian. If that makes sense." Another survivor echoed this sentiment, emphasizing the significance of his choice to reengage with his church as a crucial aspect of his healing journey. He shared, "You know for me [it] was about coming forward and, you know, especially, you know, going back into the church too, you know, really making like an effort to stay in a state of grace, um. . . . That's one of the biggest things that really helps keep me at a point."

This capability to make these types of daily choices, to "live in hope," was seen as essential to survivors' healing paths. One survivor even likened their agency to the transformative power of resurrection, saying, "I look at it as the resurrection. Taking a bad thing and turning it into a positive thing. And I have the capability . . . to do that."

Many survivors reflected on a series of choices connected to their healing journey, from the initial act of sharing their story to managing daily emotional challenges. They described these decisions as conscious and intentional steps toward recovery. For instance, one survivor detailed how the process of going to the police and consulting with a therapist enabled them to subsequently file a report with the church. While making formal reports to the police or church leaders sometimes led to further trauma, especially when the responses were unhelpful, these actions were nonetheless crucial for those who received supportive reactions. For many, joining a survivor community marked a significant milestone in their recovery. One survivor emphasized the impact of this decision, stating, "I think the first clear step that I made toward really, honestly dealing with this was when I did go to the SNAP conference."

The ability of survivors to verbalize, narrate, and comprehend their abuse was often critical for initiating their healing. Before finding this "voice," healing seemed out of reach. Reflecting on their experiences, some survivors identified moments of agency even before they fully understood their situations or began their healing journeys. These moments, though isolated, represented crucial decisions to protect themselves from further harm. One survivor recounted her decision to sever ties with her abuser at a young age, explaining, "I'm kind of glad, like really, that even at eleven years old I had the thought that I can't—there can't be any like—we can't be friends again [laughs]. . . . Like the biggest and best thing I could have done was get away."

Another survivor described leaving her Girl Scout troop, a setting that the abuser had exploited to gain access to her. She said, "So, even though I enjoyed being a Girl Scout and participating in the activities, um . . . I decided . . . I don't want that to happen." These early actions, though modest, were significant demonstrations of self-protection and autonomy amidst their overall experiences of victimization.

Many survivors experienced a transformative shift in their healing journey when they began sharing their stories with others. Michael expressed a profound sense of reclaiming their power through storytelling: "I didn't gain any of my power back until I started to share my story because then they didn't own me anymore." Another survivor described a key moment at an event with the *Boston Globe*'s Spotlight team, a group of journalists who investigated and reported on the abuse and coverup of sexual abuse in the Boston Archdiocese in 2002, saying, "I'm so grateful because finally I was strong enough to say, 'Yeah, I'm one of them that you're talking about.' It felt good to thank the reporter and the editor."

One survivor shared that, as they spoke out more about their experience, their fear of retaliation diminished and they felt less compelled to defer to priests and bishops. This individual shared a realization about challenging authority figures without consequence: "Yeah, you can challenge a bishop, and you don't die. . . . And now, not only do I challenge them, I don't have any use for them. . . . I don't have to, um, defer to anybody else." This narrative illustrates the empowerment and agency gained through the act of telling their stories, profoundly altering their engagement with the world and themselves.

Renewed Positive Identity

These new framing narratives and the language used to articulate their experiences played a critical role in helping survivors develop a renewed identity and a positive self-image. The experience of abuse and the associated moral injury had previously left many feeling burdened by guilt and shame. Understandably, healing from moral injury involves reshaping one's self-perception into one that recognizes personal goodness, empowerment, and the capacity for positive actions. Many survivors I spoke with felt that their lives and vocations were meaningfully aligned with their values.

For instance, one survivor expressed a strong vocational calling to continue working within his church, finding great fulfillment in his role and feeling that he was living out his purpose and doing God's will. He told me, "I feel fulfilled. That I'm doing the right thing. That I'm doing what I'm called to do, that I'm helping . . . or doing God's will." Overall, many survivors began to see themselves as morally upright, capable of making good decisions, and deserving of healthy relationships.

Those involved in survivor communities and advocacy felt particularly positive about their contributions. One survivor, discussing their participation in SNAP (Survivors Network of those Abused by Priests), described it as mutual support: "It's survivors helping survivors. . . . I help you. You help me. Kind of a thing. And the more involved I am, the better I feel about myself. Um, the better my mindset is. The more I think of myself as a good person." In addition to bolstering their sense of agency, this sense of mutual aid reinforced their self-perception as good individuals.

Another survivor shared that assisting others was integral to their own healing process, stating, "Working with others, helping others—I believe helping others, um, is part of my healing." Many survivors adopted an identity as advocates, which both empowered them and helped alleviate feelings of shame and guilt.

Deborah, the survivor from chapter 3, felt that joining SNAP redefined her sense of autonomy and moral clarity. She explained, "And up until [joining SNAP], I feel like there were a set of rules I had to obey whether I liked them or not. This was what is expected. This is what you must do. . . . And now, I don't feel that." Similarly, another survivor found her advocacy role, which involved "fighting back and refusing to fight within the system," as essential for maintaining her "sanity."

In addition to the personal fulfillment derived from their advocacy work, survivors were also motivated by several other factors, most notably the desire to prevent clergy sexual abuse. They viewed public storytelling as a crucial method for raising community awareness, educating others, and holding abusers accountable, thereby preventing future abuse. Nathan, the survivor from chapter 1, expressed how this purpose invigorated his efforts, stating,

"Because again, I refuse to allow what happened to me to happen to anyone else. So in that way it's actually energized me." Another survivor succinctly shared their driving force: "My bottom line is I want other victims to come forward, but I want to help others, too."

Many survivors hoped their stories would inspire and empower others in similar situations. Michael, from this book's introduction, recalled the impact of his story on fellow survivors: "These victims said that they got the courage and the strength to come forward because they heard my story through the media." The cascade effect of such disclosures was also noted by another survivor, who mentioned, "One survivor stepped forward, then three hundred followed, or 'cause the one step forward, sixty follow." Reflecting on his own experience, he added, "When I went public . . . fifteen of my classmates came forward."

Survivors found the process of empowering others both healing and energizing. One survivor humorously recalled the experience of training a group of survivors for a media interview, commenting, "It's really fun." This enjoyment was rooted in their own healing journeys and the desire to pass on effective strategies and choices to others who had similar experiences.

The unique perspective of having endured abuse themselves made many survivors feel especially equipped to advocate for others. One survivor expressed this sentiment powerfully: "Because I understand it. I can look a victim in the eye, and say, 'I know what you went through. . . . And I will help you.' And nobody else can do that. Except another survivor." This shared experience creates a profound connection and trust, enabling them to serve as potent advocates and supporters for their fellow survivors.

Alongside their advocacy, many survivors also saw themselves as protectors, a role that seemed less about their own healing and more a reflection of their ongoing moral injury. They felt a duty to shield others, including children, from abuse and their adult family members from emotional pain. This protective instinct was particularly strong when it came to their own children. One survivor explained, "You want to protect your children. . . . And that weighed heavily on me. Because I don't want my children, or any child, to endure what happened to me. And so I call that an ongoing wound or a spiritual wound."

Additionally, the role of protector extended to shielding their adult loved ones from the distress of knowing or contemplating their abuse. For example, one survivor had chosen not to disclose their abuse to their mother, believing that the knowledge would be too devastating. They said, "Because if she knew any of this, I think it would have destroyed her. That's what I think." Instead of sharing the truth with her mother, this survivor felt she had to hide her experience of abuse from her.

Taking on the roles of advocate and protector often proved challenging for survivors, not always being a straightforward or wholly positive choice. Many found themselves wrestling with exhaustion and the emotional toll of repeatedly reliving their abuse through advocacy efforts. One survivor captured this sentiment, stating, "I don't relish having to tell the story over and over again. Kind of reliving this again. But, y'know, I think it's helpful to me, and hopefully it's helpful to other people. . . . Yeah, I'd love to just stop this."

When questioned about why they would persist with their advocacy despite its detrimental effects on their mental health, the responses hinted at a sense of necessity and determination. One particularly weary survivor explained, "Nothing changes, nothing changes, all right? Gotta stop. . . . Gotta heal, gotta move on." Another survivor addressed the difficulty of moving past their experiences, asking rhetorically, "How do I just move on knowing what I know? And leaving others to experience what I have." Facing this moral conflict, many survivors feel compelled to act to prevent others from suffering as they did. This reflects the complex reality that many survivors face: the cathartic impact of their work is often coupled with significant emotional strain, yet they continue, driven by a deep-seated need for change and healing.

One survivor involved in legal reform work in multiple states expressed a personal disconnect with the benefits of his efforts, remarking, "It doesn't do me one bit of good," since his abuse occurred in a different state. Despite not personally benefiting from and expressing discomfort about the work, he recognized its necessity and was driven by a hopeful vision, stating, "I wouldn't keep doing it if I didn't have hope." Survivors disclosed complex motivations behind advocacy—actions often driven more by a sense of duty and potential impact than by direct personal gain.

Another survivor explained their acceptance of the personal costs involved in advocacy, saying, "I choose, I accept the toll, I accept these things. Because this is what it takes to get something done. Right? You can't just not put your heart and soul on the line, if you're going to get something done." Here, we can see a deep personal commitment and the heavy emotional investment that advocacy can require.

The toll of past actions—or inactions—also weighs heavily on some survivors. One individual reflected on his delay in reporting the abuse, stating, "That hurts me still to this day that I didn't. So, yeah, I feel guilt about that. And maybe that's why I'm getting so involved in this. I want to try and make up for it if I can." For survivors, guilt and shame can fuel current actions, driving survivors to engage in advocacy as a way to atone for perceived past failings and contribute positively to the future.

Affirmation from Others

Survivors repeatedly emphasized the significance of the initial responses they received when they disclosed their abuse. Articulating their experiences to others was a critical step in their healing journeys, helping them to frame, understand, and reshape their identities in light of these narratives. Support from loved ones, therapists, or spiritual advisers was equally important. Those who believed in them, offered help, and respected their decisions significantly influenced the progression of their healing. Most survivors I spoke with described their recovery as a collective endeavor rather than a solitary struggle. As one survivor expressed it, their healing involved "a lot of help from other people," relying on a support network that often included spouses, children, siblings, therapists, and trusted spiritual leaders.

Many survivors received this support from their spouses and family members. One survivor recounted a transformative shift after confiding in his wife: "Once I told [my wife], you know, I was just like, you know, it was incredible. Like everything changed after that, I mean. . . . It really helped me a lot. Just talking about it." Another described his wife's reaction as an act of "outrageous love, and compassion, and kindness" and identified this moment of disclosure as his "primary act of recovery." A third survivor credited his relationship with his current wife, who is also a sexual abuse survivor, as an important healing influence. "She really encouraged me. Because she realized this, this was a real problem. And I tended to minimize it, actually . . . [but] she really encouraged me," he explained.

In addition to spouses, many survivors received crucial support from various family members, including parents, siblings, cousins, and even their children. One survivor shared that he brought his seventeen-year-old daughter to provide support during his testimony, describing her as "my witness, my support, my advocate." Another survivor recounted an episode involving his granddaughter's first communion. Feeling unable to attend the service to avoid potential triggers, he explained his absence in a letter to his daughter. She responded supportively, assuring him that he never had to set foot in a church again if he chose not to. "She's been fantastic about it," he noted; "she's been just great. And she immediately said, without my ever saying anything, that you don't ever have to go into church again, you don't have to go to the communion, you don't have to do anything." While not all survivors had positive family reactions, those who did found such moments of understanding significant for their recovery. One survivor attributed his ability to process the abuse in adulthood to the "surroundings and the love in [his] family."

For some survivors, their path to recovery involved supportive relationships outside their immediate families. Many spoke of the important role of therapists, noting how these professional relationships facilitated their healing in different ways from family members. One survivor shared her transformative experience: "These incredible people that have just listened to my story and talking it out . . . that I finally said, 'I'm worth. I'm worth it. I'm worth having a good marriage. I'm worth somebody fighting for me.'" Additionally, survivors recovering from addiction often mentioned their AA sponsors as crucial supporters. These positive, nonfamilial relationships provided similar healing benefits to those offered by family members.

Building and practicing healthy trust is a fundamental part of these healing relationships for many survivors. One survivor explained how each positive, supportive response gradually reinforced his ability to trust others. He began by disclosing his abuse to his wife, a step that required immense trust and vulnerability. "I had to trust my wife enough that she was gonna be able to receive this in some kind of way. That's a big leap in your marriage," he

A Vision of Hope, Justice, and Resurrection

shared. After confiding in his wife, they decided to tell a few close friends. Despite his concerns about how they might react or whether they would believe him, each positive disclosure bolstered his confidence. "And because I was able to trust, y'know, my wife, our priest, and we went through the review board process, I finally was able to just take a risk, I trusted these guys and, um, I told them my story," he recounted. Another survivor shared a similar experience of building trust over time. He had initially only confided in his wife but felt the need to discuss his abuse with his spiritual director. He trusted this priest and eventually shared his story, noting, "That's what influenced me was trust. . . . I finally found someone I could trust." Trust was something that developed and strengthened over time through supportive responses and relationships.

As part of their journey to rebuild trust, several survivors came to recognize that, while they had suffered abuse at the hands of male priests, not all men or priests are abusive. One survivor noted, "There are many bad men that are using other [means to access children]; they're coaches, they're piano teachers. . . . He just chose the priesthood as his method to abuse children." Nathan, the survivor from chapter 1, shared a similar insight, reflecting on the human choices behind these heinous acts: "1 percent of the people out there, who are listening to Satan, and just don't give a damn, y'know, that's a problem." They also voiced frustration over the widespread ignorance or denial of childhood sexual abuse in society. However, through their healing process, many survivors reached a point where they could acknowledge the coexistence of good and bad individuals within the priesthood.

In addition to family and friends, support groups were important for many survivors I spoke with. They often spoke about the near-daily support they received from various survivor support groups, including Awake Milwaukee, SNAP, Healing Hearts, and Spirit Fire, among others. One survivor mentioned that their healing "exponentially increased" after joining a survivor group. For many, these groups have been and continue to be a lifeline. Gathering and discussing their experiences with fellow survivors proved immensely beneficial. As one survivor put it, "All of the sudden everybody's in a comfortable space. . . . It's very therapeutic, very healthy. And then we just talk, abuse survivors talking to other abuse survivors is what we do."

Another talked about the ease of communication within these groups, noting that there was no need to "explain yourself to anybody. You didn't have to explain how traumatic this was, or what it did to your life." This environment provided comfort by helping survivors realize they were not alone. Sharing stories and hearing about others' progress in healing helped them envision possible paths forward in their own recovery.

In addition to offering vital spaces where survivors can heal, support groups like these can offer access to resources previously unavailable to survivors. These resources include legal assistance, support during public events, and referrals to therapy and addiction counseling. However, it's essential to recognize that joining a support group is not always straightforward or beneficial for every survivor.

For instance, organizations like SNAP, known for their advocacy and legal battles, may appear too confrontational for some. One survivor noted, "I've met a lot of people that have been involved with SNAP.... I like SNAP, they do help people ... but it isn't what I need." Another shared that participating in survivor groups sometimes triggered distressing memories. Despite this, after discussing his concerns with his group, he chose to continue attending, reflecting, "I love you guys. So, I'd rather talk to you than not talk to you, you know."

Positive, supportive relationships are essential in the healing journey. Dr. Judith Herman's work in trauma recovery during the 1990s reinforced our understanding of the significance of these relationships for healing. However, forming and maintaining these relationships are often challenging for survivors. Many survivors I spoke with deliberately chose their confidantes, with varying degrees of success. One survivor described her desire to distance herself from an overwhelming circle of needy friends. Another survivor disclosed his preference for long-distance relationships, explaining, "They've lasted longer. . . . And I think that's simply because there are some inherent boundaries in those relationships that mean you can only get so far, as far as the intimacy scale goes." This sentiment was echoed by others, some of whom also grappled with setting sexual boundaries. The complexities and variety of these close relationships for survivors mirrors the multifaceted aspects of trauma recovery as a whole.

Faith after Abuse

While some survivors identified as atheists, the majority maintained some form of faith life or relationship with God, which evolved significantly through their healing journeys. This dynamic relationship often shifted in meaning and importance. For instance, one survivor recounted growing up with an image of God as "angry and vengeful" but noted that this view had transformed: "My view of God has changed; God meets me where I am, [God] meets all of us where we are." Another survivor traced her perception of God from a "figure of judgment and distance" to a deceitful figure after the abuse. Then, after she began to heal from her abuse, she saw God as a loving father, reflecting a profound shift toward a more personal and loving image. Many survivors described God as a "loving father" and felt their relationship with God was stronger than ever, influencing their daily decisions and life direction.

As discussed in the first chapter, Nathan's experience of abuse led him to feel a unique closeness to Jesus, rooted in their shared suffering. He explained, "I actually feel closer to Jesus Christ now than I ever have, because I feel like I've endured what he's enduring." He drew parallels between his struggles and the biblical narrative, saying, "If Jesus Christ can do what he did, entering Jerusalem on Palm Sunday, to a certain and known fate, then I can do this." Nathan perceived Jesus's death as a battle against institutional power, similar to his own experiences, revealing a profound theological interpretation of both their shared trials.

Some survivors noted that their experiences of abuse continue to obstruct their relationship with God, while other survivors expressed how their relationship with God remains intact, despite leaving their church. One survivor shared that leaving their church after the abuse impacted their spirituality, but their faith in God persists: "But I still have this pretty much unflappable faith in God that [God is] taking care of me and my kids. . . . My theology has changed a lot. And I shouldn't say that God's taken care of me. God is around, and I pray occasionally. . . . So . . . but it's hard."

Another survivor expressed a more profound struggle, lamenting the loss of their faith due to the abuse and its aftermath, reflecting, "I don't see that [God's] providing anything for me." This same individual continued to articulate a conflicted desire for belief, stating, "I want there to be a God, but at the same time I just don't have that belief anymore that there is." For this survivor, consciously distancing themselves from concepts like God, sin, and grace was a crucial part of their path to healing.

Many survivors struggle with understanding God's presence or role during and after experiencing abuse. Some blame God or feel abandoned. In describing their paths to healing, however, many survivors also talk about growing closer to God. For instance, one survivor shared her perspective, noting, "I've felt sort of like the need to run to God more . . . like I don't blame God for this. . . . I don't really have [a] sense of where was he in [the abuse]. I more so have the sense of this [abuse] was a man that did this that made a free will decision to do it." Despite her uncertainties about God's presence during her abuse, she emphasized the importance of maintaining a close relationship with God. She believed that blame should fall on the abuser, a sentiment echoed by many others. Another survivor expressed a similar view, saying, "I have to just reconcile myself to the good Lord, um, I don't think he did this to me, I think a really bad man did this to me. Um, I don't think anything more of it."

Other survivors perceive God's role in their experiences of abuse as actively involved, particularly in terms of grace and healing. They often describe sensing God's grace at specific points throughout their healing journey. For instance, one survivor shared, "[God] has given me the grace to enjoy a relationship with my wife and my children and others and [God's] giving me the grace to come through this . . . I am thriving. . . . The grace's help for me." This sentiment, recognizing God's grace as a sustaining force, was common among survivors. Another expressed, "For me, God's grace was present all through—because I shouldn't be alive right now. You know of all the crazy things I did. . . . [God's grace] completely overwhelmed the sin that was there." Similarly, a third survivor found grace a transformative aid, helping him positively reinterpret his experiences: "I look at it as the resurrection. Taking a bad thing and turning it into a positive thing. And I have the capability and the [indistinguishable] to do that."

Other survivors perceived God's role in their lives as even more deliberate and transformative. One survivor, who had turned to drugs and alcohol to cope with his abuse, credited God with his recovery. He viewed his journey to sobriety as a manifestation of divine grace and intervention. Reflecting on his recovery, he remarked, "That was a huge grace. I totally feel like God was the one who was just like, 'You're done. You don't need this anymore.'" He often spoke of God's intentions for his life, saying, "[God] didn't intend for me to just be a drunk and high all the time you know." He believed God wanted him to care for his children and the children in his community through his work. He shared a concept from his spiritual direction called "hard grace," explaining, "I feel like a lot of the graces I've been given are pretty much categorically a hard grace. Where it's not a . . . really, really fluffy thing. It's kind of an earned thing in a certain way. . . . Even though we don't deserve it in some ways I guess." This survivor is grappling with the complexities of atonement, feeling unworthy of God's grace due to his shame and guilt over his addiction, yet recognizing that he did not cause or deserve the childhood abuse he suffered. His experience is an example of the profound theological engagement some survivors undertake to reconcile their life experiences with their spiritual beliefs.

Other survivors experienced God's grace as a transformative force that entirely reversed their feelings of guilt and shame related to their abuse. One survivor vividly recalled a moment during a retreat when she realized that her shame was not a reflection of how God viewed her. With a smile, she shared her epiphany, saying, "God sees me as beautiful. God sees me as beautiful and perfect. And that's grace. And once you take all that stuff, . . . the disease of shame, . . . and other people's sin on me, and now you just feel grace. It's so uplifting. It's so freeing. It's truth. It's healing." This realization reshaped her understanding of the divine-human relationship, leading her to reflect, "It's how it's supposed to be. It's how human beings are supposed to be."

Deciding whether to stay or leave the Catholic Church, other Christian denominations, or organized religion altogether was a complex and challenging decision for many survivors. Often, this decision involved careful discernment with spouses, families, friends, or fellow survivors. For some, remaining within the Catholic or broader Christian Church was a crucial aspect of their healing journey. One survivor shared that his active participation in church life was integral to his decision to disclose his abuse. He explained, "For me it was about coming forward and . . . going back into the church . . . really making an effort to stay in a state of grace. . . . That's one of the biggest things that really helps keep me at a point."

Another survivor emphasized that her Christian faith, particularly her Catholic identity, was vital to her mental health and healing. I mentioned her experience of choosing to be Catholic on a daily basis earlier, and it bears repeating in the context of other survivors and their faith commitments. She simultaneously felt a strong need to identify as Catholic and the daily struggle of doing so, stating, "It's one of the hardest things. It's a daily choice to be Catholic. That's a hard part. The hard part is to be a Catholic. The easy part is to be a Christian. If that makes sense." She referred to her faith as a "lifeline," providing her with the perspective that there is more to existence than just this world.

Other survivors chose to leave their churches and organized religions, with some continuing to live out their faith independently, while others abandoned their faith entirely. Many described themselves as spiritual but not religious, opting to retain certain elements of their faith life, such as participating in the Eucharist or maintaining their prayer and contemplative practices, but they preferred to distance themselves from church hierarchy.

One survivor articulated the distinction between her faith and the institution, saying, "I'm becoming increasingly disenchanted with the church, not my faith, but the church." Her disillusionment stemmed from the clergy sexual abuse scandal and subsequent cover-ups, making her "extremely skeptical of organized religion right now." She added, "I didn't lose my faith, but faith and religion are two separate things for me, and, yes, I have always had a firm faith in God, not so much in the church." Echoing this sentiment, Deborah, the survivor from chapter 3, remarked, "To me the only way to survive this is just stay away from religion."

Many survivors who received positive responses from clergy, bishops, or other members of the hierarchy when they came forward chose to stay in their church community. Conversely, those who endured a combative, litigious, and demeaning process were less likely to feel comfortable remaining within their church community. Survivors who had favorable interactions with church authorities often reported positive and proactive responses, including encouragement to report their abuse, offers of financial assistance, or counseling services. One survivor felt that Pope Francis was personally contributing to changing the church communities' perception of survivors in positive ways. Several received written apologies from church officials, and others cited the Catholic Church's prevention efforts as a sign of hope. Many survivors expressed a desire for greater lay involvement in these reforms.

One survivor, noting significant positive changes at the hierarchical level, called for more active participation from the laity in these efforts. All agreed that the problem had not been fully resolved or healed. One survivor shared his experience of working within his church to foster change, collaborating with a group that included survivors, clergy, and staff. He described it as "a long road of healing," emphasizing the need for communal responses that involve abuse survivors, priests, and staff working together for a positive outcome. Reflecting the principles of communal justice advocated by Judith Herman, this survivor exemplifies how the effort of "building a new moral community that does not as yet exist requires community organizing, bringing together people who ordinarily do not talk to one another, and building trust based on a shared commitment to seeking a better way."[1]

Resurrected Self: Hope and Continued Healing

Due to the nature of these interviews, conducted mainly through survivor networks, most survivors we spoke with were several years into their healing journey. Yet, even among these individuals, who had at least partially processed their trauma, healing remained a continuous part of their lives. One survivor emphasized, "[Healing is] not like a done deal. It's an everyday, everyday" process. Another survivor reiterated this sentiment, stating, "Healing is just going to always be an ongoing process. It's never going to end. This is, the impact of this is never going to go away. . . . It's never gonna be totally resolved. Um, I don't think I'll ever have a resolution to it." Despite these ongoing challenges, many survivors were hopeful about their prospects for further recovery. Each had different aspirations for their next steps in healing.

One survivor wished for a day when she could interact with a priest without feeling triggered. Another was working with a

---

1. Judith Herman, *Truth and Repair: How Trauma Survivors Envision Justice* (London: Hachette, 2023), 159.

psychologist to reconnect with their body. For many, their continued healing involved support from family, therapists, and spiritual leaders. As Michael, from this book's introduction, put it, "Do I process everything today in a healthy way and share? Yes. Today. February 1st. I do. Can I tell you what I'm going to feel like next month? I can't predict that. I can't tell you. But I can tell you, if . . . I do tomorrow what I do today, I've got another good shot at it."

Many survivors also harbored hopes for change and healing within the Catholic Church itself. One survivor articulated their desire for their church to fulfill its role as "a place of hope and healing for everyone," which would require their church to be "vulnerable and true to ourselves." Many believed that healing within churches could only be achieved by openly discussing and addressing the sexual abuse crisis. One survivor pointed out, "I think that we should talk about, whether it's, it's not just abuse, because nobody wants to talk about abuse, but healing, prevention of abuse, and then healing abuse survivors now. So it's a moving forward conversation." While acknowledging some of the prevention efforts underway, all agreed that insufficient action had been taken to facilitate the healing of survivors.

In addition to churches, survivors also focused on the importance of healing within broader society. One survivor, disillusioned with the potential for change within church structures, saw greater hope for justice through secular means. They expressed, "My hope is strictly through civil authorities and educating people. The hopes of prevention." There have been some positive changes—such as more supportive parental responses to children disclosing abuse. Even so, survivors identified several areas where civil society still needs to make significant progress.

Embodied Imaginative Hope and Justice: Practicing Resurrection

If we view the experience of clergy sexual abuse as a crucifixion, then healing from this trauma can be narrated as a resurrection. In my previous book, *Fragile Resurrection: Practicing Hope after Domestic Violence*, I engaged with narratives of healing from survivors at the House of Peace women's shelter, integrating these stories with liberation theologies of the cross, resurrection, and the Empty Tomb

A Vision of Hope, Justice, and Resurrection

narrative from the Gospel of Mark. This exploration led to the concept of "embodied imaginative hope."

Embodied imaginative hope first identifies the evil that is responsible for the suffering and, then, seeks paths forward that renounce this foundational wrong. In cases of clergy sexual abuse, the root evils identified are clericalism and patriarchy. Moving forward requires that both are actively denounced and that new systems of governance and ecclesiastical practices are established. Dismantling clerical and patriarchal structures in the Catholic Church is already underway through the work of synodality. But, as we will explore in the concluding chapter of this book, there is still a significant journey ahead before new, healthy systems of governance can fully take root.

The second component of embodied imaginative hope involves envisioning an open yet uncertain future. The concept of a "fragile resurrection" from my first book acknowledges that, while healing occurs, it is not definitive. Suffering, oppression, and trauma persist. Regarding the clergy sexual abuse crisis, imagining a future where church systems are safe, accountable, and transparent is vital. We must also remain resilient and committed to seeking justice, even when progress is slow, and traumas resurface. Practices of resilience for survivors and allies within church communities are critical for this future hope work.

The third aspect of embodied imaginative hope is that it is practiced in relationships, communities, and daily interactions. It is relational and accessible, emphasizing that healing from trauma is not solely the responsibility of survivors but involves the entire community. In the context of clergy sexual abuse, this means that the entire church is implicated and must participate in the healing process. We will further explore these relationships of hope in the concluding chapter.

In addition to the practice of hope, justice is a vital component of healing after trauma. In her most recent work, *Truth and Repair: How Trauma Survivors Envision Justice,* Judith Herman argues that healing for survivors necessitates justice, which includes acknowledgment, apology, and accountability. Hope helps address the fear of harm by aiding survivors as they envision a safe and open future, and justice is essential for restoring survivors' connections to society. Herman emphasizes that, "unlike fear, shame is a social emotion, a signal of threat not to life but to human connection."[2] Justice should therefore counteract the isolation caused by clergy abuse, restoring the survivor's connection to the community.

Herman critiques our current justice systems, which prioritize punishing perpetrators over healing survivors. Instead, she proposes that justice should focus on restoring trust, fairness, and mutuality within the moral community.[3] True justice should relieve survivors of their guilt and shame, clearly exposing the perpetrator and the systems of tyranny that enable such abuses, particularly clericalism and patriarchy in the Catholic context. Moving beyond denouncing clericalism and patriarchy, new systems of governance and church practices must be established.

Herman champions the concept of a moral community, arguing that "only when a victim's resentment and demand for justice are shared by the group can the victim feel restored to full membership in the moral community."[4] This is a significant point, especially considering that, as discussed in the third and fourth chapters above, the guilt of individual perpetrators is intertwined with communal and societal structures that enable and cover up abuse. We are all, in the words of Michael Rothberg, "implicated subjects."[5] Thus, healing after clergy sexual abuse demands a response from the wider community, which has not yet fully materialized. Moral injury, which is essentially a trauma of shame, requires the restoration of an individual's honor in the community through justice.[6]

In Herman's framework, justice for survivors involves three key practices: acknowledgment, apology, and accountability. Acknowledgment of the clergy sexual abuse crisis has begun, with some dioceses releasing reports and states conducting grand juries. However, many survivors still feel unseen by the church. Herman points out, "If secrecy and denial are the tyrant's first line of defense, then public truth telling must be the first act of a survivor's resistance, and recognizing the survivor's claim to justice must be the moral community's first act of solidarity."[7] Survivors should be encour-

---

2. Herman, *Truth and Repair*, 32.
3. Herman, 15
4. Herman, 49.
5. Herman, 37.
6. Herman, 53.
7. Herman, 77.

aged to speak out, and the community must listen and affirm their experiences.

Apologies need to come sincerely from both the perpetrators and the institutions that enabled the abuse. These apologies must be made without necessitating forgiveness as a response. Additionally, reconciliation efforts can only commence after justice has been served. Accountability, according to Herman, should look beyond mere punishment. Looking to practices of "restorative justice," Herman argues that accountability involves ensuring that harm is not repeated and that the victim is restored. This is a process that requires the active involvement of the entire community.[8] Just as the communal response to our mutual implication has not materialized, communal accountability has yet to be fully implemented in the context of the clergy sexual abuse crisis.

In the absence of comprehensive victim restoration and accountability for perpetrators, the wounds of clergy sexual abuse in the Catholic Church remain grievously open.[9] Following Herman's insights, we can establish a moral community that truly supports survivors in their healing, with justice. Doing so must come through acknowledgment, apology, and accountability in the church and broader society.

---

8. Herman, 115.

9. Jonathan Madu, "Addressing Clerical Sexual Abuse through Restorative Justice: A Search for Empowerment and Collective Healing," *Journal of Transdisciplinary Peace Praxis* 3, no. 1 (2021): 75–95, 91.

11

Looking toward a Survivor-Centered Future

In the dimly lit "flex-space" of the parish hall, a group of survivors of clergy sexual abuse gathers for their monthly meeting. What started as a support group has evolved into a vibrant community of discernment. Each member, contributing their unique strengths, works democratically with the others toward their shared goal of justice.

Michael, the group's unspoken leader, begins the meeting with a moment of silence, his voice steady and tender. "We gather here not just to mourn and remember the past, but to shape our future," he says. He updates the group on advocacy efforts in neighboring communities and reads a supportive letter from the bishop regarding an upcoming memorial for survivors.

James, always skeptical of church authority, shares his past experience of being dismissed by the previous bishop when he reported his abuse. He questions the group's decision to seek the bishop's approval at all.

Rebecca, deeply rooted in her faith, supports including the bishop in their memorial plans. "We need to bridge the gap between clergy and laity. This will provide a space for dialogue and healing, and may even encourage more community members to get involved," she explains, hoping the group will grow to include nonsurvivors, clergy, and laity.

Nathan, who often mediates between James and Rebecca, sees both sides. "While we don't *need* the bishop's support, I agree with Rebecca. His presence could help ease community tensions," he says.

Deborah, with wisdom and patience honed from years of advocacy, listens carefully. Their group is used to debate and the slow, yet intentional, discernment process. Although retired from teaching, Deborah can't help but mediate the discussion. After more debate, she summarizes the consensus: "It sounds like we should invite the bishop to the opening ceremonies of the memorial, but any speaking opportunities should prioritize survivor voices." The group nods in agreement, and even James seems satisfied with the compromise.

Mary Ann, the youngest member, excitedly shifts the meeting, sharing a compelling dream she had the previous night. As she recounts her vision, everyone listens intently, some nodding, others closing their eyes. When she finishes, a few have tears in their eyes, and they sit in silence, absorbing the revelation.

Finally, Michael breaks the silence gently, saying, "This is our shared hope: to create *that* world."

* * * * *

Narratives of suffering and healing are powerful resources for trauma survivors. A meaningful narrative can help survivors articulate their experiences, providing the language to understand what happened to them and guiding them toward post-traumatic growth. Conversely, a toxic narrative can retraumatize and further injure a survivor, compounding their sense of powerlessness, shame, and guilt. The Christian tradition is rich with these narratives, the most central being the crucifixion and resurrection of Jesus as the Christ.

As discussed throughout this book, Christian atonement traditions are complex and can often reinforce hierarchical or toxic interpretations of the relationship between humanity and God. Has Jesus's death on the cross lost its ability to symbolize God's radical solidarity with those who suffer? In many ways, within popular Christianity in the United States, it no longer represents the call to center the experiences of the poor and oppressed. Instead, Christ's death on the cross has become sanitized or, worse, a tool used by the powerful to reinforce the coerced self-sacrifice of the powerless in our society.

This does not have to be the case. The narratives of Jesus's crucifixion and resurrection hold within them powerful and radical examples of the reality of evil, critiques of self-sacrifice, God's suffering solidarity, and the communal role in suffering and healing. The reimagined narratives presented in the previous chapters challenge us to consider: How do these renewed theological narratives impact the way we "do" church? If survivors of clergy sexual abuse, as the crucified peoples of today, were at the center of the Catholic Church, how would things change? One survivor poignantly expressed, "If [the church] would just understand the beauty of what we could have as a church—if we were vulnerable and true to ourselves— . . . we could be a place of hope and healing for everyone."

Healing from Clergy Sexual Abuse Today

The clergy sexual abuse crisis is ongoing. Even if the structural changes that have been implemented were completely effective in stopping future abuse, generations of Catholics have already been directly or indirectly impacted by this abuse and its cover-up. The body of Christ has been wounded, and the work that is required to heal those wounds has yet to be seriously undertaken by the Catholic Church hierarchy. Considering that many enabling systems, such as clericalism and patriarchy, continue to exert powerful influences within church structure, structural changes are still needed to ensure parishioners' safety. Addressing the moral injury experienced by survivors and laity alike requires dedicated work, reform, and conversion.

To summarize, the moral injury of survivors and laity begins with moral confusion. The experience of clergy sexual abuse, whether directly or indirectly, contradicts deeply held beliefs about the world. For example, someone may believe that priests are sinless, but experiencing or hearing about clergy sexual abuse shatters that belief. The person is faced with a new, disorienting reality that they lack the language to describe or understand. This lack of understanding impacts their sense of self, leaving them feeling powerless and burdened with guilt and shame. Moral injury also manifests in the survivor's relationships with others, their spirituality, and their relationship with their church. Recognizing the trauma of clergy sexual abuse as including moral injury helps us name the wound that has been inflicted on the church community. By understanding this damage and hurt, we can begin to imagine and understand how healing and post-traumatic growth can take place.

The survivors of clergy sexual abuse who were quoted in the previous chapter help us understand healing from this type of trauma as a moral healing. New language and narratives are needed for a survivor to begin to understand their experience as abuse. Being able to name the evil of sexual abuse provides moral clarity for survivors. This clarity enables survivors' agency and renews their identity as survivors. It also allows them to move forward in their relationships with others, their spirituality, and their church community.

A survivor who has begun their healing journey should be encouraged to practice embodied imaginative hope. This includes naming and denouncing the evil and suffering they experienced while envisioning a future that is open, acknowledging the potential for the return of trauma and doubt. This hope is practiced in relationships with others, in communities, and through everyday actions. Practices of embodied imaginative hope from the survivors interviewed included leading and participating in survivor groups, attending protests and activism events to change legal statutes of limitations, mentoring other survivors, participating in and leading their church's healing circles, holding bishops accountable, making documentaries, attending survivor conferences, practicing healthy relationships in parenting and marriage, and protecting their own and others' children.

Part of this healing journey must include justice at both personal and institutional levels. Justice will only be possible through acknowledging the individual survivors and perpetrators and addressing the institutional problems and dark history. Survivors need personal apologies from the perpetrators of the abuse, church leaders, and church communities for the cover-up, denial, and retraumatization. There must also be contrition from the Catholic Church as a whole for allowing this to persist for so long. Accountability must extend from individual perpetrators to the bishops who denied survivors or moved perpetrators to new parishes, to the generations of popes who were either ignorant of or willfully blind to the corruption in their church.

Finally, part of the Catholic Church's institutional healing will involve wrestling with the central theological narratives of suffering and healing. We must engage our atonement theologies and narratives of the cross at all levels of Christian life, from personal spirituality and what we teach our children to what is preached from the pulpit and stated doctrinally. The cross is a symbol of divine solidarity and should influence how we understand our own agency and nonagency, consent and coercion, and healthy and unhealthy forms of trust.

The crucifixion narrative can become an empowering story, illustrating the complexities of human nature made in the image and likeness of God. Jesus's crucifixion exemplifies how humanity is empowered to resist evil and corruption, yet it also shows our ultimate fragility and dependence on others and society for our agency and safety. Our language and narratives of the crucifixion should stress "suffering discipleship" as resistance to evil rather than glorified self-sacrifice. Spiritual, emotional, and physical coercion, perpetrated by others and systems of domination, impinge on our agency and consent, making self-sacrifice unattainable. Instead, we are called to resist these death-dealing forces and advocate for systemic change.

These renewed narratives can also bring comfort to those in situations of abuse and suffering by helping them reimagine God's work in the world as embodied in others and accessed through healthy relationships and systems. We may mourn the loss of our comforting images of God as a supernatural, impenetrable father figure who protects the good from all harm and punishes the wicked. In return, we gain a more complex understanding of how the Divine and evil work in this world, removing the guilt and shame from survivors and holding the perpetrators, the systems of power they used, and the community accountable. As we move into a future that is increasingly interconnected and sensitive to justice, the church will cease to be the body of Christ unless these systems of corruption, power, and control are dismantled.

Future Practices of Church

Recognizing survivors of clergy sexual abuse as today's crucified allows the Catholic Church to confront its darkest legacies directly and with transformative intent. A renewed vision of the church, led by the community of abuse survivors and their allies, may be our only hope for the church's survival and relevance. If we understand clergy sexual abuse survivors as one of the crucified peoples of today, we must center them in our church communities for Catholicism to continue in any meaningful way. Churches need to bring about justice through acknowledgment, apology, and accountability, and survivors should be at the forefront of this movement. Having borne the cross of the church communities' failings, survivors bring the wisdom and integrity that is needed to lead churches toward genuine repentance and renewal.

Parishioners should hear about clergy sexual abuse from the pulpit. Every church member should know their rights and power within the body of Christ. Each church community should have clear protocols for handling abuse of all kinds. Children must be educated about their rights, bodily autonomy, and the nature of consent. Church leaders who committed, enabled, or ignored abuse must repent, apologize, and be held accountable.

The extent of the corruption is unknown, and some fear that dismantling the Catholic Church's hierarchy could lead to its complete destruction. However, our choices are to remain ignorant, perpetuating abuse, trauma, and moral injury until these are synonymous with "church" or to begin the hard process of healing. Choosing healing requires naming the problem and discerning a way forward, with survivors at the center.

What does a survivor-centered, renewed church, free of clericalism and patriarchy, look like? What ways are there for church governance and decision-making to be shared? To answer this, we explore both the current shift in ecclesial culture, focusing on the movement toward synodality, and the ancient Christian community's application of democratic dialogue and practices. Synodality, championed by Pope Francis, invites every level of the Catholic Church into a dialogic and decision-making process, taking steps toward sharing authority and responsibility within church structures. The practices of democracy and dialogue within the early Christian church, represented by the word *ekklēsia* in ancient texts, provides a countervision of the church community as a public space for dialogue and debate. These two practices of synodality and *ekklēsia* help us as we imagine how the church community can center survivors and ensure safe and healthy churches in the future.

Synodality: Pope Francis and a Renewed Vision of Church

Centering survivors of abuse will require a "listening church," a church hierarchy that is willing to hear from the laity. The recent

Synod on Synodality (2021–2024) signals a shift in how the church hierarchy "listens" to the people of God. This shift began in the writings of the Second Vatican Council (Vatican II), which focused on the Catholic Church's self-understanding in relation to the world. Vatican II emphasized the role of the entire Catholic Church—including all baptized members, both laity and clergy—in discerning divine revelation, embodying the mission of the church, and participating in the teaching, sanctifying, and governing offices of Christ.[1] This renewed sense of the church as the people of God has profoundly influenced Pope Francis and his theology of the church.

Both Vatican II and Pope Francis depict the church as a pilgrim people, not yet fully realized but continually moving toward perfection.[2] This sense of ongoing growth, renewal, and reform encourages church leaders and communities to actively practice "being church." In his writings and public speeches, Pope Francis focuses on synodality as a holistic way for the structural church to "be the church," often grounding this practice in the documents and theological insights of Vatican II.

Pope Francis expands synodality beyond its original meaning and use in Vatican II, emphasizing not only papal–bishop relationships but also two-way communication within the church community. He uses the image of the "inverted pyramid" to describe renewed church structures, with the laity at the top and the bishops and pope at the bottom. For Francis, synodality involves more than teaching and governing. It encompasses listening and creating pathways for laity engagement. As he insists, "a synodal Church is a Church which listens, which realizes that listening is more than simply hearing."[3]

Listening to survivors of clergy sexual abuse at all levels of the Catholic Church is a crucial step toward healing the moral injury and trauma that is still present in our communities. This dialogue must occur not only at the level of the survivor or the pope. It must happen throughout the entire church community. Synodality is

---

1. Ormond Rush, "*Dei Verbum* and the Roots of Synodality," *Theological Studies* 84, no. 4 (2023): 570–91.

2. Second Vatican Council, Dogmatic Constitution *Lumen Gentium*, chap. 7, nos. 48, 50, www.vatican.va.

3. Pope Francis, "Address Commemorating the 50th Anniversary of the Synod of Bishops," October 17, 2015, www.vatican.va.

not a unidirectional relationship. Pope Francis defines a healthy, synodal church as "the faithful people, the college of bishops, the Bishop of Rome: all listening to each other, and all listening to the Holy Spirit."[4]

The vision of a synodal church, as articulated by Pope Francis, includes several key themes that connect to the shifts in the church community that are necessary to address the sexual abuse crisis. First, the ecclesial relationships within church structures must be transformed. By the grace of their baptism, the laity are equal to the clergy. "A failure to acknowledge the priority of baptism has led, Francis is convinced, to the evils of clericalism and a ubiquitous clerical culture," Richard Gaillardetz writes.[5] Francis has identified clericalism as a perversion and the root of many evils in church communities today, calling for the creation of conditions that would prevent clericalism from continuing.[6] This is an important step in dismantling the systems that caused and allowed the sexual abuse crisis to persist.

Another important aspect of synodality that promises to help with the healing process from the clergy abuse crisis is giving authority to more laity. This restructuring would create more checks and balances on the clergy, making it harder for the toxic aspects of clericalism to thrive. Pope Francis has advocated for reforms that create more recognized positions of authority for the laity within churches, bringing more laity into roles where their voices can be heard by clergy and bishops. He has also reformed the Roman Curia to include more nonclergy members.

A synodal church is called to go to the margins. This book has consistently argued that survivors of clergy sexual abuse are among the marginalized of our church communities. As a church, we are called beyond our comfort zones, to build a culture of encounter with the poor. Caring for and encountering the poor have been central themes of Pope Francis's papacy. A culture of encounter with survivors would include giving them platforms to share their expe-

---

4. Rush, "*Dei Verbum*," 590.

5. Richard R. Gaillardetz, "Synodality and the Francis Pontificate: A Fresh Reception of Vatican II," *Theological Studies* 84, no. 1 (March 2023): 44–60.

6. Pope Francis, "Address at the Opening of the Synod of Bishops on Young People, the Faith and Vocational Discernment" Speech, October 3, 2018, www.vatican.va.

riences and insights on the evils of clericalism, toxic atonement narratives, and the impact of theological themes of shame and guilt.

Many survivors interviewed for this project spoke of early childhood formation that focused on obedience, the goodness and authority of priests, and their own inherent fallen nature. A synodal church focuses on the essentials of living out a Christian faith as disciples of Christ, without dogmatism or indoctrination. Pastoral and moral formation of the entire church community is crucial to its future. A synodal church will empower all levels of church communities, helping to guide individuals and communities toward moral clarity and developing their powers of discernment.[7]

Renewed Sources of Revelation: Discerning the Spirit

Beyond just "being listened to," survivors must play an important role in the work of discerning structures and practices of the Catholic Church. The future of the work started in the Synod on Synodality and the role for laity in governance of the Catholic Church is unknown. While a deeper theological expression of synodality continues to be realized, the current theological justification for more discernment toward reform and robust democratic church structures is rooted in the Holy Spirit and the sense of the faithful (*sensus fidei*).

The role of the Holy Spirit in shaping the church cannot be overstated. At the beginning of the Synod on Synodality, Pope Francis declared, "The Synod is an ecclesial event and its protagonist is the Holy Spirit. If the Spirit is not present, there will be no Synod."[8]

---

7. Much of the discussion on synodality, encouraged by Pope Francis, focuses on decentralizing church authority. Catholic theologian Richard Gaillardetz argues that the pope's use of the term "decentralization" aligns with the concept of "subsidiarity." This concept, rooted in the earliest writings of the Christian tradition, holds that our Christian vocations should be lived out at the most local level. Individuals and local churches govern themselves and their faith, and higher levels of church authority are involved only in matters threatening the church's unity. Gaillardetz contends that while Pope Francis has initiated many of these reforms, the church is still far from becoming truly synodal (Gaillardetz, "Synodality and the Francis Pontificate," 57).

8. See Jos Moons, "The Holy Spirit as the Protagonist of the Synod: Pope Francis's Creative Reception of the Second Vatican Council," *Theological Studies* 84, no. 1 (March 2023): 61–78; Pope Francis, "Address of His Holiness Pope Francis for the Opening of the Synod," October 9, 2021, www.vatican.va.

The Catholic Church understands the Holy Spirit as a guide for the pilgrim church, mediating the development of apostolic tradition through theological scholarship, the sense of the faithful, and the oversight of the Magisterium.

This book has focused extensively on the role of theological scholarship in shaping atonement thinking and responses to the clergy sexual abuse crisis. Part II emphasized the sense of the faithful and the role of survivors of clergy abuse in churches. One of the roles of theologians in the Catholic Church is to facilitate dialogue between tradition, scholarship, and the lived experience of the faithful.[9] This book aims to contribute to that conversation by empowering people outside of the theological academy with an overview of theological tradition, clergy sexual abuse history, and current survivor experiences.

In addition to theological scholarship, the sense of the faithful provides another vital avenue for revelation. The discernment and forward movement of the church toward the full realization of the Kingdom of God involves listening for the Holy Spirit, promised by Jesus, in the hearts of church members (both lay and clergy). The divine–human relationship, maintained through communication with the Holy Spirit, is connected to our baptism and grants all of the faithful access to knowledge about God and God's will for humanity.[10]

The sense of the faithful produces new insights over time based on our human context. In this way, divine revelation is ongoing, shaped by humanity's ability to interpret, understand, and discern the will of God. This does not mean there is *new* revelation beyond the Christ event, but rather our interpretations and contextual understandings of those truths are continuously evolving. Our perceptions, knowledge, questions, and cultures grow and change, always influenced by the past, shaped by the present, and looking toward an imagined future. Our understanding and discernment of our faith and God's will also shift accordingly.[11]

In addition to theological scholarship and the sense of the faithful, the Magisterium plays a role in revelation. While much of this book

---

9. Ormond Rush, "Inverting the Pyramid: The *Sensus Fidelium* in a Synodal Church," *Theological Studies* 78, no. 2 (June 2017): 322.

10. Rush, "*Dei Verbum*," 573.

11. Rush, "*Dei Verbum*," 573.

has sought to uncover the problems of clericalism, patriarchy, and hierarchical structures, it should be noted that Pope Francis does *not* argue for the complete decentralization of church authority. He believes there is a purpose for hierarchical leadership within a synodal framework. The two-way listening promoted by Pope Francis "offers us the most appropriate interpretive framework for understanding the hierarchical ministry itself."[12]

Given this tension, how will the Magisterium work to avoid repeating the sins of clericalism? To what measures of discernment will clergy be held? Considering that synodality can be a framework by which church leaders and communities listen to one another and discern the Spirit through consensus, implementing practices of right discernment, conscience formation, and communal dialogue will be essential. Discerning these spirits requires the moral and pastoral growth and formation called for by the critique of clericalism that I made in the fifth chapter of this book. A truly synodal church necessitates an entire cultural shift within church communities, empowering all members, especially the most vulnerable, to develop practices of discernment.

The narratives of clergy abuse survivors show how children, despite often sensing something was wrong, ignored their gut feelings due to dominant narratives around obedience. Mary Ann's renewed resurrection narrative highlights the need to empower children with knowledge about their bodies, autonomy, and agency to make them less vulnerable in our churches and other spaces. Empowering children in these ways strengthens the church's collective health.

Practicing our communal discerning of the spirits is essential for developing a resilient church body. Our churches must become spaces of communal dialogue, debate, and discernment. While there are many styles and practices of discernment within church tradition, such as the Ignatian Spiritual Exercises, these often focus on individual discernment. Theologians like Jos Moon have simplified this practice into a litmus test of gut feelings, discerning the "aftertaste" of a statement or experience. He writes: "Is there depth, peace, love, wisdom . . . ? Or rather, does it give a blunt, sharp, or cynical sensation."[13] Practices that encourage us to listen to our

---

12. Pope Francis, "Address Commemorating the 50th Anniversary."
13. Jos Moons, "A Comprehensive Introduction to Synodality: Reconfigur-

inner selves are crucial. However, a synodal church requires communal spaces to share these insights and discern paths forward together.

We can look to tradition to find a variety of ways our churches have practiced communal discernment throughout history. Movements of *ressourcement* scholarship, which return to the earliest texts of the tradition, seek to understand biblical and patristic writings and the historical centralization of power in church structures. While the common scholarly narrative suggests that power and authority have become increasingly centralized in the bishops and the pope, many feminist and liberation scholars highlight parts of the tradition that have been overlooked, silenced, or ignored due to their more communal and less hierarchical focus.

Counternarratives exist and are told by Christian communities throughout history as they have practiced communal discernment with principles of equality, freedom, and even democracy. The plurality of the Gospels and epistles of early churches illustrates the discerning work that has been and continues to be the core of the Christian community. Discerning "the living voice of the Gospel"[14] has always been the work of each Christian within their church community.

Ekklēsia: Democratic Practices and Spaces in the Early Church

In order to garner insights into early church community formation and leadership, biblical scholars study the earliest texts about the first Christian communities found in the Gospels, epistles, and writings of early church fathers and mothers. These documents do not describe a single, unified church. Instead, they reveal a community that was deeply engaged in discussions and debate about structure and authority as they practiced their faith.

Scholars such as Anna C. Miller use rhetorical analysis and compare these early texts with other writings from the first and second centuries, shedding light on these discussions. Historically, the dominant narratives have focused on the voices of elite men who were shaping the early church's structure. However, for every

---

ing Ecclesiology and Ecclesial Practice," *Roczniki Teologiczne* 69, no. 2 (February 2022): 84.

14. Second Vatican Council, Dogmatic Constitution *Dei Verbum*, chap. 2, no. 8.

letter written by an early church leader, there was a community on the receiving end, working hard to navigate their new religion. These communities used the structures of governance and tools of organization they knew and understood. These communities also included women and the enslaved, who knew through their baptism that they were equal to their elite male counterparts.

These early Christian communities were called the *ekklēsia*, a term linked to the ancient Greek concept of democracy, where free citizens participated in civic life. From the time of Athens into the first century, the *ekklēsia* was the governing body of the democratic *polis*. The use of the term *ekklēsia*, along with democratic language and dynamics found in early church writings, shows that these communities saw themselves as civic and political bodies.[15]

Using the example of 1 Corinthians, Miller shows the active negotiation between Paul and the Corinthian Christian community over leadership, freedom, and gender roles. The letter shows Paul working rhetorically to convince the community to endorse his authority and vision of the *ekklēsia*. Even as Paul uses gender hierarchies of speech and speaker that disenfranchise free women and the enslaved, the letter evidences women and the enslaved asserting their own egalitarian vision within the context of the *ekklēsia*. Whether the Corinthians had equality among men, women, and the enslaved in the *ekklēsia* is not certain, but Paul feared that their democratic practices, in line with the baptismal promise of equality (Gal 3:28), might lead to that radical equality.[16]

These insights challenge both the traditional view of Paul as the sole authority in early churches and the false narrative of early Christian churches as relegated to the "private sphere." By reading these early texts against the grain, we encounter not just Paul's vision for the church, but a larger community that was participating in debate and dialogue. This practice of reading positions Paul

---

15. Anna C. Miller, *Corinthian Democracy: Democratic Discourse in 1 Corinthians* (Eugene, OR: Wipf & Stock, 2015), 2–11. Miller challenges the idea that the term *ekklēsia* was just a metaphor or reference to Jewish texts. She shows that democratic principles were a strong part of Hellenistic culture and identity in the first century, reinforced through education focused on free speech and equality. This democratic spirit was evident in civic assemblies, *ekklēsiai* that were convening at the time, writings of first-century Jews, and early Christian communities.

16. Miller, *Corinthian Democracy*, 9–13.

as one voice among many in the early church's discussions. The decision-making power held by the Corinthians as a community is evidenced by Paul's intensive work to convince this community of his vision. It is also clear that early Christians were not confined to private, religious spheres but, through democratic debate and discussion, formed public, civic spaces.[17]

The "traditional" separation of ancient private/public and religious/secular spheres, often assumed by scholars, has been mobilized in antiquity and today to control and silence certain voices. Scholars have long assumed that early Christianity blurred these lines uniquely, allowing women and the enslaved to participate in "house churches." Some claim this inclusiveness faded as churches became more public and Greco-Roman. However, ancient texts show that democratic discourse and practice—including the civic *ekklēsia* itself—existed well into the third century. These civic *ekklēsia* were spaces that early Christians would have known and participated in. The "citizens" of ancient Christian churches navigated a world with multiple "publics," where debate and discernment were common.

Today, the false dichotomy of private/public and religious/secular spheres continues to hinder church communities in their work for reform. Bringing survivors of clergy sexual abuse to the center of our communal discernment on the functioning of church structures and polity is often portrayed as a controversial move. Clergy sexual abuse is a topic that, at the very least, makes people uncomfortable and, at worst, inflicts moral injury and secondary trauma. Conversations in church communities on this topic are often relegated to small, self-selecting working groups, or seminars. Rarely is this a problem that is addressed from the pulpit or brought up in discussions on church structures. Survivors and the topic of clergy sexual abuse must be at the center of these conversations, acknowledging that the church community is a public that must be discerned and shaped by all.

The Future of the Church: A Vision of a Survivor-Centered Church

The above conversation on synodality, the theologies of the Holy Spirit and the sense of the faithful, and democratic debate and

---

17. Miller, 5.

practice found in the early Christian *ekklēsia* give us other models of church, counternarratives to fixed hierarchical church structures that are often assumed by modern Catholics. The church is a pilgrim people, not yet fully realized, and has been on a path of communal discernment since its beginning. We can see examples from across history of this journey; from the current discussions around synodality to the early *ekklēsia*, communal discernment is at the heart of church formation. As we move into the future, we must creatively engage with tradition and reimagine our practices in light of our lived experiences and historical context.

Theologian Thomas O'Loughlin offers a hopeful and imaginative proposal for what a truly synodal church might look like in practice. In his recent scholarship, O'Loughlin envisions the daily life and community of local synodal churches.[18] He suggests that local churches might be a community of around 75 people, as this size is sociologically supported. Communities larger than 150 people tend to develop hierarchies or stratifications, as we saw in early Christian churches, such as in Paul's letter to the Corinthians.[19] Much of the Catholic Church's response to clergy abuse has been top-down, but there is a need and desire for local communities to find their own ways of healing and moving forward intentionally together.

O'Loughlin also emphasizes that leadership roles should be based on individual gifts rather than status symbols. In these synodal churches, roles would be expanded to include lectors, acolytes, and deacons, in addition to clergy. This expansion of positions of authority could provide checks and balances against the rise of clericalism. The more transparency, and the more voices of laity, women, and survivors involved in important conversations, the less likely it is for abuse of authority to occur.

O'Loughlin argues for a renewed practice of communal penance and reconciliation, rather than individual confession. These practices acknowledge the community's collective guilt. Instead of the quick, production-line style of Eucharist, there would be a shared meal at a table. This practice is crucial for future churches that are sensitive to clergy abuse for several reasons. First, individual

---

18. See Thomas O'Loughlin, "Celebrating Synodality: Synodality as a Fundamental Aspect of Christian Liturgy," *New Blackfriars* 104, no. 1110 (March 2023): 161–78.

19. O'Loughlin, "Celebrating Synodality," 168.

confession has been a site of abuse and can be triggering for many survivors. Second, a Eucharistic table can become a space for the communal discernment needed to heal churches at the local level.

A church that centers the voices and experiences of sexual abuse survivors will become a church of listening, discernment, debate, and reform. Drawing insights from the discussions above, we see a path forward for the Catholic Church to heal the wounds caused by clericalism and the clergy sexual abuse crisis. This church will be a listening church, a community where all members are heard and acknowledged. It will be guided by the Holy Spirit and the sense of the faithful, with every member developing habits of discerning the spirits and embracing lifelong vocations of both interior and exterior listening. Furthermore, this church will foster debate and democratic dialogue, ensuring that every voice is heard and engaged in public discourse.

Future Implications to Faith

The healing after clergy sexual abuse that is depicted in Mary Ann's dream, the discussion of embodied imaginative hope, and the proposed future practices of church structure and communities, all speak to the significant theological and structural changes needed in the Catholic Church to truly become the body of Christ. In this conclusion, I aim to expand the conversation around atonement beyond traditional views to consider their practical implications. Atonement theology has remained too theoretical and focused on scriptural debates for too long. By examining how atonement theories affect the lives of clergy sexual abuse survivors, I hope to inspire others to reevaluate their assumptions. Today's atonement theologies should be shaped by contemporary knowledge, insights, and challenges.

I renew the nearly thirty-year-old call made by Lucy Tatman in her chapter on atonement in *An A to Z of Feminist Theology* (1996). Tatman argues, "It is probable that no one will agree entirely with any one theologian's revision of at-one-ment."[20] My midrashic interpretation of clergy sexual abuse as crucifixion may not resonate with everyone, or even all survivors. However, the Gospel message

---

20. Lucy Tatman, "Atonement," in *An A to Z of Feminist Theology*, ed. Lisa Isherwood and Dorothea McEwan (Sheffield: Sheffield Academic Press, 1996), 12.

contains multiple perspectives, and our images and narrations of crucifixion and salvation should reflect this diversity. Tatman also says, "It is vital that this task be shared and thereby enriched by the contributions of many women, none ever claiming to speak for all."[21] I encourage you, reader, to consider how your own experiences of suffering and healing, as well as those of your community and—even more radically—distant communities, should influence our understanding of atonement, salvation, and crucifixion.

Insights on the Crucifixion

In this book, I argue that we can better understand the cross today through the experiences of clergy sexual abuse survivors. The historical crucifixion of Jesus is distant from our modern context, making it challenging to fully grasp its meaning and connection to our salvation. But we can renew our atonement and salvation theories by renarrating Jesus's death in our own context, just as the Gospel writers did. This practical theological approach and the idea that clergy sexual abuse survivors are the crucified people of today have broader implications for our understanding of Christology.

In this renewed narrative, Jesus's life, death, and resurrection are salvific. Classical atonement theories claimed that these events healed and reunited humanity with the Divine. Similarly, this renewed narrative shows how Jesus saves us, not through sacrifice or torture, but by reminding us of our true nature and calling us to embody it throughout our lives, unto death, and after death.

The cross symbolizes not self-sacrifice but an encounter with and testimony to the suffering of the poor. Mary Ann's crucifixion narrative is a "true fiction" because it reveals the real evils of sexual abuse, clericalism, and power imbalances in the church. These practices deny our core humanity: we are each created in the image and likeness of God. Mary Ann's suffering, like Jesus's on the cross, illustrates the impact of these evil structures. Suffering does not negate our salvation. Instead, the presence of the Divine as a co-sufferer in the narrative shows that God is an active companion on our journey, not a passive observer or retributive father.

Mary Ann's crucifixion narrative also reveals the community's guilt. These evils are systemic, supported and perpetuated by larger

---

21. Tatman, "Atonement," 12.

societal structures. Communities allow these evils to continue by ignoring survivor testimonies. The community is also traumatized and experiences moral injury from being complicit in the abuse. Crucifixion symbolizes all unjust suffering caused by the world's evil powers, not just one sacrificial death.

The above theological insights become clear and understandable when we recontextualize Jesus's crucifixion today through the narrative of Mary Ann. But there remains the scholarly and discerning work of returning to the tradition to see how these new insights might deepen other theological concepts. For example, how do we understand the difference in nature between the crucified people of today, like Mary Ann, and that of Jesus as the Christ? Our understanding of the Incarnation and the hypostatic union differs from our understanding of Christian anthropology. Though we are made in the image and likeness of God, how does our humanity differ, if at all, from that of Jesus as the Christ? The victims of sexual abuse have been stripped of their agency and ability to consent by corrupted systems of power. Do we say the same of Jesus? Does this impinge on Jesus's divine nature, and is the Divine impacted by circumstance and history?

Insights on the Resurrection

Mary Ann's resurrection narrative, encompassing both her healing journey and her dream, helps us recontextualize the resurrection for today. Through her story and the development of both her personal and the community's moral clarity and agency, we see how suffering and evil can be resisted. Mary Ann begins to reimagine and narrate her life as a survivor, much like the Gospels narrate Jesus's resurrection. She becomes an advocate, working against the powers that once dominated her. In the Gospels, Jesus's ministry and community do not end at the cross. Similarly, Mary Ann's narrative presents an uncertain future, but one filled with hope.

Mary Ann's resurrection required the accompaniment and support of others. Our salvation is a communal realization. This insight can be read back into the Gospel narratives: the resurrection required Jesus's relationships and community. The Catholic Church's resurrection from the sexual abuse crisis will require the entire body of Christ to work toward justice. This work is beginning to take place in the discernment of the synodal church but is far from fully realized. If churches are to experience resurrection, justice—requiring acknowledgment, apology, and accountability—will be at the center.

Similar to the insights garnered from Mary Ann's crucifixion narrative, reinterpreting the larger systemic models of Christology is an ongoing task that is not completed in this book. When recontextualizing the resurrection into our modern world, theologians and the faithful struggle with the supernatural aspects of the Gospel narratives, particularly the nature of the resurrected body of Jesus. It has long been understood that the resurrection is not the same as "resuscitation." Can Mary Ann's dream give us insight into the imaginative hope of the Gospel writers and communities?

The final dream sequence of Mary Ann's narrative—imagining a reality untouched by abuse—may offer us a beautiful way to recontextualize the resurrection of Jesus. It might reframe the resurrection as a vision of what will be, rather than a historical event. Just as Mary Ann's dream offers a revelation of a healed future, the resurrection narratives of the Gospels offer hope and a call to transformative action to their communities.

This book has sought to bridge the gap between ancient atonement theories and the pressing realities of modern-day clergy sexual abuse survivors. By renarrating the crucifixion and resurrection of Jesus through the lens of Mary Ann's experience, we gain fresh insights into the meaning of salvation, community, and divine presence. These renewed narratives challenge us to reimagine our theological frameworks and church practices, emphasizing the importance of justice, communal healing, and the active participation of survivors in leading churches toward genuine repentance and renewal. As the church moves forward on our pilgrimage, let us seek to embody a faith that is responsive to the suffering and hopes of our time, committed to building a more just and compassionate church for all.

Index

Abbott, Curtis, on atonement and transference, xiv
Abelard, Peter, and moral influence atonement theory, 14, 27, 29, 144
abuse
    experience of, as warning sign of future behavior, 86, 87
    impact on faith, 101, 102, 199, 200
    theological support for, 21
    See also clergy sexual abuse, sexual abuse
abusive priests
    alignment of hierarchy with, 79, 99, 100
    failure to screen for, 70
    fatherly role of, 58
    institutionalization of, 89
    perceived holiness of, 67
    rehabilitation of, 90, 91
    relocation of, 81, 89, 90, 125, 126
accountability
    of hierarchy, 125, 126
    and recovery from abuse, 113, 114
    and rehabilitation of abusive priests, 90, 91
    and restorative justice, 206, 207, 211
    as support for sexual abuse, 56, 186, 187
acknowledgment
    by church of harm caused, 117
    and restorative justice, 206, 207, 211

Ad Hoc Committee on Sexual Abuse (1994, USCCB), 69
adult victims, and allegations of complicity, 73, 74
Against Heresies (Irenaeus), 8
age, of victim, and safety, 111, 112
agency (survivor), through moral clarity, 189–91
aggression, and sexual desire, 86
Alsford, Sally
    on feminist theology, 18
    on sin and salvation, 30
    on a theology of Incarnation, 147
Anselm of Canterbury, on substitutionary/satisfaction model of atonement, 10, 11, 22, 151
anti-Catholicism, and allegations of abuse, 122
apology, and restorative justice, 206, 207, 211
atonement language, and experience of trauma and healing, xvii, xviii
atonement
    and crucifixion of Jesus, 3
    harmful interpretations of, 37
    through the Incarnation, 147, 148
atonement narratives
    abusive environment perpetuated by, xvi, xvii
    and hierarchical relationship between humanity and the Divine, xvi, xvii

atonement narratives (*cont.*)
  influence on abuse survivors, 54, 211, 212
  as narratives of healing, xvii, xviii, 211, 212
  and psychological well-being, xiv
  and worldview, xiv
atonement theories
  classical theories, 6–15
  and sacred moral injury, xvi
atonements, necrophilic, 27
Aulén, Gustav, on human salvation owing to Jesus's Incarnation and death, 8
Awake Milwaukee, 197

Baxter, Christina, on suffering and salvation, 20
Beste, Jennifer, proposals for church response to abuse, 123
betrayal, personal and institutional, 99, 100, 101
bishops
  response to allegations of abuse, 70
  See also abusive priests, alignment of hierarchy with; church leadership, ignorance of nature and impact of abuse
Black women, surrogate roles of, 25, 26
Boersma, Hans
  on *Christus Victor* atonement theory, 143
  on self-sacrifice in Christian life, 25
Boston Globe, investigation of clergy sexual abuse, 4, 5, 69, 122, 123
boundary maintenance, in priestly formation, 88, 89
Brock, Rita Nakashima
  on atonement narratives, trauma, and guilt, xv
  on communally focused Christology, 33
  on community's role in salvation, 153
  on God as abusive father, 21, 22
  on a theology of the Incarnation, 147, 148
Brown, Joanne Carlson
  on church's relationship to women as abusive, 22
  on glorification of suffering, 23
  on Jesus's suffering as divinely ordained, 21
  on redemptive suffering, 58
Cahill, Lisa, on sexuality in Christian tradition, 56
Calvin, John
  on Jesus as criminal, 12
  on punishment and suffering of Jesus, 12
  on substitutionary theory of atonement, 11, 12, 19, 21
Catholic Church
  and compensation for victims, 71
  future practices for survivors of abuse, 212–13
  future response to abuse, 123, 124, 125
  historical response to abuse, 118–23
  and the media, 122, 123
  as pilgrim people, 214, 222
  prioritizing institution over victims, 119,–22
  vision of future, 221–23
celibacy, and clergy abuse, 79, 80
Charter for the Protection of Children and Young People (2002, 2005, 2006), 69, 70, 119, 120, 125
children, inferior status of, 83, 84
Christ, maleness of, 30–32
Christology, communal focus in, 33, 34

Index

Christus Victor theory, 7–9, 24, 28
   and contemporary theologies of salvation, 9
   critique of, 9
   nonviolent interpretation of, 141–43
   and recapitulation theories, origins in Hebrew and Christian Scriptures, 7, 8
church, separation from world and sexual abuse, 78, 79
church leadership, ignorance of nature and impact of abuse, 121
clergy
   authority of, and sexual abuse, 65, 66, 67
   conflation with the Divine, 65, 66
   See also priests, exalted view of
clergy sexual abuse, 36
   in Boston Archdiocese, 5, 69, 123
   of children, statistics, 71, 72
   as crucifixion, 177, 204
   as exercise of power, 64–67
   and family abuse, 76, 77
   gender dynamics of, 73, 74
   history of, in US, 68–71
   impact on parishes, 105, 106
   in Los Angeles Archdiocese, 71
   during medieval period, 68
   mental health impact of, 175, 176
   and moral injury, 52–53
   prevalence, 164
   public dimension of, 91
   as systemic evil, 15
   See also abusive priests; confession, as setting for clergy abuse; John Jay Report; Spotlight investigation; media, role in uncovering; moral injury; secrecy and silence, as support for; sexual abuse

clericalism, 215, 218
   in Catholic Church structure, 77–80, 121
   as enabling clergy abuse, 80–85, 121, 158
   as support for sexual abuse, 56, 158
Collins, Marie, on church leaders covering up abuse, 119
communal discernment, 218, 219
communal penance and reconciliation, 222, 223
community
   recovery after abuse, 116–17
   role in healing and transformation, 179, 180
   significance of, in Christology, 32–34
   support for abuse survivors, 195–98
   See also religious community
compensation, of victims, 119, 120
confession
   reduced participation in, 107
   as setting for clergy abuse, 79, 157
coping mechanisms, 188, 189
Cornwell, John, on childhood confessions, 79
counseling
   of abusive priests, 91
   and recovery, 112, 113
   See also therapists, role in healing
credibility, loss of, 106
cross
   in atonement theories, 27, 28
   co-sufferer model of, 26, 178, 179
   reevaluation as symbol, 177, 178, 224
   as symbol of salvation, 149, 150, 224
crucifixion, and reconciliation of God and humanity, 9–13, 224, 225

crucifixion narratives, and suffering discipleship, 138, 212
Crysdale, Cynthia, on an ethic of risk, 151
Cur Deus Homo (Anselm), 10

Daly, Mary, on sexism and salvation, 30, 31
Damian's Book of Gomorrah, 68
Day of Atonement rituals, 9–10
De Jesu Christo servatore (Faustus Socinus), 14
death of Jesus
  meaning of, in Mark's Gospel, 136–39
  as true fiction, 139, 140
democratic practices, in early church, 219–21
Dewey, Arthur, on historicity and Mark's Gospel, 133
Dill-Shackleford, Karen E., on narrative fiction and worldview, xiii
disability status, and sexual abuse, 43
disbelief, 170, 175
  of authorities, 73, 100, 109, 118, 164, 181
  of family and friends, 100, 101, 103
Doyle, Rev. Thomas P.
  and "The Manual," 68, 69
  on re-imaging God, 111

Eid, Michael, on experience and postevent growth, xviii
ekklēsia, and democratic practices of early church, 220, 221
ephebophiles, 72
evil
  and classical atonement theories, 18–19
  confrontation with, 183; in Mark's Gospel, 151, 152
  endurance model of, 55
  naming and resisting, 179, 211
  problem of, and a loving God, 54, 55

faith
  after abuse, 199–203
  impact on healing, 102, 103
  loss of, as consequence of clergy sexual abuse, 171–72
  restoration through healing, 171, 199–203
  of survivors, 101, 102, 189, 200
families of survivors, 100–105
family support, for abuse survivors, 184, 195–96
Farley, Margaret, on sexuality in Christian tradition, 56
feminist theologians
  challenge to glorification of suffering, 20
  critique of gender as essential characteristic, 32
  perspectives on atonement, 140–48
  on substitutionary and satisfaction atonement models, 13
Finger, Rita, on Jesus's relationships with women, 32, 33
forgiveness, and recovery from abuse, 115, 163
forgiveness of sins, in Mark's Gospel, 138
formation, of nonabusive priests, 88–89
Fortune, Marie
  on clergy sexual abuse as incest, 59, 60
  on clergy sexual abuse as theft of innocence, 64, 65
  on clergy sexual misconduct with parishioners, 72
  on endurance model of evil, 55
  on forgiveness and recovery from abuse, 115
  redefinition of sin by, 56
  on sexual abuse as exercise of power, 65

Index

Francis (Pope), and synodality, 213–16, 218

Gaillardetz, Richard, on Pope Francis and clericalism, 215, 216n7
Gauthe, Fr. Gilbert, trial for abuse of children, 68
gender, and experience of survivors, 99
Girard, René, on Jesus as scapegoat, 26, 142, 143, 144
God
    as abuser, 21–23, 37, 59, 60
    as divine co-sufferer, 145, 178, 179
    loving, and problem of evil, 54, 55, 187, 188
    and problem of suffering, 21
    re-imaging notions of, 111, 187, 188
    role in experience of abuse, 200, 201
    solidarity and compassion of, 151, 178, 179
    trinitarian nature and atonement theories, 22
God image, of survivors, 101, 102, 187, 188
Gonsiorek, John, on warning signs of abuse, 86
Gospel of Mark
    historical backdrop, 133
    passion narrative in, 133–40
    on sacrificial purpose of Jesus's mission, 10
grooming, 97, 98
guilt, and moral identity, 167, 168

Haas, David, 103
healing
    after clergy sex abuse, xi
    importance of articulating the experience, 53
    through justice, 205–7
    as lifetime journey, 186, 203, 204
    and response of religious community, 103, 104
    as resurrection, 204–7, 225
    through religious narratives, 47, 209
    See also recovery
healing circles, 119
Healing Hearts, 197
Heim, Mark, on Jesus as scapegoat, 26
Herman, Judith
    and healing through justice, 205–7
    on relationships for healing, 198
    on sexual abuse and PTSD, 50
    on stages of recovery, 110
hierarchy
    alignment with abusive priests, 79, 99, 100
    dilution of authority of, 81, 82
Holy Spirit, role in synodal church, 216, 217
homophobia, 171
homosexual attraction, and abusive behavior, 87, 88
homosexuality, Catholic Church's stance on, 99
hope, embodied imaginative, 204, 205, 211
House of Peace women's shelter, 204

Iadicola, Peter, on clerical power, 77
Incarnation
    and *Christus Victor* atonement theories, 8
    and reversal of Adam's fall, 7
    significance in atonement theories, 27–28
    as vital for salvation, 147, 148
Institutes of the Christian Religion (John Calvin), 11, 12
institutionalizing, of abusive priests, 89

Irenaeus
    on God and evil, 54
    on human salvation owing to Jesus's Incarnation and death, 8

Jamieson, Penny, on structural reform, 84, 85
Jeffery, Steve, on penal substitution, 37
Jesus
    as active participant in salvation, 24
    as divine victim, 23–25
    idealization of, and human imperfection, 23, 24
    as lone superhero, 32–34
    as male symbol of salvation, 31
    maleness of, and marginalization of women, 31, 32
    as Messiah, in Mark's Gospel, 136
    as model of acceptance of suffering, 39, 40
    as moral exemplar, 14, 144
    as new Adam, 7
    as obedient/passive victim, 24, 37
    as scapegoat, 26, 142, 143, 144
    as Suffering Innocent One, 137–39, 148, 159
    relationship with Jewish temple, 135
    solidarity with the oppressed, 20
    significance of suffering of, 28, 29
Joh, Wonhee Anne
    critique of self-sacrifice, 150, 151
    on the meaning of the cross, 146, 147
John Jay Report, on clergy sexual abuse, 69–72
Johnson, Elizabeth, on influence of God language, xii, 54

Jordan, Mark, on medieval clergy abuse, 68
judicial system, use by church leaders against victims, 120–22
justice, and recovery from abuse, 113, 205–7

Keshgegian, Flora, and substitutionary atonement, 22, 24

laity
    impact of clergy abuse on, 105–7
    moral injury to, 107, 108, 225
    sidelining of, in abuse events, 119
    subordination to clerical class, 83
    See also religious community
Lakeland, Paul, on defensive stance of church, 82
liberation theologians, challenge to glorification of suffering, 20
Linnane, Brian, on loss of credibility in Catholic Church, 106
listening church, 213, 214
    See also synodality, as renewed vision of church
liturgical practice, and priestly authority, 79
Litz, Brett, on moral injury, 48
Llewellyn-Beardsley, J., on mental health recovery narratives, xvii, xviii
Lucado, Max, and purposeful suffering, 38, 39, 40, 41
Luhmann, Maike, on experience and postevent growth, xviii

Magisterium, role in revelation, 217, 218
male sacrifice, and salvation, 31
male savior, and salvation of women, 31, 32

Index

Mangelsdorf, Judith, on experience and postevent growth, xviii
"The Manual," 68, 69
martyrs and martyrdom, 137
Mass attendance, and clergy sexual abuse crisis, xvi, 107
McCarrick, Fr. Theodore, investigation of, 71
meaning-making, through narratives, 140, 209–12
media
　role in uncovering abuse, 187
　See also Boston Globe, Spotlight investigation
mental health issues, and survivors of abuse, 46
Metz, Johannes, on God as beyond suffering, 146
midrash, and Gospel of Mark, 133, 134, 148
Miller, Anna C., on democratic practices in early church, 219, 220
Miller, Sarah Clark, on impact of rape on survivors, 51
Moltmann, Jürgen, on the suffering of God, 145, 146
Moon, Jos, on synodality and communal discernment, 218
moral agency, as consequence of clergy sexual abuse, 164–66, 189–91
moral clarity, through articulation of experience, 186–89
moral confusion, as consequence of clergy sexual abuse, 161–64, 210
moral identity, and clergy sexual abuse, 167–68, 191–95
moral influence and moral example theories of atonement, 13–15, 28, 29, 144
　modern interpretations, 144, 145
　origins in Hebrew and Christian Scriptures, 14
　strengths and weaknesses, 15

moral injury, 48
　cultural and spiritual context, 50–52
　impact on crucifixion narratives, 154, 155
　and PTSD, 50
　and sexual abuse, 51, 52, 107, 108, 210
　symptoms, 49, 50
moral repair, after moral injury, 116
mourning, and trauma healing, 113
Mouton, F. Ray, and "The Manual," 68, 69

narratives
　of Christian theology, and worldview, xiii
　moral impact of, xii–xv
　See also atonement narratives, crucifixion narratives, religious narratives, resurrection narratives
National Review Board, 69, 70
Nawaz, Sabahat, on attitudes toward redemption and justice, xiv

obedience
　to authority of priests, 162, 163
　as virtue, 21, 22
O'Loughlin, Thomas, on synodal church, 222
Ortiz, Dianna, on purpose of suffering, 38
Ott, Kate, on formation in sexual ethics, 89
Ovey, Michael, on penal substitution, 37

parental pressure, and moral expectations, 163
parents
　strained relationships with, 169
　See also families of survivors, family support

parishes, impact of clergy abuse on, 105, 106
Parker, Rebecca
　on God as abusive father, 21, 22
　on redemptive suffering, 58
passion narrative, in Gospel of Mark, 133–40
passion of Jesus, purpose of, 139–40
patriarchy
　and classical atonement theories, xvi
　and clergy abuse, 76–85, 158
　and salvation, 31
Paul (apostle), on substitutionary aspect of Jesus's death, 10
pedophiles, 72
peer support, and recovery from abuse, 114, 182, 183, 185, 192, 195–98
penal substitution, 37
Pennsylvania Grand Jury Report (2018), 71
perpetrators, protection of, 89, 98, 99, 118, 124, 125
Peterson, Rev. Michael R., and "The Manual," 68, 69
Plante, Thomas, on destructive nature of clericalism, 80, 81
Plaskow, Judith, and problem of sin, 29
Poling, James, on clergy sexual abuse as incest, 59, 60
positive identity, through healing after abuse, 191–95
power, sexual abuse as exercise of, 64–67
power imbalance, between clergy and laity, 66, 67, 73, 76
powerlessness, and inability to verbalize experience, 164–66
priesthood, sacramental view of, 79
priests, exalted view of, 161, 162
psychopathologies, as consequence of sexual abuse, 43–45

PTSD (post-traumatic stress disorder), and clergy sexual abuse, xvi
purity culture, focus on abstinence and marital procreation, 56, 57

race, and clergy abuse, 98, 99
Rahner, Karl
　on God as beyond suffering, 146
　on relational aspect of sin, 30
　on a theology of the Incarnation, 147
Raslau, Flavius, on atonement narratives and cognitive restructuring, xiii
Ray, Darby Kathleen
　on communally focused Christology, 33
　on confrontation with evil, 152, 153
　critique of *Christus Victor* theory, 141
recapitulation theory, 7–9
reconnection, stage of recovery, 114–16
recovery
　of community after abuse, 116–17
　of survivors of abuse, 110–16
　See also healing
rehabilitation, of abusive priests, 90, 91
reintegration, of abusive priests, 90
relationships, damaged, as consequence of clergy sexual abuse, 168–71
religious belief
　challenged after sexual assault, 46
　effect on trauma from abuse, 51, 52
religious community
　connection with, after abuse, 115

impact of clergy abuse on, 105–8
influence on post-trauma religious identity, 47
reaction to clergy abuse, 103, 104
role in salvation, 153, 154
religious institutions, decision to stay/leave, 201–3
religious narratives
　as aids in recovery and healing, 132, 209
　effect on victims, 131, 132, 209–12
religious settings, as triggering for survivors of abuse, 46, 47
relocation, of abusive priests, 81, 89, 90, 125, 126
remembrance and mourning, stage of recovery, 112–14
Report to the People of God (2004), 71
restitution, monetary, based on nature of abuse, 174
restorative justice, and rehabilitation of abusive priests, 91, 92
resurrection, and salvation, 147, 225
resurrection narratives, and healing, 225, 226
Riaz, Saima, on attitudes toward redemption and justice, xiv
Riswold, Caryn, on Jesus's resistance to his fate, 24
Rosetti, Stephen, on warning signs of abuse, 86
Ross, Susan
　on atonement theologies and acceptance of suffering, 36, 37
　on patriarchal power of church institutions, 67
Ruether, Rosemary Radford
　on community's role in salvation, 153, 154
　on Divine goodness and omnipotence, 18, 19
　on maleness of Jesus and patriarchal dominance, 31
　on teaching and actions of Jesus, 32

Sach, Andrew, on penal substitution, 37
sacramental worldview, and clericalism, 78, 79
sacrifice, in Christian Scriptures, 10
safety, stage of recovery, 111
Saiving, Valerie, and problem of sin, 29
salvation, participatory, 12
Satan, role in clergy sexual abuse, 8, 9
satisfaction model, in Anselm of Canterbury, 10, 11, 151
scapegoat/scapegoating, 26, 142, 143
　and Jewish understanding of atonement, 9
Schüssler Fiorenza, Elisabeth
　on communally focused Christology, 33
　on suffering discipleship, 138
screening, of clergy candidates, 85–88
secrecy, culture of, 79, 80–83
secrecy and silence, as support for sexual abuse, 56, 163–66, 169
secularization, after sexual assault, 45, 46
self
　crucified, 175, 176
　damage to, 167–68
self-blame, 44, 45, 187
self-image, affect of clergy abuse on, 97, 191–95
self-sacrifice
　critique of, 150, 151, 178
　of Jesus, 24, 25, 57
　as virtue, 21, 22, 24
sense of the faithful, 217
sex, cultural beliefs about, and sexual abuse, 51, 52

sexism
  and classical atonement theories, xvi
  as support for sexual abuse, 56
sexual abuse
  beyond Catholic Church, 84
  child and adult, 68
  as exercise of power and control, 64–67
  impact on survivors, 43, 44, 45, 96–105
  and moral injury, 48–52, 210
  as personal and social sin, 56, 57
  and PTSD, 50
  statistical prevalence of, 43–45
  as theft, 64, 65
  See also clergy sexual abuse
sexual assault, impact on spirituality, 45
sexual confusion, 52, 53
sexual identity/orientation, and clergy sexual abuse, 5, 6, 43
sexuality, priestly formation in, 88, 89
shame
  and cultural views on dignity, 51
  and moral identity, 167, 168
Shay, Jonathan, on moral injury, 48
Sherman, Robert, on trinitarian theology of atonement, 148
Shupe, Anson, on clerical power, 77
siege mentality, among church leaders, 81, 82, 83
silencing, of victims, 119, 120
sin
  problem of, and sexual abuse, 55–57
  as rebellion against creation, 57
  relational aspect of, 29, 30
  and salvation, 29, 30
  social and systemic aspects of, 55–57
Sipe, A. W. Richard, on celibacy and culture of secrecy, 80

SNAP (Survivors Network of those Abused by Priests) 70, 190, 192, 197, 198
Socinus, Faustus, and moral example theory, 14, 27, 29
sodomy, and clergy abuse, 68
Soelle, Dorothee
  on God as abusive father, 146
  on understanding of God, 19
Spanish Inquisition, and abuse of religious women, 68
Spirit Fire, 197
spiritual trauma, of clergy abuse survivors, 97
Spohn, William, on accountability of bishops, 125, 126
Spotlight investigation (*Boston Globe*), 4, 5
stigmatization, of survivors, 170, 171
storytelling, moral agency through, 191–93
structural reform, opposition to, 84, 85
substitutionary atonement theories
  critique of, 18, 19
  limitations of, 13
  origins in Hebrew and Christian Scriptures, 9, 10
substitutionary and satisfaction theories, 9–13
substitutionary language in early Christian theologians, 10
Suchocki, Marjorie, redefinition of sin by, 56, 57
suffering
  as divinely sanctioned, 54
  glorification of, 19–21, 39, 40, 41, 57, 58
  passive endurance of, 24
  purposeful, in Christian literature, 38–42
  reality of, 28–29
suffering discipleship, 138, 212
suffering of Jesus
  and human suffering, xiv

Index

and solidarity with human suffering, 20
survivor identification with, 5
suicide, among sexual abuse survivors, 44, 50, 100, 118, 175
Summa Theologica (Thomas Aquinas), 11
surrogacy, and Black women, 25
survivor advocacy, 5, 183, 184, 192–95
survivor groups, connection with, 114, 182, 183, 185, 192, 197, 198, 208
survivor (amalgamated) stories: Michael, xi–xii; Deborah, 35–38; James, 94, 95, 97, 99-104; Mary Ann, 156–59, 181–86; Nathan, 3–6, 15–16; Rebecca, 95, 97, 98, 100–105, 112–15, 119, 120
survivor stories, as reflections of Jesus's suffering, 159, 160
survivors
  as crucified people, 212, 213
  damaged relationship to church, 172–75
  denial of abuse, 170
  families' attitude toward abuser, 98
  impact of sexual abuse on, 43–45, 96–105
  inability to form relationships, 168–70
  methodology in studying, xix
  mistreatment by church authorities, 100
  sacred moral injury suffered by, xvi, 107, 108
  testimony of, xi, xii
  See also faith, healing, recovery, religious narratives
Synod on Synodality (2021–2024), 214, 216
synodality, as renewed vision of church, 213–16, 221–23

Taking Responsibility project, 52, 94, 107, 160, 160n2, 186
  and moral injury, 107, 108
Tanner, Kathryn
  on Incarnation-centered atonement, 28
  on a theology of the Incarnation, 147
Tatman, Lucy, on abuse as crucifixion, 223, 224
temple
  critique of, in Mark's Gospel, 135, 136
  destruction of, and Gospel of Mark, 135–36
TerKeurst, Lysa, and purposeful suffering, 38–41
Terrell, JoAnne Marie
  critique of Delores Williams, 145
  on cross as symbol of salvation, 149, 150
  on the cross in atonement theology, 26
  on God as divine co-sufferer, 145
theology of transformation, 55
therapists, role in healing, 196
Thomas Aquinas
  on substitutionary/satisfaction model of atonement, 11, 19
  on the suffering and death of Jesus, 11
transparency, effect on community healing, 116–17
trauma
  of friends and family, 104, 105
  and religious identity, 45, 46, 47

Vatican, attitude toward clergy abuse crisis, 122, 123
veterans, and moral injury, 48, 49
victim profiles, 95–96
victim-blaming, 47
victims of abuse, ages, 72

vulnerability, and power imbalance between clergy and laity, 66, 67, 73

Weger, Stephen Edward de, on clergy sexual misconduct against adults, 72, 73
Welch, Sharon, on an ethic of risk, 151
Williams, Delores
   critique of surrogate language in atonement theories, 25, 26
   on modern moral influence theory, 144, 145
Wink, Walter
   on confronting evil, 153
   on a nonviolent atonement narrative, 142

womanist theologians
   challenge to glorification of suffering, 20, 144, 145
   critique of atonement theories, 25, 26, 144, 145
women
   exclusion from church leadership, 119
   prevalence of sexual abuse against, 43
   as victims of clergy sexual abuse, 72

Young, Pamela Dickey, on modern moral influence theory, 144